THE FIELDS
WERE GREEN

Who were too carefree or careful, who were too many
Though always few and alone, who went the pace
But ran in circles, who were lamed by fashion,
Who lived in the wrong time or the wrong place,
Who might have caught fire had only a spark occurred,
Who knew all the words but failed to achieve the Word—

Their ghosts are gagged, their books are library flotsam,
Some of their names—not all—we learnt in school
But, life being short, we rarely read their poems,
Mere source-books now to point or except a rule,
While those opinions which rank them high are based
On a wish to be different or on lack of taste.

In spite of and because of which, we later
Suitors to their mistress (who, unlike them, stays young)
Do right to hang on the grave of each a trophy
Such as, if solvent, he would himself have hung
Above himself, these debtors preclude our scorn—
Did we not underwrite them when we were born?

—LOUIS MACNEICE, "Elegy for Minor Poets"

Child of our children's children yet unborn,
　　When on this yellow page you turn your eyes,
Where the brief record of this May-day morn
　　In phrase antique and faded letters lies,
　　How vague, how pale our flitting ghosts will rise!

Yet in our veins the blood ran warm and red,
　　For us the fields were green, the skies were blue,
Though from our dust the spirit long has fled,
　　We lived, we loved, we toiled, we dreamed like you,
　　Smiled at our sires and thought how much we knew.

Oh might our spirits for one hour return,
　　When the next century rounds its hundredth ring,
All the strange secrets it shall teach to learn,
　　To hear the larger truths its years shall bring,
　　Its wiser sages talk, its sweeter minstrels sing!

—OLIVER WENDELL HOLMES, "American Academy
Centennial Celebration"

THE FIELDS WERE GREEN

A New View of Bryant, Whittier,
Holmes, Lowell, and Longfellow,
with a Selection of Their Poems

BY

GEORGE ARMS

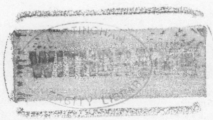

Stanford University Press, Stanford, California

B53 13714

STANFORD UNIVERSITY PRESS, STANFORD, CALIFORNIA

PUBLISHED IN GREAT BRITAIN, INDIA, AND PAKISTAN BY GEOFFREY CUMBERLEGE,
OXFORD UNIVERSITY PRESS, LONDON, BOMBAY, AND KARACHI

THE BAKER AND TAYLOR COMPANY, HILLSIDE, NEW JERSEY
HENRY M. SNYDER & COMPANY, 440 FOURTH AVENUE, NEW YORK 16
W. S. HALL & COMPANY, 457 MADISON AVENUE, NEW YORK 22

Library of Congress Catalog Card Number: 53-6445

Preface

FROM A WORK of this kind critical principles and methods ought to emerge clearly and naturally. It may be well to remark, however, that I have been conscious of the pitfalls that beset an attempt to revalue neglected poets. If I have fallen into any of these traps, it is rather from faulty maneuvering than from ignoring their existence.

I believe that we ought to apply contemporary standards to literature of the past as long as we remain aware of the always important fact of its pastness. I also believe that the "reading *into* the work" of complexities, ironies, ambiguities, and other critical passions of the moment is worth risking. Essays of the sort here undertaken are easily tempted into ambitiousness and overvaluation, but if one must err (as I suppose is inevitable) it seems better to do it in that direction than in the direction of banality.

Throughout the book I have named a number of writers on the schoolroom poets who have helped me. To those critics mentioned by name I owe a great debt, and to them and the unnamed others whose use was either incidental or unrealized I am glad to make acknowledgment. I also want to record my personal thanks to Thomas A. Bledsoe, William M. Gibson, Norman Holmes Pearson, Randall Stewart, Arthur Voss, and C. V. Wicker, who read the manuscript in whole or part and offered many valuable suggestions.

The passage by Donald A. Stauffer is reprinted by permission of *The Hudson Review*. The poems of Whittier, Holmes, Lowell, and Longfellow are reprinted from the authorized editions of these poets by permission of Houghton Mifflin Company; and the poems of Bryant are reprinted by permission of Appleton-Century-Crofts and through the courtesy of Tremaine McDowell, whose text of the 1876 edition, as published in his *William Cullen Bryant* (1935), has been followed.

The chapter on Bryant originally appeared in *The University of Kansas City Review*; a few sentences from other chapters first appeared in *The Explicator, Modern Language Notes*, and *The New England Quarterly*. The courtesy of the editors in allowing me to print this material is gratefully acknowledged.

G. A.

THE UNIVERSITY OF NEW MEXICO
ALBUQUERQUE, NEW MEXICO
April 20, 1953

Contents

The Schoolroom Poets

I CALL THEM the schoolroom poets because they were a literary staple of the curriculum in schools until the last two decades and because they are still a familiar serving. Their faces in steel engravings have long gazed benignly—though to many students with torpidness and enmity even—from the schoolroom walls. And not merely the schoolroom belonged to them but often the whole building. At some time or other most Americans have attended a school named Bryant, Whittier, Holmes, Lowell, or Longfellow.

No matter what we think of these poets they are probably more widely known from early learning and general currency than any other group of authors in America. That is the great literary fact about them—their pervasiveness. If a person of average education is asked to name the authors of *Thanatopsis*, of *Snow-Bound*, of *The Chambered Nautilus*, of *The Vision of Sir Launfal*, and of *A Psalm of Life*, his score will be higher than if he is asked to name the authors of such a distinguished group of modern poems as *Stopping by Woods on a Snowy Evening*, *Peter Quince at the Clavier*, *Tract*, *Gerontion*, and *Captain Carpenter*. Whether a good thing or bad, that may not be so in another twenty years. Our nineteenth-century poets are being almost completely ignored by present-day criticism. As for the schoolroom, if they are not being displaced by Frost, Stevens, W. C. Williams, Eliot, and Ransom, they are yielding to picture books and television. In 1881 Holmes wrote to Lowell, "When the school-children learn your verses they are good for another half century at any rate." As far as school children were concerned he was just about right; for the literary public he overestimated by about twenty years; and for the general public he may have fallen short by twenty.

No voices protest the passing of these schoolroom poets unless in petulant argument against our moderns. The scholarly magazines run a few articles on them, but the literary quarterlies have all but forgotten they existed. Anthologies of American poetry, whether for students or general readers, trim their offerings more and more. But when Oscar Williams' *Little Treasury of American Poetry* appeared in 1949, one New Critic noticed the way that the early poets were being slighted. This was Donald A. Stauffer, who raised a question in *The Hudson Review*:

Mr. Williams is severe on the nineteenth century, so that Longfellow gets fewer pages than Frankenberg, Lowell (James Russell) less than Coman Leavenworth, and Whittier less than a third as much as Eberhart. Was the nineteenth century as bad as all that? Or are our current standards of taste—*l'art pour l'art*, irrationality, allusion, compression, mystery, expressionism, suggestion—somewhat limited? . . . It is a grave charge to dismiss the New England School as "sentimental and largely meretricious" and to suggest that omitting them entirely might have been an even more courageous effort to raise the standard of taste and to educate the young "through serious poetry." Such an attitude intimates again, what the world is always too willing to believe, that truth and beauty have been discovered in our own day for the first time.

Is this a sign of a revival of interest? One could name other instances, but they have not happened often enough to argue a change.

Thus American poets of the last century occupy a paradoxical place. They have unequaled currency in the national mind and their poems have constituted a large part of the formal study of American literature. Yet critical response to them is generally nonexistent, or if expressed, antipathetic. My belief is that there has been a failure to do justice to these poets and that in dealing with them as it does criticism is either inadequate or wrongheaded.

The result seems extremely unhappy in its disowning of a large segment of our literary experience. We are aware of the importance to us of the American nineteenth century in politics and other kinds of social inquiry. Upon our backgrounds in the fine arts we place less emphasis, though we recognize the historical relevance of our early architecture and are increasingly aware of our past in painting and in the useful and folk arts. But in intellectual matters certainly and in the fine arts probably the interest is cultural rather than aesthetic. For a concern with poetry the easy argument is also its importance as an aspect of our society, and in most histories and anthologies of American literature it is so presented.

Without denying it significance in our history and without urging an absolute isolation of an aesthetic from a cultural appreciation, I feel that the ultimate justification of our nineteenth-century poets must depend upon their literary worth. It is just that, of course, which has been denied. The denial parallels a dismissal of nineteenth-century poetry in general and of much British and American prose fiction. But there has been a revival of interest in the British poets and novelists of the period; and the enthusiasm for Melville and James among American authors has not been equaled by enthusiasm for any other authors of any time or place. Among American poets Emily Dickinson has received a permanent place in the rank of great poets of Western civilization. But with a great author we usually find contemporaries of extraordinary merit if not equal value, yet our treatment of Melville, James, and Dickinson is often as if they existed in a literary vacuum. Partisans might contend for Poe and Whitman, though even with these two the last few years have been less than kind. And not even a partisan could at the moment contend that Bryant, Whittier, Holmes, Lowell, and Longfellow occupy a place of any significance in the literary tradition of Western civilization. It is not my argument that they should be awarded a place at the summit. I do not claim their absolute greatness, but feel that a just consideration will cause us to appreciate these schoolroom poets as of a real literary worth.

As a preliminary step in such appreciation we must recognize that certain differences exist between their work and that of the moderns or of many other poets of the past. Most of these differences place them at some disadvantage in my own critical view and in that of modern readers. But within these limits we can enjoy and praise much of their poetry, for the differences belong more to the realm of fashion than of principle. For example, a literary rather than a colloquial diction, the use of poetical-picturesque subject matter, and an effect of relaxation are three differences which are major drawbacks to most of us. But none of these can be regarded as elemental in literary art, and as we shall see throughout this book they need some qualification as judgments of all the work of the poets.

In using a traditional literary language rather than a colloquial language the schoolroom poets were following the neoclassical tradition of Dryden and Pope, with the modifications proposed by Wordsworth for simplicity and the real language of real men. The shift was less great than the traditional dichotomy of neoclassic and romantic has made it, for recent studies have revealed how startlingly close the vocabulary of Blake, Shelley, and Keats was to that of the Dryden-Pope tradition. Wordsworth and Pope were closer to each other than either to Shakespeare before them or Eliot afterward. "My salad days, When I was green in judgment, cold in blood," says Cleopatra. Or Prufrock: "And when I am formulated, sprawling on a pin, When I am pinned and wriggling on the wall . . ." Compare Wordsworth's Matthew: "Where are your books?—that light bequeathed To Beings else forlorn and blind!"

We must admit the superiority of Eliot and Shakespeare for our ears. Yet in using a diction more literary and more abstract than we like it, Wordsworth stands closer to the center of the literary tradition than to its edge. There is no *reason* for preferring one kind of diction to the other, and the arguments in classical criticism are all on the Wordsworth-Pope side. Effectiveness and not level of usage should be the test, and this effectiveness we find again and again in our American poets. Thus by playing off the idea of circularity in the planting of trees and in the coronation of a monarch, the following lines of the pre-schoolroom poet Philip Freneau achieve poetical distinction:

> A hermit's house beside a stream
> With forests planted round,

Whatever it to you may seem
More real happiness I deem
Than if I were a monarch crown'd.

The figurative nicety of this unexceptional—and even nonsyntactical—
stanza can be duplicated again and again in the American poets who follow.
They and their readers found in well-worn words an enrichment to which
we are nearly deaf. But they are not always traditional: quite properly
Henry W. Wells has spoken of the "burly expression" of Freneau, and
Emerson's preference for "a rattling oath in the mouth of truckmen and
teamsters" to "a page of the *North American Review*" is known to every-
one. Though except for Lowell we see little of this in the schoolroom
poets, we find some of it in all but Bryant. And in the language of Bryant
and the rest we find great precision.

The tendency of the schoolroom poets to limit themselves to the
poetical-picturesque in subject matter also gives us pause, and can be less
fully excused by pointing to the tradition. Largely they neglect the whole
contemporary scene, or the sordid and illicit. Their selection from history
is patriotic (*Barbara Frietchie*), domestic (*The Courtship of Miles Stan-
dish*), and melodramatic (*The African Chief*). When they come into their
own time or when their content is meditational, the same glosses of pa-
triotism, domesticity, and melodrama are often present.

Such excuse as can be made for this order of treatment is slight; but
I think it is worth remembering that a closely knit culture with large areas
of ethical and emotional agreement is inclined to yield such moods. The
poet took as his province the normal matter and feeling of polite society.
Though he thereby lost a good deal, he also gained by possessing a poetical
security largely unknown today. The almost immediate use that the people
made of many of Whittier's poems as songs, the acceptance of the devo-
tional poetry of all these poets as hymns shows that these men had large
and immediate (if not "great") audiences. To have a Cape Ann fishing
boat named after one (as Whittier did) or to have spontaneous celebra-
tions of your birthday in nearly all the schoolrooms of the country (as
Longfellow had) must have meant a good deal more to a poet than a
committee's awarding a prize. Poetry suffers in some ways from popular
suffrage, but it also gains immensely. How long is it since any of us have
seen, as Lowell did, a man reading Burns' poetry to casual traveling ac-
quaintances in a railroad coach?

We should not forget also that a good many poems exist not tainted
by fashions verging on the sentimental and that others show a technical
firmness that keeps them far from being an emotional wallow. The ex-
amples mentioned from history suggest still another consideration. More

often than not the poet chose the commonplace incident instead of the tapestried event—*Barbara Frietchie* rather than the surrender of Lee to Grant. So in nonhistorical matter. Whittier gives context to his grief by the use of an old folk custom in *Telling the Bees*. Longfellow's *The Building of the Ship* uses the major New England industry to give substance to his allegory. The material is not altogether diverse from that of Frost's *Mending Wall* or Shapiro's *University*.

It is a smart trick of historians in American literature to point out that Longfellow's *The Day Is Done* was written for a volume of sentimental poets which he edited and that it does not fairly represent his own attitude toward the function of poetry.

> Come, read to me some poem,
> Some simple and heartfelt lay,
> That shall soothe this restless feeling,
> And banish the thoughts of day.

The response expressed here, however, must be admitted not only as a major one in Longfellow but as general for the American poets of his century. Yet some discrimination should be made in the means of soothing. Partly the method was of the kind that resulted in the "most delicious tears" that Longfellow elsewhere spoke of. Before Holmes got through one of Whittier's poems "the tears were rolling out of my eyes." The reading of another, he said, "brought the tears into my eyes—and out of them"; and Lowell too reports weeping over still another poem by Whittier. Such displays are remote from us as aesthetic judgments, but there is another kind of soothing that we can appreciate more fully—one which results in smiles rather than tears. A great deal of the poetry of these authors aimed at a solution of conflicts through good social sense. It comforted not by asking for tears but by being urbane and witty, and we can understand it better here than in its other moods. Partly because we can immediately respond to this kind of poetry and partly because it is an essential element of schoolroom poetry too much neglected, we may rightly emphasize the polite and humorous tone of much of the work.

Even so the poetry is more relaxed—intellectually, emotionally, and metaphorically—than we care to have it. Though ethical, the didacticism is often of an easy sort. Seldom do its figures provide that fine shock of Eliot's "When the evening is spread out against the sky, Like a patient etherized upon a table." It contents itself with nonambiguous simplicity too much. But I am not certain that the schoolroom poets erred on that side farther from an ideal norm in literature than our moderns err on the side of tension and complexity; and many modern poets and critics of the most advanced wing have already recognized the error of this extremity in poetry of our time. Yet a behavior is not virtuous because it differs from a particular kind of misbehavior, and the early American poets are not to be construed as better, or even less worse, in having gone to another extreme. Quite properly they have lost much interest because of it. What I can say is that they do not deserve to lose all their interest for us and that they never did relax quite as much as we are apt to think.

These then appear to be the three main literary differences that have caused the present marked devaluation of our schoolroom poets and that keep us from a more favorable reconsideration. Since no one of them appears decisive, I should also like to suggest another reason which, though adventitious to their literary worth, nevertheless has utmost importance. By long exposure too fully aware of the poetry and having customarily become acquainted with it before much literary sensitivity has been developed, we read carelessly and imperceptively. If we can bring ourselves to read this poetry with the freshness and flexibility with which we read less familiar poems, we shall find much that we otherwise miss. In spite of the differences of fashion that will often detract from these poets, we shall find that they wrote poems of much firmer texture than we realized, poems of considerable and controlled effect.

Usually our fault is to expect a superficial didacticism, and so we get no farther than that. An adult reading of *Maud Muller* will however show that Whittier has not sentimentalized the situation and that the sadness of "It might have been" points as much to the thoughtless reader's wish fulfillment as to Maud's self-recriminations. We make the same error in oversimplifying point of view, image, and tone. Thus the speaker in Emerson's *Days* who is scorned for accepting substance when he might have had spirit is not a facile moralizer but a person in a dramatic situation fully aware of the ironic implications of his act. The image of Holmes' *The Chambered Nautilus* suggests expansive self-fulfillment on one level, but on another alludes to a triumph realizable only in death ("from thy dead lips a clearer note"). The tone of Longfellow's *The Children's Hour* is no less whimsical than that of Eliot's *Old Possum's Book of Practical Cats*.

Something more of these matters appears in the essays on the individual poets; but later comment does not try so much to "place" the poets definitively as to suggest probabilities for placing. Important problems remain unanswered. At times it seems impossible for us to cross the gap between the sensibility natural to our generation and that natural to theirs. What for instance made Tennyson call Whittier's *My Playmate* "a perfect poem," or what gave rise to Sarah Orne Jewett's deep feeling for *The Homestead* (and more particularly for the "line about the squirrel in the forsaken house")? These judgments also point to an occasional difference in the ranking of poems, though usually there is a large agreement between the contemporaries of the schoolroom poets and modern readers as to which poems are best. But the fact of this agreement raises a still more difficult question: Why has such a large proportion of poetry that seems indubitably bad been produced by these authors when at their best by the standard of their time they are also at their best by our standard?

The reasons that I have so far given for the lowness of the low estate of Bryant, Whittier, and the others have been mainly ones directly literary. It must be admitted that biographical background is an important contributing cause as well. By general belief and frequent accusation these poets were optimists in theology, romantics in philosophy, progressives in politics, and dissociationists in sensibility—all attitudes that many readers would rather have less than more of today. With these descriptions one must in general agree, though at the same time making certain reservations. The romanticism of these poets is seldom the "spilt religion" of many of their British and continental contemporaries and is usually modified by a strong neoclassical sense of order. Optimists in religious outlook, their view was nevertheless shadowed by a marked survival of Puritanism in their heritage. Though of dissociated sensibilities in their separation of the rational and emotional, their constant awareness of the correspondences between nature and spirit seems to foreshadow such integration as our age has been able to achieve and extends the unified sensibility of Renaissance poetry. This last point has been thoroughly discussed in a study of the revival of the metaphysicals from 1800 to 1912 by Joseph E. Duncan, who appropriately cites Thoreau, when in referring to Donne's words "one might almost say, her body thought" he affirmed: "I quite say it." "In fact," Mr. Duncan continues, "during the nineteenth century the passage about Elizabeth Drury's speaking soul and almost thinking body was quoted much more than any other lines from Donne . . ."

In our consideration of the lives of these poets we have been still less fair, influenced by pious filial biographies in one generation and by debunkers in another. The consensus seems to be that they were unsophisticated in either a good or bad sense. Though in making a literary estimate I have consciously avoided biography, a few generalizations may not be amiss. The fact that they loved their wives and children should not mark them down as fools, and the fullness and depth of their love seems adequate assurance of a healthy sense of sex. Lacking the novels of James M. Cain and Erskine Caldwell, they still read Aristophanes, Boccaccio, and Rabelais. Though they had their genteel reticences, they escaped the protective facilities of modern medicine: the same rooms in their houses that served for daily living were also rooms of childbirth and of death. Finally, if provincial in their sensing of the newness and cultural insecurity of their milieu, they made up for it by a breadth of learning and an awareness of the life of their time that most of us may well envy. Thus Longfellow was offering a course at Harvard exclusively devoted to Goethe five years after Goethe's death; and those academicians who scorn Longfellow's intellectual attainments will do well to examine their own college's curriculum in modern continental authors with this fact in mind.

If the position taken here is substantially right, a more thorough examination of the schoolroom poets ought to result in a revaluation that will award greater approval than they have customarily received. But it should be clear that such approval is of them as minor and not major poets. A great part of the twentieth century's hesitancy in accepting them arises from the assumption that we must approve of them as major poets or not at all. Though as their long careers began to reach their end the poets themselves were sometimes betrayed into thinking of themselves as greater than they were, it is generally true that neither they nor their more informed contemporaries lost perspective. The five schoolroom poets may indeed be matched by five American poets of their own time who, though still not all major, are clearly their superiors. In addition to Emerson, Poe, Melville, Whitman, and Dickinson (whom I should regard as the superior five), such other nineteenth-century Americans as Tuckerman, Very, Thoreau, and Lanier deserve our attention as much or more.

There is no need to compare the poets in our time except to deny a desire to challenge their literary worth in this attempt to claim important virtues for the schoolroom poets. If indeed the old habit of naming schools for poets were revived, it should not be our hope to see buildings called after the nineteenth-century poets. From our modern living poets now past sixty we have ready at hand the names of Frost, Sandburg, Stevens, W. C. Williams, Eliot, and Ransom. At the same time, while granting these as more fit for the new schools, there is no need to change the names of the old ones.

Bryant

"A RESPECTABLE STATION on the Parnassian mount" was prophesied for Bryant in a review of his first printed volume. That early judgment remains sound. To such a midpoint, not one but most of Bryant's contemporaries assigned him; as Poe wrote, "It will never do to claim for Bryant a genius of the loftiest order." But he continued, "Mr. Bryant has genius, and that of a marked character."

Most historians of American literature have concurred with Bryant's contemporaries, yet today we may justly suspect that even their modest estimate has resulted from a nostalgic desire to honor an early native poet, and not from an objective facing up to his real accomplishment. Only one distinctly modern critic, Yvor Winters, has written well of Bryant, and his remarks have been limited to two poems. William Ellery Leonard, of an earlier generation, wrote respectfully in *The Cambridge History of American Literature*. But there are few other authoritative witnesses for the defense. The question then is: "What may Bryant amount to for the modern reader?"—not "What *does* he amount to?" for that is quickly answered with "Nothing at all."

Though the thought of Bryant is his least significant aspect, it has nevertheless been best handled, notably by Norman Foerster and Tremaine McDowell. Dissenting from Foerster in his emphasis upon Puritanism, McDowell agrees in hinting Bryant's shortcomings as a thinker. Yet neither follows up the implications. In religion Bryant was a Unitarian who regularly worshipped in a Presbyterian church. In politics he was a laissez-faire liberal who helped found the Republican party. In philosophy he affirmed natural goodness but not the goodness of natural man. Such inconsistencies, which are common enough, should not cause dismay. But more completely than seems possible in a man of intelligence, Bryant was not only unconcerned by the difficulties of his position but was oblivious of them. And this lack of complexity harms his poems.

While a brooding sympathy helps to clothe the bareness of thought, sentimentalism too often marks sympathy that lacks texture. Perhaps *The Greek Boy* shows best how much complexity is needed. The poet addresses a Greek youth brought to this country to be educated and envisions in him the revival of classical culture. But a note in the collected poems suggests that the boy was being educated to be a missionary. Nearly fifty years after the poem was published he sent Bryant a letter largely confined to telling of his debt to Christianity: "My country is free and I am free, and what is more, I am a believer in Christ, thanks to those who taught me." Here then is the vivifying circumstance that the poem lacks; and without insisting that Bryant should have used *this* circumstance in his poem, I hold that the evasion of *this kind* of circumstance makes much of Bryant's poetry as flaccid as a gift annual.

Lack of complexity in thought is closely related to thinness of diction. A part of this further disappointment is peculiar to the demands of readers today. Used to the sharp bite of colloquialism in our poetry, we can hardly understand how a contemporary reviewer, Hugh Swinton Legaré, would dare to call Bryant's language "idiomatic and racy—the language of people of this world such as they use when they utter home-bred feelings in conversation with one another around the fireside or the festive board." Even though we may grant that the reviewer was thinking of language akin to Wordsworth's "language really used by men," examples of such language in our own sense are rare. A phrase in *The Ages* when America is described as "lifter-up of proud sky-mingling mountains" is perhaps the most striking; but even here the raciness is of a literary rather than colloquial sort.

The language does have a justness about it, a justness that reminds us of the eighteenth-century tradition at its best. Not infrequently the niceties are too unpretentious for the dulled sense of today's readers, yet as I hope to show when we examine certain poems later on, those niceties fully exist. In recalling how a minister told him as a boy that his parents were ready to make any sacrifice, even to taking the bread out of their own mouths to give their children, Bryant concludes: "I remember being disgusted with this illustration of parental kindness." The anecdote only reinforces what is widely known—that both in the revisions of his own poems and in the criticism of others Bryant showed a scrupulous interest in the choice of the right word.

The diction is just and has dignity, and it lends itself to a satisfactory if not unique rhythm. But the diction is often trite and clumsy, too. Beginning at his first poems, we can end up with a crammed bagful of clichés when we reach *A Lifetime*, which is almost solidly built up of trite phrasing. Frequently also Bryant depends upon the assumption that his words must be dignified just because they are his words, and partly he suffered from a static view of language. "Let us congratulate ourselves," he once said, "that we have such an author as Shakespeare, so admired, so loved, to protect our noble language against the capricious innovations of those who read only the authors of yesterday." Even though he elsewhere fought against weak imitation, his diction is often outworn.

Bryant may also have suffered from being put into a false position by what he thought were the proper conventions of his time, as is suggested by descriptions of him in his old age when he appears to have returned to a boyhood rusticity of manners and language. "He had a strange fondness for talking with queer and common people—farmers, woodmen, and stage-drivers," an early acquaintance remembered. The dichotomy of artificial and natural speech emerges from an examination of the humorous poetry. Bryant half-regretted that the humor "found lurking in the dialogue of Harvey Birch, and of Leatherstocking" was not more abundant in Cooper. In another contemporary, Halleck, he praised the wit, the "irresistible stroke of ridicule," and the "ludicrous contrasts." But his own familiar poems that depend upon verbal wit are notably poor. He is more successful when as in *Robert of Lincoln* and *The Planting of the Apple-Tree* he makes use of colloquial situations, depending only slightly for development upon vocabulary.

Bryant's critical writing makes clear that his faults in ideas and diction are not fortuitous but basic. Although his criticism is not to be despised, parts of it give uneasy pause. Poetry, he believed, differs from prose "by excluding all that disgusts, all that tasks and fatigues the understanding, and all matters which are too trivial and common to excite any emotion whatever." This is what Bryant said in 1826, and though in an essay of 1871 he was more polished in condemning "subtilties of thought, remote from the common apprehension" and in praising the "luminous style," the practical upshot is the same. Bryant's goal was less the functional simplicity of a great building than the homely simpleness of a one-room cabin.

Partly related to thought and diction, partly to imagery, is Bryant's misprizing of the metaphysical poets. He did not possess the shy but secure love for them of many nineteenth-century American writers. Late in life he wrote an essay on Cowley, which he began as one of a projected series on "the less known British poets" (among them Donne, Vaughan, Herbert, and Crashaw!). In the Cowley essay he praised the skill and ingenuity of the poet, and showed at least an antiquarian pleasure in him. Yet in an essay of about the same date he made his most extensive declaration against the metaphysicals: "For what they regarded as poetic effect they depended, not upon the sense of beauty or grandeur, not upon depth or earnestness of feeling, but simply upon surprise at quaint and strange resemblances, contrasts, and combinations of ideas. These were delivered for the most part in rugged diction, and in numbers so harsh as to be almost unmanageable by the reader."

Even more relevant to his practice in imagery are Bryant's remarks on imagination in his 1826 lecture *On the Nature of Poetry*. He begins by challenging the principle of mimesis. "Instead of a visible or tangible imitation," poetry employs "arbitrary symbols, as unlike as possible to the things with which it deals." Yet later in the lecture he subordinates imagination to feeling and understanding. With this emphasis *The Old Man's Counsel* agrees:

> 'Tis an old truth, I know,
> But images like these revive the power
> Of long familiar truths.

Bryant's own poems largely reflect this ultimate indecisiveness of theory. If the image of his poem is in relatively small compass, it is apt to lack vigor. When Holmes burlesqued the famous "Truth, crushed to earth" quatrain ("Does not Mr. Bryant say, that Truth gets well if she is run over by a locomotive, while Error dies of lockjaw if she scratches her finger?"), he was writing more lively, though not better, poetry than that of the original passage. But when Bryant himself attempts sharp images, they are often unintentionally gauche. The final lines of *Oh Fairest of the Rural Maids* are ludicrous if image is realized as image:

> The forest depths, by foot unpressed,
> Are not more sinless than thy breast.

(They come too close to the Morley-Cooglerian couplet for comfort! "My feet are so tired, they must have rest: I'll pillow them on a maiden's breast.") Yet in deprecating *Oh Fairest of the Rural Maids*, I do so with a certain doubt of my own response as against that of Poe with his well-known praise for other parts of the image and for its total effect.

When the image is neither short nor sharp, when it rather consists in the event of the poem or when it belongs to what Leonard calls the "three or four huge and impressive metaphors" that "underlie a great part of his poetry," Bryant achieves success. Sometimes the fundamental metaphors become badly scrambled ones, as in *The Past*. Bryant prided himself upon this poem, and he may have consciously juxtaposed his two figures of the past as prison and as womb. But if he knew what he was doing, he still did not work out the relationship upon as full terms as he ought to have. He lapsed particularly if the woman "who, still and cold, fills the next grave" is not the poet's mother, as the context suggests, but his sister, as biographical circumstance indicates. In other poems, as *The Flood of Years*, there is a looseness in handling metaphors similar to that of *The Past*, but the closeness of pattern in other respects and the large-ness of vision assist in our acceptance.

Another indictment against the poems is that frequently they have scarcely any image when an image seems to be demanded. In *The Poet*, for instance, I judge that Bryant allowed a metaphor of weaving to languish because he could not come to terms with it. Yet it is hard to reduce a poet's practice to generality without exception, as one stanza in this same poem shows. The sudden shift to the image of the sea from that of a dusty street (recalled by "windless") could hardly be more happily handled:

> Yet let no empty gust
>   Of passion find an utterance in thy lay,
> A blast that whirls the dust
>   Along the howling street and dies away;
> But feelings of calm power and mighty sweep,
> Like currents journeying through the windless deep.

Here, as elsewhere, Bryant produces poetry of a high order. In another poem, *Green River* (p. 19), the dual use of the river as a symbol of peacefulness and of poetry makes for a fine structural intensity. We begin with a set piece of nature description. Then at line 35 the speaker is characterized, but as dreamer and not as poet—poetry is restricted to the birds and to the river either in itself or in its likeness to a singing traveler:

> Or haply, some idle dreamer, like me,
> To wander, and muse, and gaze on thee,
> Still—save the chirp of birds that feed
> On the river cherry and seedy reed,
> And thy own wild music gushing out
> With mellow murmur of fairy shout,
> From dawn to the blush of another day,
> Like traveller singing along his way.

As for his own relation to the river, the speaker wishes for its peace and envies the song, but he presents himself as a poet only by hint or negation. Finally in the last couplet the poem is brought into focus in a manner perhaps forced by the words "image" and "greener," but also with dazzling clarity: "An image of that calm life appears That won my heart in my greener years."

Those poems which contain the image in the event are also likely to be poems with a dramatized occasion. Even in *Green River* the narrator is there ("I steal . . . I often come") in a series of scenes. His presence lends vigor to the meditation. This aspect of *Green River*, partially realized as it is, may serve to introduce one of the two great virtues of our poet. As we shall see, dramatization is frequently indirect, often so indirect as to make its presence doubtful in a single poem. But a reading of all the poems assures us that Bryant works dramatically more often than not. Though I do not find this method clearly recognized by Bryant's contemporaries, like most critics of their time they took a great deal for granted. With later critics, whose method is more fully interpretative, the oversight probably results from schoolroom conditioning to Bryant's poetry as familiar and dull.

The obliqueness of Bryant's dramatization serves his purpose better than a full and direct presentation of scene and character. He was apparently unable to achieve complete objectivity. Thus his better work results either from self-dramatization or dramatization of nature, for unconsciously he may have recognized the danger of too obviously posing or too flagrantly personifying. He must also have realized his inability to characterize others, either through examining his own poetry or through reading reviews unfavorable to this aspect of his work. Several remarks on Cooper's Harvey Birch seem to show that Bryant knew what constituted successful characterization. But in practice he fell short, for those poems in which Bryant made a direct dramatization of characters other than himself are his worst. Among the best known of this group are *The Indian Girl's Lament* and *Song of Marion's Men*; and similarly wooden displays make up a solid bulk of his poetry.

At its most successful, the method is dramatization of self or of nature, as I have said. The two familiar instances of the latter are *Thanatopsis* and *Inscription for the Entrance to a Wood*. About both of these early poems this fact is notable: Bryant reached his final dramatic form only after revision. The available evidence shows only one redraft of *Inscription*, but the changes are significant. As it originally appeared in the *North American Review*, the poem was entitled *A Fragment* and lacked the last three lines of the final version:

> The cool wind,
> That stirs the stream in play, shall come to thee,
> Like one that loves thee nor will let thee pass
> Ungreeted, and shall give its light embrace.

These lines enforce the sense of a particular occasion, of which the final title (traditional as it is in concept) gives the scene.

With *Thanatopsis* (p. 21) we have several drafts, which show that Bryant could not decide whether to make the major part of the poem the voice of his better genius or the meditation of the author or the voice of nature. The final use of nature has annoyed two of the best students of the revision, Van Doren and McDowell, but neither states convincing reasons. In the course of redating the poem and proposing a different order of drafts, a more recent writer, William Cullen Bryant II, seems to favor the final version. Indeed the poem gains much of its force because nature, and not the poet, speaks to the reader:

> Go forth, under the open sky, and list
> To Nature's teachings, while from all around—
> Earth and her waters, and the depths of air—
> Comes a still voice . . .

But does the poet play no part other than that of introducing nature's words? I should like to suggest that the poet resumes with his own voice in the didactic close, beginning "So live, that when thy summons comes to join." Bryant first added the closing lines when he returned to the dramatic introduction of the "better genius," and he revised them when he finally settled upon the "still voice" of nature. In their final form (separated by spacing only after several editions) they do not destroy either the symmetry of the poem or the objectivity of nature if they are regarded as balancing lines 1–17. In those earlier lines the poet gives general promise of gladness, beauty, and sympathy. But when nature speaks, she offers at best cold comfort:

> The oak
> Shall send his roots abroad, and pierce thy mold.

> . . . As the long train
> Of ages glide away, the sons of men . . .
> Shall one by one be gathered to thy side,
> By those, who in their turn shall follow them.

Where is the gladness, beauty, sympathy in this? It is again necessary for the poet to comment, to defend nature; and so I believe he does:

> . . . but, sustained and soothed
> By an unfaltering trust, approach thy grave,
> Like one who wraps the drapery of his couch
> About him, and lies down to pleasant dreams.

In spite of the term "self-dramatization" the poems of which it is used have their own integrity and do not depend upon Bryant's life for their effectiveness. We have as narrator a man like Bryant, but a man who is presented to us independently in a poem. By using detail from outside, drama may be diminished rather than heightened. Thus in emphasizing biography commentators upon *Hymn to Death* (p. 23) have done it a disservice. This is the poem in which Bryant hymns death as a deliverer:

> God hath anointed thee to free the oppressed
> And crush the oppressor.

In a series of vivid pictures the poet presents death in this guise, when suddenly he breaks off: his father has died. Now, the death of Bryant's father is not mere coincidental event; rather, by the fact of that death in the poem the speaker has called his father an oppressor, extortioner, perjurer, and felon.

> Shuddering I look
> On what is written, yet I blot not out
> The desultory numbers; let them stand,
> The record of an idle revery.

Whether or not the death of Bryant's father occurred during composition (and sole evidence for dating seems to be internal), we have here one of the most impressive examples of countersuggestion in nineteenth-century poetry. "Let them stand, The record of an idle revery"—yet revery most dramatically and sharply conceived.

In *The Prairies* (p. 27) Bryant again dramatizes an event recognizably from his own life. Again, also the presentation is obliquely dramatic. Actual details of the poet on the scene are few, yet they are indubitably there:

> As o'er the verdant waste I guide my steed,
> Among the high rank grass that sweeps his sides
> The hollow beating of his footstep seems
> A sacrilegious sound.

But the poet is conscious of this mingling of revery with scene ("And my *heart* swells, while the dilated *sight* . . ."). From this duality he achieves his symbol, as he stands between two worlds.

> Thus arise
> Races of living things, glorious in strength,
> And perish, as the quickening breath of God
> Fills them, or is withdrawn.

The present uncultivated plain heralds through the bees a new civilization, which Bryant elegiacally hints will perish like the older civilization that the prairies had once known. Out of this kind of dramatization comes a richness which compensates for the generally naïve single-mindedness of Bryant's thought, and even gives complexity to the thought itself.

In his better poems Bryant also achieves intensity by structure. His technique may well remind us of his close connection with the eighteenth century, and it helps to make him available to the twentieth. But we overlook it in Bryant because of the same historical stock response, additionally complicated by the poet's smooth vocabulary, that has made us blind to his use of drama. Yet indubitably Bryant has structure, not only as any poet must have it, but as one of his two major ways of achieving poetry. In discounting poetry as a mimetic art, he was thrown back upon the alternative of form probably more than a man of his time wanted to be. Yet he accepted the consequence boldly with his definition of poetry in the 1826 lecture: "Poetry is that art which selects and arranges the symbols of thought in such a manner as to excite it [imagination] the most powerfully and delightfully." And at the close, after he had extolled feeling and understanding, he asked: "Is there anyone . . . who will confess himself insensible to the beauty of order or to the pleasure of variety—two principles, the happy mingling of which makes the perfection of poetic numbers?"

We have already seen closely patterned verse in such poems as *Green River* and *Hymn to Death*. Two more poems, both of which likewise make use of image and drama, may be examined as further examples. These are *To a Waterfowl* and *The Evening Wind*.

During Bryant's lifetime *To a Waterfowl* (p. 30) was regarded as one of his greatest achievements, but both then and now the didactic ending has caused uneasiness. Yvor Winters has defended it as "an explicit statement, and a fine statement, of the idea governing the poem, an idea inherent, but insufficiently obvious, in what has gone before." More defense of its integrity within the poem may still be offered. No one, indeed, has pointed out that in *To a Waterfowl* there is not merely one didactic passage, but two, and that the relation of the first to the second and the gradual growth toward the second make the final stanza inhere in the poem. The symmetrical placing of two morals (one in the fourth stanza and the other in the eighth) gives in itself a pleasing framework. But more subtle is their interrelation. The first statement reads, "There is a Power whose care Teaches thy way along that pathless coast," and by natural expansion what is taught by God in the fourth stanza gives its lesson to the poet in the eighth. Other anticipations lead into the final passage with a technical nicety that surely contributes to the intangible emotion. Immediately following the first statement the poet calls our attention to the air (through "pathless coast" he has led into it from lake, river, and ocean of stanza three), and he follows this scene with a reference to land ("Yet stoop not, weary, to the welcome land"). When we come to the moral of the last stanza, we find it predicated upon the same contrast.

> He who, from zone to zone,
> Guides through the boundless sky thy certain flight,
> In the long way that I must tread alone,
> Will lead my steps aright.

Tonally indeed "sky" and "steps" (especially "steps") receive major emphasis in their lines. Here too the poem reaches its moment of dramatic revelation: it is just before the line in which the lesson is announced that the first reference to the poet is made—"yet, on *my* heart, Deeply has sunk the lesson." And not until we are at the climax of the lesson itself does the poet use "I," revealing himself upon the scene at the same moment he voices his final idea. This idea is bound to the scene as much emotionally as the poet is bound to the idea dramatically.

Though the number of Bryant's poems which have moral pendants are relatively few in his total work, most readers think otherwise. Because of this false impression, it is appropriate to turn to *The Evening Wind* (p. 31), which concludes not with a moral but a picture. *The Evening Wind* also differs from *To a Waterfowl* in that it begins with the poet ("Spirit that breathest through *my* lattice") and after the first stanza deals with material beyond his direct vision.

> Go, rock the little wood-bird in his nest,
>   Curl the still waters, bright with stars, and rouse
> The wide old wood from his majestic rest,
>   Summoning from the innumerable boughs
> The strange, deep harmonies that haunt his breast:
>   Pleasant shall be thy way where meekly bows
> The shutting flower, and darkling waters pass,
> And where the o'ershadowing branches sweep the grass.

The idea of the poem is recurrent in Bryant, that of the wind as a part of the "elemental harmony" (a phrase Bryant used in translating a part of Boethius), bringing life to men and nature. The wind comes to the poet from the sea; from him it goes into "the vast inland stretched beyond the sight"; finally it returns to the sea with an announcement, merging idea and form, of "the circle of eternal change." With a technical deftness Bryant reinforces the concept of the circle by using detail of an earlier stanza in the last line of his end-note:

> Sweet odors in the sea-air, sweet and strange,
>   Shall tell the homesick mariner of the shore;
> And, listening to thy murmur, he shall deem
> He hears the rustling leaf and running stream.

Highly wrought structure, while not present in all of Bryant's poems, occurs in many. The preparation in *Monument Mountain*, though inept, is at least meticulous. In *Autumn Woods* and *The Death of the Flowers* careful cross reference helps to control excesses in sentimentalism and moralizing. When in other poems there is no deficiency lurking as in these,

Bryant's consciousness of form brings a certain greatness. The syllogistic structure of *An Evening Revery* produces a fine poem; in conjunction with oblique dramatization and ironical interplay of thought, it yields a work that belongs with Bryant's best. In the sonnet *October* we find a neat joining of octave and sestet, and the introduction of a new figure in the final couplet gives the power of appropriate variety to the smooth unity of what has gone before.

In spite of manifest deficiencies in Bryant, there are then great compensating merits. He had the quality essential to poetic success, a sense of form; and his deficiency in ideas, diction, and imagery are less important than they might otherwise be because of a highly personal yet valid means of dramatization. Certainly, as do most poets of any time, Bryant wrote much that is worthless. Not a little of such dispensable stuff still appears in anthologies, partly through custom and partly for biographical and historical reasons. But if we go to the best of his poetry and use a taste critically fastidious but tolerant to older fashions, we find in Bryant a pleasure and a power. He has his place on Parnassus, surely; and what is more, he still speaks to us from it.

GREEN RIVER

When breezes are soft and skies are fair,
I steal an hour from study and care,
And hie me away to the woodland scene,
Where wanders the stream with waters of green,
As if the bright fringe of herbs on its brink
Had given their stain to the wave they drink;
And they, whose meadows it murmurs through,
Have named the stream from its own fair hue.

Yet pure its waters—its shallows are bright
With colored pebbles and sparkles of light,   *10*
And clear the depths where its eddies play,
And dimples deepen and whirl away,
And the plane-tree's speckled arms o'ershoot
The swifter current that mines its root,
Through whose shifting leaves, as you walk the hill,
The quivering glimmer of sun and rill
With a sudden flash on the eye is thrown,
Like the ray that streams from the diamond-stone.

Oh, loveliest there the spring days come,
With blossoms, and birds, and wild-bees' hum;   20
The flowers of summer are fairest there,
And freshest the breath of the summer air;
And sweetest the golden autumn day
In silence and sunshine glides away.

Yet, fair as thou art, thou shunnest to glide,
Beautiful stream! by the village side;
But windest away from haunts of men,
To quiet valley and shaded glen;
And forest, and meadow, and slope of hill,
Around thee, are lonely, lovely, and still,   30
Lonely—save when, by thy rippling tides,
From thicket to thicket the angler glides;
Or the simpler comes, with basket and book
For herbs of power on thy banks to look;
Or haply, some idle dreamer, like me,
To wander, and muse, and gaze on thee,
Still—save the chirp of birds that feed
On the river cherry and seedy reed,
And thy own wild music gushing out
With mellow murmur of fairy shout,   40
From dawn to the blush of another day,
Like traveller singing along his way.

That fairy music I never hear,
Nor gaze on those waters so green and clear,
And mark them winding away from sight,
Darkened with shade or flashing with light,
While o'er them the vine to its thicket clings,
And the zephyr stoops to freshen his wings,
But I wish that fate had left me free
To wander these quiet haunts with thee,   50
Till the eating cares of earth should depart,
And the peace of the scene pass into my heart;
And I envy thy stream, as it glides along
Through its beautiful banks in a trance of song.

Though forced to drudge for the dregs of men,
And scrawl strange words with the barbarous pen,
And mingle among the jostling crowd,

Where the sons of strife are subtle and loud—
I often come to this quiet place,
To breathe the airs that ruffle thy face,   60
And gaze upon thee in silent dream,
For in thy lonely and lovely stream
An image of that calm life appears
That won my heart in my greener years.

THANATOPSIS

To him who in the love of Nature holds
Communion with her visible forms, she speaks
A various language; for his gayer hours
She has a voice of gladness, and a smile
And eloquence of beauty, and she glides
Into his darker musings, with a mild
And healing sympathy, that steals away
Their sharpness, ere he is aware. When thoughts
Of the last bitter hour come like a blight
Over thy spirit, and sad images   10
Of the stern agony, and shroud, and pall,
And breathless darkness, and the narrow house,
Make thee to shudder, and grow sick at heart;—
Go forth, under the open sky, and list
To Nature's teachings, while from all around—
Earth and her waters, and the depths of air—
Comes a still voice—Yet a few days, and thee
The all-beholding sun shall see no more
In all his course; nor yet in the cold ground,
Where thy pale form was laid, with many tears,   20
Nor in the embrace of ocean, shall exist
Thy image. Earth, that nourished thee, shall claim
Thy growth, to be resolved to earth again,
And, lost each human trace, surrendering up
Thine individual being, shalt thou go
To mix for ever with the elements,
To be a brother to the insensible rock
And to the sluggish clod, which the rude swain
Turns with his share, and treads upon. The oak
Shall send his roots abroad, and pierce thy mould.   30

Yet not to thine eternal resting-place
Shalt thou retire alone, nor couldst thou wish
Couch more magnificent. Thou shalt lie down
With patriarchs of the infant world—with kings,
The powerful of the earth—the wise, the good,
Fair forms, and hoary seers of ages past,
All in one mighty sepulchre. The hills
Rock-ribbed and ancient as the sun,—the vales
Stretching in pensive quietness between;
The venerable woods—rivers that move   40
In majesty, and the complaining brooks
That make the meadows green; and, poured round all,
Old Ocean's gray and melancholy waste,—
Are but the solemn decorations all
Of the great tomb of man. The golden sun,
The planets, all the infinite host of heaven,
Are shining on the sad abodes of death,
Through the still lapse of ages. All that tread
The globe are but a handful to the tribes
That slumber in its bosom.—Take the wings   50
Of morning, pierce the Barcan wilderness,
Or lose thyself in the continuous woods
Where rolls the Oregon, and hears no sound,
Save his own dashings—yet the dead are there:
And millions in those solitudes, since first
The flight of years began, have laid them down
In their last sleep—the dead reign there alone.
So shalt thou rest, and what if thou withdraw
In silence from the living, and no friend
Take note of thy departure? All that breathe   60
Will share thy destiny. The gay will laugh
When thou art gone, the solemn brood of care
Plod on, and each one as before will chase
His favorite phantom; yet all these shall leave
Their mirth and their employments, and shall come
And make their bed with thee. As the long train
Of ages glide away, the sons of men,
The youth in life's green spring, and he who goes
In the full strength of years, matron and maid,
The speechless babe, and the gray-headed man—   70
Shall one by one be gathered to thy side,
By those, who in their turn shall follow them.

So live, that when thy summons comes to join
The innumerable caravan, which moves
To that mysterious realm, where each shall take
His chamber in the silent halls of death,
Thou go not, like the quarry-slave at night,
Scourged to his dungeon, but, sustained and soothed
By an unfaltering trust, approach thy grave,
Like one who wraps the drapery of his couch   80
About him, and lies down to pleasant dreams.

HYMN TO DEATH

Oh! could I hope the wise and pure in heart
Might hear my song without a frown, nor deem
My voice unworthy of the theme it tries,—
I would take up the hymn to Death, and say
To the grim power, The world hath slandered thee
And mocked thee. On thy dim and shadowy brow
They place an iron crown, and call thee king
Of terrors, and the spoiler of the world,
Deadly assassin, that strik'st down the fair,
The loved, the good—that breathest on the lights   10
Of virtue set along the vale of life,
And they go out in darkness. I am come,
Not with reproaches, not with cries and prayers,
Such as have stormed thy stern, insensible ear
From the beginning; I am come to speak
Thy praises. True it is, that I have wept
Thy conquests, and may weep them yet again,
And thou from some I love will take a life
Dear to me as my own. Yet while the spell
Is on my spirit, and I talk with thee   20
In sight of all thy trophies, face to face,
Meet is it that my voice should utter forth
Thy nobler triumphs; I will teach the world
To thank thee. Who are thine accusers?—Who?
The living!—they who never felt thy power,
And know thee not. The curses of the wretch
Whose crimes are ripe, his sufferings when thy hand

Is on him, and the hour he dreads is come,
Are writ among thy praises. But the good—
Does he whom thy kind hand dismissed to peace,   30
Upbraid the gentle violence that took off
His fetters, and unbarred his prison-cell?

  Raise then the hymn to Death. Deliverer!
God hath anointed thee to free the oppressed
And crush the oppressor. When the armed chief,
The conqueror of nations, walks the world,
And it is changed beneath his feet, and all
Its kingdoms melt into one mighty realm—
Thou, while his head is loftiest and his heart
Blasphemes, imagining his own right hand   40
Almighty, thou dost set thy sudden grasp
Upon him, and the links of that strong chain
Which bound mankind are crumbled; thou dost break
Sceptre and crown, and beat his throne to dust.
Then the earth shouts with gladness, and her tribes
Gather within their ancient bounds again.
Else had the mighty of the olden time,
Nimrod, Sesostris, or the youth who feigned
His birth from Libyan Ammon, smitten yet
The nations with a rod of iron, and driven   50
Their chariot o'er our necks. Thou dost avenge,
In thy good time, the wrongs of those who know
No other friend. Nor dost thou interpose
Only to lay the sufferer asleep,
Where he who made him wretched troubles not
His rest—thou dost strike down his tyrant too.
Oh, there is joy when hands that held the scourge
Drop lifeless, and the pitiless heart is cold.
Thou too dost purge from earth its horrible
And old idolatries;—from the proud fanes   60
Each to his grave their priests go out, till none
Is left to teach their worship; then the fires
Of sacrifice are chilled, and the green moss
O'ercreeps their altars; the fallen images
Cumber the weedy courts, and for loud hymns,
Chanted by kneeling multitudes, the wind
Shrieks in the solitary aisles. When he
Who gives his life to guilt, and laughs at all

The laws that God or man has made, and round
Hedges his seat with power, and shines in wealth,— 70
Lifts up his atheist front to scoff at Heaven,
And celebrates his shame in open day,
Thou, in the pride of all his crimes, cutt'st off
The horrible example. Touched by thine,
The extortioner's hard hand foregoes the gold
Wrung from the o'er-worn poor. The perjurer,
Whose tongue was lithe, e'en now, and voluble
Against his neighbor's life, and he who laughed
And leaped for joy to see a spotless fame
Blasted before his own foul calumnies, 80
Are smit with deadly silence. He, who sold
His conscience to preserve a worthless life,
Even while he hugs himself on his escape,
Trembles, as, doubly terrible, at length,
Thy steps o'ertake him, and there is no time
For parley, nor will bribes unclench thy grasp.
Oft, too, dost thou reform thy victim, long
Ere his last hour. And when the reveller,
Mad in the chase of pleasure, stretches on,
And strains each nerve, and clears the path of life 90
Like wind, thou point'st him to the dreadful goal,
And shak'st thy hour-glass in his reeling eye,
And check'st him in mid course. Thy skeleton hand
Shows to the faint of spirit the right path,
And he is warned, and fears to step aside.
Thou sett'st between the ruffian and his crime
Thy ghastly countenance, and his slack hand
Drops the drawn knife. But, oh, most fearfully
Dost thou show forth Heaven's justice, when thy shafts
Drink up the ebbing spirit—then the hard 100
Of heart and violent of hand restores
The treasure to the friendless wretch he wronged.
Then from the writhing bosom thou dost pluck
The guilty secret; lips, for ages sealed,
Are faithless to their dreadful trust at length,
And give it up; the felon's latest breath
Absolves the innocent man who bears his crime;
The slanderer, horror-smitten, and in tears,
Recalls the deadly obloquy he forged
To work his brother's ruin. Thou dost make 110

Thy penitent victim utter to the air
The dark conspiracy that strikes at life,
And aims to whelm the laws; ere yet the hour
Is come, and the dread sign of murder given.

    Thus, from the first of time, hast thou been found
On virtue's side; the wicked, but for thee,
Had been too strong for the good; the great of earth
Had crushed the weak for ever. Schooled in guile
For ages, while each passing year had brought
Its baneful lesson, they had filled the world   120
With their abominations; while its tribes,
Trodden to earth, imbruted, and despoiled,
Had knelt to them in worship; sacrifice
Had smoked on many an altar, temple-roofs
Had echoed with the blasphemous prayer and hymn:
But thou, the great reformer of the world,
Tak'st off the sons of violence and fraud
In their green pupilage, their lore half learned—
Ere guilt had quite o'errun the simple heart
God gave them at their birth, and blotted out   130
His image. Thou dost mark them flushed with hope,
As on the threshold of their vast designs
Doubtful and loose they stand, and strik'st them down.

  . . . .

    Alas! I little thought that the stern power,
Whose fearful praise I sang, would try me thus
Before the strain was ended. It must cease—
For he is in his grave who taught my youth
The art of verse, and in the bud of life
Offered me to the Muses. Oh, cut off
Untimely! when thy reason in its strength,   140
Ripened by years of toil and studious search,
And watch of Nature's silent lessons, taught
Thy hand to practise best the lenient art
To which thou gavest thy laborious days,
And, last, thy life. And, therefore, when the earth
Received thee, tears were in unyielding eyes
And on hard cheeks, and they who deemed thy skill
Delayed their death-hour, shuddered and turned pale
When thou wert gone. This faltering verse, which thou

Shalt not, as wont, o'erlook, is all I have 150
To offer at thy grave—this—and the hope
To copy thy example, and to leave
A name of which the wretched shall not think
As of an enemy's, whom they forgive
As all forgive the dead. Rest, therefore, thou
Whose early guidance trained my infant steps—
Rest, in the bosom of God, till the brief sleep
Of death is over, and a happier life
Shall dawn to waken thine insensible dust.

Now thou art not—and yet the men whose guilt 160
Has wearied Heaven for vengeance—he who bears
False witness—he who takes the orphan's bread,
And robs the widow—he who spreads abroad
Polluted hands in mockery of prayer,
Are left to cumber earth. Shuddering I look
On what is written, yet I blot not out
The desultory numbers; let them stand,
The record of an idle revery.

THE PRAIRIES

These are the gardens of the Desert, these
The unshorn fields, boundless and beautiful,
For which the speech of England has no name—
The Prairies. I behold them for the first,
And my heart swells, while the dilated sight
Takes in the encircling vastness. Lo! they stretch
In airy undulations, far away,
As if the Ocean, in his gentlest swell,
Stood still, with all his rounded billows fixed,
And motionless forever. Motionless?— 10
No—they are all unchained again. The clouds
Sweep over with their shadows, and, beneath,
The surface rolls and fluctuates to the eye;
Dark hollows seem to glide along and chase
The sunny ridges. Breezes of the South!
Who toss the golden and the flame-like flowers,

And pass the prairie-hawk that, poised on high,
Flaps his broad wings, yet moves not—ye have played
Among the palms of Mexico and vines
Of Texas, and have crisped the limpid brooks   20
That from the fountains of Sonora glide
Into the calm Pacific—have ye fanned
A nobler or a lovelier scene than this?
Man hath no part in all this glorious work:
The hand that built the firmament hath heaved
And smoothed these verdant swells, and sown their slopes
With herbage, planted them with island-groves,
And hedged them round with forests. Fitting floor
For this magnificent temple of the sky—
With flowers whose glory and whose multitude   30
Rival the constellations! The great heavens
Seem to stoop down upon the scene in love,—
A nearer vault, and of a tenderer blue,
Than that which bends above our Eastern hills.

As o'er the verdant waste I guide my steed,
Among the high rank grass that sweeps his sides
The hollow beating of his footstep seems
A sacrilegious sound. I think of those
Upon whose rest he tramples. Are they here—
The dead of other days?—and did the dust   40
Of these fair solitudes once stir with life
And burn with passion? Let the mighty mounds
That overlook the rivers, or that rise
In the dim forest crowded with old oaks,
Answer. A race, that long has passed away,
Built them; a disciplined and populous race
Heaped, with long toil, the earth, while yet the Greek
Was hewing the Pentelicus to forms
Of symmetry, and rearing on its rock
The glittering Parthenon. These ample fields   50
Nourished their harvests, here their herds were fed,
When haply by their stalls the bison lowed,
And bowed his manèd shoulder to the yoke.
All day this desert murmured with their toils,
Till twilight blushed, and lovers walked, and wooed
In a forgotten language, and old tunes,
From instruments of unremembered form,

Gave the soft winds a voice. The red-man came—
The roaming hunter-tribes, warlike and fierce,
And the mound-builders vanished from the earth.   60
The solitude of centuries untold
Has settled where they dwelt. The prairie-wolf
Hunts in their meadows, and his fresh-dug den
Yawns by my path. The gopher mines the ground
Where stood their swarming cities. All is gone;
All—save the piles of earth that hold their bones,
The platforms where they worshipped unknown gods,
The barriers which they builded from the soil
To keep the foe at bay—till o'er the walls
The wild beleaguerers broke, and, one by one,   70
The strongholds of the plain were forced, and heaped
With corpses. The brown vultures of the wood
Flocked to those vast uncovered sepulchres,
And sat, unscared and silent, at their feast.
Haply some solitary fugitive,
Lurking in marsh and forest, till the sense
Of desolation and of fear became
Bitterer than death, yielded himself to die.
Man's better nature triumphed then. Kind words
Welcomed and soothed him; the rude conquerors   80
Seated the captive with their chiefs; he chose
A bride among their maidens, and at length
Seemed to forget—yet ne'er forgot—the wife
Of his first love, and her sweet little ones,
Butchered, amid their shrieks, with all his race.

Thus change the forms of being. Thus arise
Races of living things, glorious in strength,
And perish, as the quickening breath of God
Fills them, or is withdrawn. The red-man, too,
Has left the blooming wilds he ranged so long,   90
And, nearer to the Rocky Mountains, sought
A wilder hunting-ground. The beaver builds
No longer by these streams, but far away,
On waters whose blue surface ne'er gave back
The white man's face—among Missouri's springs,
And pools whose issues swell the Oregon—
He rears his little Venice. In these plains
The bison feeds no more. Twice twenty leagues

Beyond remotest smoke of hunter's camp,
Roams the majestic brute, in herds that shake   100
The earth with thundering steps—yet here I meet
His ancient footprints stamped beside the pool.

    Still this great solitude is quick with life.
Myriads of insects, gaudy as the flowers
They flutter over, gentle quadrupeds,
And birds, that scarce have learned the fear of man,
Are here, and sliding reptiles of the ground,
Startlingly beautiful. The graceful deer
Bounds to the wood at my approach. The bee,
A more adventurous colonist than man,
With whom he came across the eastern deep,
Fills the savannas with his murmurings,
And hides his sweets, as in the golden age,
Within the hollow oak. I listen long
To his domestic hum, and think I hear
The sound of that advancing multitude
Which soon shall fill these deserts. From the ground
Comes up the laugh of children, the soft voice
Of maidens, and the sweet and solemn hymn
Of Sabbath worshippers. The low of herds   120
Blends with the rustling of the heavy grain
Over the dark brown furrows. All at once
A fresher wind sweeps by, and breaks my dream,
And I am in the wilderness alone.

TO A WATERFOWL

    Whither, midst falling dew,
While glow the heavens with the last steps of day,
Far, through their rosy depths, dost thou pursue
    Thy solitary way?

    Vainly the fowler's eye
Might mark thy distant flight to do thee wrong,
As, darkly seen against the crimson sky,
    Thy figure floats along.

Seek'st thou the plashy brink
Of weedy lake, or marge of river wide,   10
Or where the rocking billows rise and sink
    On the chafed ocean-side?

There is a Power whose care
Teaches thy way along that pathless coast—
The desert and illimitable air—
    Lone wandering, but not lost.

All day thy wings have fanned,
At that far height, the cold, thin atmosphere,
Yet stoop not, weary, to the welcome land,
    Though the dark night is near.   20

And soon that toil shall end;
Soon shalt thou find a summer home, and rest,
And scream among thy fellows; reeds shall bend,
    Soon, o'er thy sheltered nest.

Thou'rt gone, the abyss of heaven
Hath swallowed up thy form; yet, on my heart
Deeply has sunk the lesson thou hast given,
    And shall not soon depart.

He who, from zone to zone,
Guides through the boundless sky thy certain flight,   30
In the long way that I must tread alone,
    Will lead my steps aright.

THE EVENING WIND

Spirit that breathest through my lattice, thou
    That cool'st the twilight of the sultry day,
Gratefully flows thy freshness round my brow;
    Thou hast been out upon the deep at play,
Riding all day the wild blue waves till now,
    Roughening their crests, and scattering high their spray,

And swelling the white sail. I welcome thee
To the scorched land, thou wanderer of the sea!

Nor I alone; a thousand bosoms round
    Inhale thee in the fulness of delight;   10
And languid forms rise up, and pulses bound
    Livelier, at coming of the wind of night;
And, languishing to hear thy grateful sound,
    Lies the vast inland stretched beyond the sight.
Go forth into the gathering shade; go forth,
God's blessing breathed upon the fainting earth!

Go, rock the little wood-bird in his nest,
    Curl the still waters, bright with stars, and rouse
The wide old wood from his majestic rest,
    Summoning from the innumerable boughs   20
The strange, deep harmonies that haunt his breast:
    Pleasant shall be thy way where meekly bows
The shutting flower, and darkling waters pass,
And where the o'ershadowing branches sweep the grass.

The faint old man shall lean his silver head
    To feel thee; thou shalt kiss the child asleep,
And dry the moistened curls that overspread
    His temples, while his breathing grows more deep:
And they who stand about the sick man's bed,
    Shall joy to listen to thy distant sweep,   30
And softly part his curtains to allow
Thy visit, grateful to his burning brow.

Go—but the circle of eternal change,
    Which is the life of Nature, shall restore,
With sounds and scents from all thy mighty range,
    Thee to thy birthplace of the deep once more;
Sweet odors in the sea-air, sweet and strange,
    Shall tell the homesick mariner of the shore;
And, listening to thy murmur, he shall deem
He hears the rustling leaf and running stream.   40

Whittier

AMONG BOOKMEN, though not among critics, our present decades have shown more attention to Whittier than to most other schoolroom poets. No other American author has received as full-scale a bibliography as that published of Whittier's works in 1937. Two biographies have shown an affection for their subject that does not exist in recent biographies of Longfellow, Holmes, and Lowell. *Barbara Frietchie* is the subject of a forty-five-page monograph. But the monograph is concerned with historical accuracy rather than literary merit, and as the subtitles of the two biographies show (*Bard of Freedom* and *Friend of Man*), their interest, too, lies with Whittier's place in the political events of his time.

A more convincing tribute to the poetry than either biography is the memorial by Winfield Townley Scott, whose poem *Mr. Whittier* appeared in 1948. This is more concerned with the man than his poetry, if one must choose an emphasis. But with an informed tenderness Mr. Scott writes about the poetry too:

It is easier to leave *Snow-Bound* and a dozen other items in or out of
The school curriculum than it is to have written them . . .
It is so much easier to forget than to have been Mr. Whittier.
He put the names of our places into his poems and he honored us
with himself;
And is for us but not altogether, because larger than us.

In much that will be written here I hope that Mr. Scott, who also published an essay on Whittier in 1934, would agree with me. With everyone else we would admit that for prosiness, emotional flatness, and intellectual emptiness some of Whittier's poems can be surpassed only by diligent search. Yet in one long poem his "largeness" is questioned by few, and for other poems a rereading may lead to the admission that we have good reason to remember him. The poet is seldom more imperfectly and infrequently a poet than are those of us who write about him inadequate as critics.

Customarily scholars have divided Whittier's poems into the legendary, antislavery, personal, and religious. Though a simplification of the ten divisions in the collected works, the categories are more logical and useful as a description of subjects than are Whittier's own. Yet both classifications are delusive, for all the poems are personal and transform into personal reminiscence even matter that is remote. We should not confuse this personalizing with romantic confession, for neoclassical restraint

made Whittier hesitate to publish poems too "near my heart." But without
seeking to unveil the intimately personal, at his best Whittier must make
his material relevant to himself. Against his stated preference for "farmer
boy and barefoot girl" in the poem on Robert Burns, he frequently writes
of "lands of gold and pearl, Of loving knight and lady." Yet he always
brings the foreign home and brings the local to his heart—often, it must
be admitted, by plain didacticism, but at his most successful with intensity.
Thus the New England custom of *Telling the Bees* is presented in terms
of the poet's own experience; the antislavery *Ichabod*, one of the few propa-
ganda poems that retain power, transforms a public betrayal into an occa-
sion for private pity; and *The Brewing of Soma* concludes, after eleven
stanzas describing Asiatic religious ritual, with the devotional hymn, "Dear
Lord and Father of Mankind." The poems are not better because they
are about the author; rather Whittier could make them better only when
they fuse with his own experience. Much like Mark Twain's, his artistry
functioned best in a personal frame of reference.

As the subjects of the poems tend to one motif, their philosophy focuses
at one place—the Quaker view of man. Though consciously deistic and
nonsectarian, his faith was informed in its particulars by specific Christian
dogma. He better deserves to be called trinitarian than many present-day
Episcopalians or Baptists, and with good reason an able orthodox theo-
logian, A. H. Strong, found in him an impressive leaven of Calvin. Again,
Whittier's inner light depends upon Christian revelation. He says that he
turns from

> Dark creed, and mournful eastern dream
> Of power, impersonal and cold,
> Controlling all, itself controlled

to the "still witness in my heart." But this opposition has no logic. The
inner light feeds upon a New Testament Christianity that has undergone
small dilution.

Dilution did exist, for Whittier was affected by the romanticism of
his time, traces of which we most easily discern in the relationship he felt
between man and nature and in his view of evil. The healing and reju-
venating power of nature, expanded fitfully to identification and even
pantheism, finds place in many of the poems. On Wordsworth he writes,
perhaps with a connotation in the second word that identifies English ro-
manticism with Quaker insight:

> Dear friends, who read the world aright,
>   And in its common forms discern
> A beauty and a harmony
>   The many never learn!

With Wordsworth he insists upon "common, natural things," but unlike Wordsworth he uses nature as little more than the basis of hope. Too often, as in *Summer by the Lakeside*, he expresses the hope with a wearying verboseness; once (*Storm on Lake Asquam*) the hope so permeates the description that he almost suppresses prose exegesis; and upon another occasion (*Pentucket*) he wistfully contrasts the hope of nature with human depravity and achieves greater effectiveness for not trying to explain. Thus in spite of his titling a large section of the collected work "Poems of Nature" and in spite of the presence of many other poems indulging in natural description and philosophizing, neither Wordsworth nor other more radical romantic thinkers entered deeply into Whittier's pages. Though one poem makes us aware that he knew Rousseau, it equally assures us that he did not know him as a revolutionary philosopher.

In treating evil Whittier shows less the challenge of romantic-transcendental concepts than the superficial benignity of his age. To read *The Reformer* against Hawthorne's *Earth's Holocaust* or *The Fisherman* against *Moby-Dick* makes it plain that Whittier belongs with the easy theologians of the time. He recognized evil, but in the narrative poems he thrust it aside or treated it melodramatically. In the poems on Robert Burns he admits moral faults, and then goes on to declare that they are inessential or to ask forgiveness. Yet when it does not suggest failure to recognize man's full nature, the sense of man's glory in the face of his debasement conveys solid belief at best. Whatever shortcomings we may find here, Whittier does not offend for his affirmation of human dignity and for his ideal of man. His favorite bywords are "order" and "symmetry"—"calm beauty of an ordered life," "the flawless symmetry of man." His early American heroes and heroines exhibit such qualities: on an exalted plane, Cassandra Southwick and Abraham Davenport; on a homely one, Cobbler Keezar and Abram Morrison.

Most biographers have found in Whittier the man this moral symmetry that he prizes in others, but in his work an ordered art confesses beauty less often than we should like. The reason certainly does not arise from an unwillingness to revise, since Whittier was constantly making changes in both his early drafts and late printings. Unfortunately the changes often went toward greater diffuseness; and the main part of *Among the Hills*, for example, grew from forty-two to eighty-six stanzas between its periodical and book publication. Whittier's lack of hesitation in accepting the suggestions of others must also be held against him. When he took suggestions from Lowell or H. E. Scudder, we blame him less. But when he instantly accepted a revision proposed by the politician James G. Blaine, we can only wonder. The truth seems to be that Whittier is an uneasy poet in spite of frequent pronouncements which limit, and hence might strengthen, the scope and practice of his muse.

Probably the main trouble is not didacticism, for although Whittier indulges in digressive moralizing he shows no more of it than his background might lead us to expect. In theory he does not incline toward it at all. His critical writing thus neglects and even spurns didactic elements: a review of *Evangeline* commends Longfellow for not displaying social censure; one on Holmes recognizes without rebuke that, far from being a reformer, Holmes almost sympathizes with folly; and an essay on Marvell praises the Puritan poet for being genial, polite, and fashionable. Though Whittier defends didacticism in his own poetry, he also recognizes its limitations. In *The Tent on the Beach* the Traveller (Bayard Taylor) upbraids him because

> You check the free play of your rhymes, to clap
> A moral underneath, and spring it like a trap.

True art, according to the *Proem* and *Dedication*, requires no direct moralizing, though that may find place in lower levels. Morality can get along without the didactic tag: "The whisper of the inward voice Is more than homilies."

Whether Whittier was willing to accept art as an essential expression of life remains at best an open question. No doubt his modest recognition of his own shortcomings influences his scale of values for others. Speaking of an illustrated edition of his poems, he found the pictures "often better than the verses they illustrate." "My vehicles," he admitted on another occasion, "have been of the humbler sort—merely the farm wagon and buckboard of verse, and not likely to run so long as Dr. Holmes's 'One Hoss Shay' . . ." As he looked over the proofs of his collected works he wanted to drown some of the poems there "like so many unlikely kittens."

As a part of this self-sacrificing modesty, one finds a depreciation of art which not only tends to place it low on a scale of values but to split it off altogether. Hawthorne saw such a split in a frequently quoted passage that has sometimes been used to praise the poet: "Strictly speaking, Whittier did not care much for literature. He loved men and things and books of biography and travel . . ." Whittier's poetry opens the gap still further: art there is the "mockery" of nature. In tributes to contemporary poets the men are divorced from their work, and of himself Whittier wrote, "I am a *man* and not a mere verse-maker." When he condemned the "specious counterfeit Of sentiment or studied wit" we are not quite sure whether he reproached a particular kind of art or all art as he knew it.

Yet in spite of the doubts that Whittier's miscellaneous judgments raise, we need not decry the essential view. As he has it humorously:

> Ah well!—The wreath the Muses braid
> Proves often Folly's cap and bell;
> Methinks, my ample beaver's shade
> May serve my turn as well.

Or seriously and definitively in the *Proem* with which he introduces his collected poems:

> O freedom! if to me belong
> Nor mighty Milton's gift divine,
> Nor Marvell's wit and graceful song,
> Still with a love as deep and strong
> As theirs, I lay, like them, my best gifts on thy shrine!

The sense of dedication rescues Whittier from what could be an offensive artistic position. Though the split is there, though all too often the Quaker garb hanging loosely over his "restless wings of song" keeps him from happy flights, the man and poet have secured a reconciliation.

Still, the gifts of which Whittier wrote in *Proem* are not those for which we enjoy knowing him. Mostly he was thinking of his antislavery poems, to which he insistently gave a large part of his volumes. At the time he was not justifying such poems as *Telling the Bees, Skipper Ireson's Ride*, and *The Pennsylvania Pilgrim*, for none of these had yet been written. But in retrospect he probably saw, as the retaining of the *Proem* in later collections suggests, that these poems were more acceptable gifts at the shrine of freedom than antislavery propaganda.

The "legendary" poems, however, immediately raise another problem. Just as Whittier was uneasy with art, so he was uneasy with the past that was so much a part of him. He believed in the epic quality of his own age and saw "ancient myth and song and tale" as inadequate to the great political question of his time. The unbalance of this attitude may account for the ludicrous attempt to heroicize a certain Conductor Bradley for his actions at a railroad wreck and for the smug praise of the "moral steam enginery" of his age. Perhaps because he lacked an integrated view of the past, he often introduced the legendary poems with long preludes. These afford a dramatic setting and prepare the readers' emotion for the story that follows, but primarily (as he hints in *The Bridal of Pennacook*) they serve to justify the stories by the personal associations of their scenes.

Birchbrook Mill (p. 48), one of the less-known poems, illustrates a happier use of legend. Whittier describes the stream where a mill once stood and the superstitious awe in which local inhabitants hold it.

Its birches whisper to the wind,
 The swallow dips her wings
In the cool spray, and on its banks
 The gray song-sparrow sings.

But from it, when the dark night falls,
 The school-girl shrinks with dread;
The farmer, home-bound from his fields,
 Goes by with quickened tread.

Whittier refuses to specify the "nameless horror of the past" that is attached to the mill, content instead to concentrate his effect in the word "grinding": "What ghost his unforgiven sin Is grinding o'er and o'er?" Though he leaves the subject with little grace (the last two stanzas are supernumerary), he has presented materials directly. Again, in *Telling the Bees* he makes the past a part of the present, using the old custom of announcing a death to the bees as the dramatic center of an experience. With *Skipper Ireson's Ride* and *The Pennsylvania Pilgrim* the experiences are presented in their own terms, even though Whittier relates the latter poem to the antislavery struggle. But against these successful evocations we can contrast such poems as *The Robin, How the Women Went from Dover*, and *Chalkley Hall*. In itself the legend of *The Robin* involves folklore quite as charming as *Telling the Bees*—that the fires of hell, which the robin mercifully tries to quench, have scorched the bird's breast to redness. But this matter is set in a foolish poem that meanders between a dialogue opposing cruelty to animals and the poet's more general plea for lovingkindness. *How the Women Went from Dover* contains the same (though more accurate) historical stuff as *Skipper Ireson's Ride*, both vigorous and vengeful. But unlike the tale of Marblehead the poet tries to argue that of Dover into contemporary meaning.

Less obvious distinctions exist between *Chalkley Hall* and *The Pennsylvania Pilgrim*. Both describe early Friends in the Philadelphia area; both are related to antislavery. Yet Thomas Chalkley is subordinated to a particular use in his poem, while Daniel Pastorius in his own right permeates the work of which he is an integral part. Along with this difference—and as a result of it, since the accompaniment is inevitable in Whittier—*The Pennsylvania Pilgrim* (p. 50) overflows with virtues not present in *Chalkley Hall*. A prelude, not as so often one of discursive anecdote and natural description, states the subject in these terms:

. . . over fields of harvest sown
With seeds of blessing, now to ripeness grown,
I bid the sower pass before the reapers' sight.

This metaphor of sowing and reaping is constantly picked up and illuminated throughout the poem and reinforced by reference to a century plant.

> And Anna's aloe? if it flowered at last
> In Bartram's garden, did John Woolman cast
> A glance upon it as he meekly passed?

The resultant poem does not have the directness and economy of *Telling the Bees* and *Skipper Ireson's Ride*, but it absorbs naturally all that Whittier puts into it: homely humor, antiquarian detail, rebukes to New England harshness, and the inception of the antislavery movement. Like the immigrant Pastorius, whose "Memory, while he trod the New World's strand, A double ganger walked the Fatherland," Whittier has here achieved a rare fusion of sensibility.

In this poem Whittier comes up to his best, liberating himself from merely topical interests and from a simplified code of good or bad. In attaining the first of these freedoms he has centered his focus upon the immediately personal, and in attaining the second he has given depth to his material. Of such paradoxes art is made, yet not without ultimate resolution; and in Whittier there emerges from the concentration and diffusion an essential poetry unaffected by formal loyalties.

In the relatively small group of poems in which this happens, certain other qualities also emerge as distinctive values in his art. He successfully conveys a complex view of character, a control of narrative technique, and a just proportion of parts.

The most memorable poems of character present no stock figures of virtue or evil, but people to whom Whittier gives depth and solidity of understanding, even while he passes moral judgment. Most are "bad" characters, yet bad characters redeemed by nobility. Webster, in *Ichabod* (p. 67), is the most moving, because he is worst and greatest. This poem on his betrayal in the Seventh of March speech has its inconsequential oratory ("Revile him not, the Tempter hath A snare for all"); but for the greater part diction and imagery are used with dignity. What sustains the poem is the central image of the fallen angel, not presented with metaphorical outspokenness as ornament, but slowly expanded from the "So fallen! so lost!" of the first line to the "fallen angel" in the latter part.

> Of all we loved and honored, naught
>   Save power remains;
> A fallen angel's pride of thought,
>   Still strong in chains.

One critic has spoken of the use of Dante, who in the *Inferno,* XXXIII,

121–35, describes a friar whose soul falls into hell before his earthly body dies. This does not appear to involve the main effect of the poem, the great power of which derives from an allusive use of Milton's Satan as a fallen angel and of the Biblical reference to "departed glory." Lowell's use of the latter four years earlier reminds us of its literary currency: "Shall not the Recording Angel write *Ichabod* after the name of this man in the great book of Doom?" Again we have a likely source, but there is a more significant one in Whittier's own use of Ichabod as a pseudonym for certain poems of his boyhood. Had he only referred then to Irving's country schoolmaster, or had he sensed the Biblical connotation of the name? If his reference was Biblical, which seems likely, the connection would underline Whittier's infusion of his own personality into this poem. A later and kindlier treatment of Webster, *The Lost Occasion*, also shows an unusual control of the images in the contrast of the mountains and the seaside grave.

In *Skipper Ireson's Ride* (p. 68) one feels solid structure too. Perhaps this happens because the material springs from an evil man and situation and because Whittier has drawn upon his own boyhood. "My verse," he wrote, defending the inaccuracy of his knowledge of the event, "was founded solely on a fragment of rhyme which I heard from one of my early schoolmates . . ." It is well to point out that the mob action against Ireson does not receive the moral approval of Whittier, himself by the time of this poem's composition a man who had experienced mob violence. Mediating thus between two forces of evil, Whittier takes time for little more than vivid presentation of the action in the early stanzas. The first stanza with its allusions to the Golden Ass of Apuleius, to the Arabian Nights, and to Mohammed highlights the picturesque with an irresponsible humor that is carried into the later stanzas and the whole tone of the poem:

> The strangest ride that ever was sped
> Was Ireson's, out of Marblehead!
> Old Floyd Ireson, for his hard heart,
> Tarred and feathered and carried in a cart
> By the women of Marblehead!

Until the last two stanzas, all is vigor, and the reader is allowed to draw his own conclusion of the horror beneath it. But at the end Whittier comes close to negating his fine effect when the skipper, crying that the sense of his own evil is greater punishment than tar and feathers, repents with a confession that works well as an indirect plea for his liberation. Though it may be argued that Whittier in thus ending the story merely follows such historical source as he knew, one suspects that if this is so he would not have chosen the story had it ended otherwise. But I am not sure that the genteel intention, made plain by the shift in refrain from "old Floyd" to "poor Floyd," is conveyed in the poem.

> So with soft relentings and rude excuse,
> Half scorn, half pity, they cut him loose,
> And gave him a cloak to hide him in,
> And left him alone with his shame and sin.
> Poor Floyd Ireson, for his hard heart,
> Tarred and feathered and carried in a cart
> By the women of Marblehead!

After the skipper's supposed repentance the refrain still speaks of his hard heart; and it is with "half scorn, half pity" that the women give him his freedom. The modern reader, at least, skeptically wonders whether the repentance of this Son of Wrath is for the sake of his eternal life or immediate escape, and the poem retains its brutally humorous effect without weakening.

In his *Literary History of America* Barrett Wendell regarded *Skipper Ireson's Ride* and *Maud Muller* as "so commonplace that one finds critical admiration out of the question." Most of those who now read Whittier would differ from Wendell, finding more poetic value in the first of these than in most other poems by Whittier. But they would solidly agree in the dismissal of *Maud Muller*. Furthermore they would have close sympathy with its own author's judgment—for losing patience at the persistent questions of well-intentioned readers, Whittier once wrote that he didn't think the poem worth "serious analysis." To most readers today the poem has become the epitome of all that is bad in Whittier. The contrast between this critical situation and the esteem which the nineteenth century had for the poem suggests *Maud Muller* (p. 71) as an important exhibit in Whittier's treatment of character.

Probably the average reader did make an emotional debauch of the poem. What is more, the materials in the poem lent themselves to the same kind of attitude in Whittier. The poor unbred country dweller rescued by a rich and cultivated lover appears close to what he had earlier wished for himself and to what he later piously endorsed in *Among the Hills*. But in *Maud Muller* he shows consciousness of the corrosive sentimentality implicit in such a situation. Of this view, the reputedly infamous couplet is at the heart:

> For of all sad words of tongue or pen,
> The saddest are these: "It might have been!"

For the casual reader the words are sad because a country Cinderella has missed her chance, but in the context they are sad because of the emotional waste that the judge and Maud suffer by giving these words their allegiance. In the lines that go before, Whittier says this as plainly as he needs to:

> Alas for maiden, alas for Judge,
> For rich repiner and household drudge!
>
> God pity them both! and pity us all,
> Who vainly the dreams of youth recall.

The qualification that immediately follows the crucial "might have been" ("Ah, well! for us all some sweet hope lies Deeply buried from human eyes") does not weaken by excuse. Rather, it strengthens by urging an extenuation of vain mortality as an imperfect type of spiritual yearning. In the characterization of the man and girl, Whittier has prepared us for this with an insight that commands respect. At the time he does it one is not altogether sure whether he attempts irony in having the judge look back at Maud and think of her wisdom and goodness just when she indulges in an egocentric daydream of herself as a grand lady. But as the story continues and as the judge and Maud marry with members of their classes, the suspicion becomes a certainty. Not desiring to make his heroine a monster, he still makes her an object of pity—and this not for her rural marriage but for her false dream.

For our own delight as well as for the poet's repute, it is a pity that Whittier could not treat his good characters more often in this mood. On one or two other occasions he does it less sharply, as with the members of the family circle in *Snow-Bound* or with Pastorius in *The Pennsylvania Pilgrim*. But in the better of these two poems, it must be remembered that the picture of rural innocence secures effective relief from the exotic Harriet Livermore. In many others, whether the characters are out of a legendary past or out of childhood experience, unrelieved sweetness causes the reader to fret not only for that in itself but for the apparent license to artistic abandonment that it bestows upon the poet. *In School-Days* shows what may happen, and is a better spot for making an attack against Whittier than *Maud Muller*. Mindful of Matthew Arnold's recognizing *In School-Days* "as one of the perfect poems which must live" and remembering the tears of Oliver Wendell Holmes when he read it, I still cannot see how a defense may be made.

On the other hand, when character is realized, the whole poem emerges integral and direct. Something more might be desired for *Skipper Ireson's Ride*, but within their kind *Ichabod* and *Maud Muller* are perfect. In the poem on Webster we have seen Whittier's ability in sustaining his metaphor; and in that on Maud he shows precision in his handling of the main issue. Given the ingredients, Whittier can make a poem on many counts, and in *Maud Muller* we may properly suspect a pun when the girl dreams, thinking of the judge as taking the place of her real husband, that "joy was duty and love was *law.*" Also in this poem we find a sense of narrative technique that could hardly be bettered. Instead of the long introductory description typical in Whittier, the scene is set in a single couplet.

> Maud Muller on a summer's day
> Raked the meadow sweet with hay.

To the "meadow sweet with hay" in the first stanza, a "mock-bird" and a "far-off town" are added in the next few, both properties that anticipate the demands of the drama. The judge enters, talks with Maud, rides away. Paralleling the immediate response of the two, glimpses are given of their later regret. And the story, with a quotation drawn from Maud's own musing, is quickly concluded.

Something about economy of narrative has already been said for *The Pennsylvania Pilgrim*, and a good deal more will be said for *Snow-Bound*. But perhaps *Barbara Frietchie* (p. 75) affords the most convincing example. The setting, a little more discursive than that of *Maud*, is still far from leisurely. Rather than using properties with symbolic intent, Whittier mostly prepares for the story by a remarkable use of prepositions: "*Up* from the meadows," "*Round about* them," "*Over* the mountains." With another step toward the main action, we come back to the first preposition and get it three times more—"*Up* rose old Barbara Frietchie," "She took *up* the flag," "*Up* the street came the rebel tread"—and conclude the sequence with its reverse as Stonewall Jackson appears:

> *Under* his slouched hat left and right
> He glanced; the old flag met his sight.

In eight rapid couplets the flag is fired upon, rescued, and its rescuer defended by the general. In the remaining nine, day ebbs, the two protagonists die, and the poem concludes with an elegiac fitness that contrasts the repose with the earlier action, the evening with the "pleasant morn" that began the story, and the stars of the flag with those of the scene. In this closing couplet the vertical movement of the "up" prepositions is also recalled:

> And ever the stars above look down
> On thy stars below in Frederick town!

The poem has blemishes—why Whittier had to resort to such wooden phrasing to achieve rhyme as "fruited deep" and "royal will" when in the same poem he rhymed "staff" and "scarf" challenges explanation. Nor can I excuse Whittier for attributing to Jackson "a blush of shame," in spite of the later couplet honoring Jackson and the sense that throughout the poem Jackson plays a more interesting part than Barbara Frietchie and emerges the better from it. Yet with its faults, the poem seems to me as fine as any done of a Civil War episode, belonging with Melville's *Sheridan at Cedar Creek* and with no other narrative poem of the war.

Another genre of Whittier does not result in poetry that strikes deeply, but deserves mention because it shows the same sort of workmanlike control that we have seen elsewhere. Certain inscriptive pieces of Whittier show him at his technical best; not particularly personal even when they have a personal background, they omit the emotional sense of his best work. But though lacking impact and offering only public sentiments, they still show a rhetorical balance and metaphorical pointedness that pleasantly surprise. Two may be quoted, one written for the Powers bas-relief of the last Indian and last bison, the other for the sundial of Whittier's friend Bowditch:

> The eagle, stooping from yon snow-blown peaks,
> For the wild hunter and the bison seeks,
> In the changed world below; and finds alone
> Their graven semblance in the eternal stone.
>
> With warning hand I mark Time's rapid flight
> From life's glad morning to its solemn night;
> Yet through the dear God's love, I also show
> There's Light above me by the Shade below.

There are a few others, more extensive and more immediately personal in their occasion. In propriety and wit, *Flowers in Winter: Painted upon a Porte Livre* takes us back to the preceding century. A final one deserves mention as not only successful in itself but as evidence of the closeness between the poet and the common reader in Whittier's generation. This is *To a Cape Ann Schooner*, verses on a fishing boat named in honor of the poet. None of these perhaps deserve places in anthologies, none at least get them; but they serve to remind us that when an artificial occasion is approached without the enervating doubts of art versus life and reform versus beauty, Whittier consistently shows technical accomplishment.

The one poem by which Whittier is almost universally esteemed, even in our reaction against him, remains for consideration. With *Snow-Bound* (p. 77) he reached for once on a large scale that harmony in art which he seems to have achieved during the greater part of his life only in spirit. For this poem belonged to his being as much as *Huckleberry Finn* to Mark Twain's, and we shall not err by regarding it with the same love and honor.

In the *Shelburne Essays* Paul Elmer More touches upon a similarity he perceives in New England's creed and life, both snowbound but both also warmed by the domestic hearth. "Whittier was recalling a true incident of his childhood," he says, "and was writing also an allegory of New England's inner life, when he described that night of storm and snow . . ." Though this remark is a preachment from the poem rather than a full interpretation, More shows greater wisdom than those critics who have followed the subtitle of "A Winter Idyl" too exclusively and valued the poem as a simple image of farm life—realistic if limited, "Flemish pictures of old days" as the poem itself describes the material, but without the fullness of life that a Teniers painted.

It is true that Whittier consciously sought this response, not only using the terms "winter idyl" and "Flemish pictures" but also invoking the recognition of the city businessman dreaming of his boyhood. A substantial part of the poem consists in its pastoralism, which made its special appeal to the reader of a nineteenth-century America that was becoming urban. Perhaps less than the reader realized when the effects of urbanization upon family ties were not so evident as they are now, the picture of a domestic circle had a compelling attraction; and it may indeed have meant much personally to the bachelor author. But though the poem as picture of farm and family life is not to be thrust aside, the larger effect of that picture is what determines its artistic validity.

Beyond the realistic details but arising from them is a symbolic richness that More's statement recognizes, though not in an immediately accurate way. Epigraphs—the woodfire of Cornelius Agrippa that "drives away dark spirits" and the radiant fireplace of Emerson's *Snow Storm* that provides a haven against the cold—make plain the major symbol. The building of the fire on the third night expands it, as does the covering of the fire when the evening ends.

> Sit with me by the homestead hearth,
> And stretch the hands of memory forth
>   To warm them at the wood-fire's blaze!

But if the hearth gives us the major symbol and scene of the central action, the poem does not limit itself to this. So completely has the poet felt his material that all is fused. Even the coat of "homespun stuff" and the "low rhythm" of the ocean in the first strophe take on overtones. Furthermore, the poet shows so much certainty in his use of the fireplace as symbol that he is able to suggest qualification when at the end of the week the family is no longer a unit in its isolation.

> The chill embargo of the snow
> Was melted in the genial glow,

but the glow this time belongs to the world and not the domestic hearth.

The poem has led into this insight—one which prevents it from being disposed of as sentimental—by the mother's prayer for uncomforted strangers and by the summons she receives to help a neighbor. The schoolmaster and the eccentric guest have also furnished preparation in their contrast with the family group. Both represent a culture which though indigenous contrasts with the rustic family's "common unrhymed poetry Of simple life and country ways." Each receives a greater number of lines than any member of the family. The schoolmaster is a kind of Dionysus, bringing culture to the family and giving to classic scenes "all the commonplace of home," while Harriet Livermore rebukes their "homeliness of words and ways." In contrast with "The sharp heat-lightnings of her face," his laughing countenance is lit by the warm light of the woodfire.

Another difference between these two guests helps us to see why Whittier has introduced antislavery sentiment into the poem, matter generally regarded as an excrescence. There are three major passages in which it appears: the first, at the beginning of the characterizations of the family circle when a schoolbook poem that is recited allows digression into the poet's later abolitionist activity; the second, when the schoolmaster is described as the type of those who will lead the postwar settlement of the issue; and the third, in the epilogue, when social responsibilities are contrasted with private reverie. The first passage is most out of context and can only be justified by its shock of surprise and by its later reinforcement. The last passage is stated in terms so general that if we did not see the connection between its closing line ("The century's aloe flowers to-day") and the aloe of the later *Pennsylvania Pilgrim*, its reference to the slavery issue might escape us.

The second passage is the crucial one and explains why the others are not outside the bounds of the poem. The schoolmaster and the eccentric are both of the world and both destined to play an important part in it. One enters into a course that represents a sterile and self-indulgent religious fanaticism, while the other vigorously rights social wrong. Though we may well wish that Whittier had followed Emerson in recognizing the potential self-indulgence of reformers and though the second coming of Christ (which Harriet Livermore prophesied) has more potential significance than the Thirteenth Amendment, we should recognize that for Whittier and most of his contemporaries slavery was the moral issue of the age, "the century's aloe," just as the absolute state is of ours. Even if we differ from his implication that the moral issue must be public or from his choice of this particular issue, we may regard it as a poetical counter that serves its purpose in the poem. Using both the genial glow of the world and its sufferings as countersuggestion to domesticity, Whittier has also modified the idyllic dream for one of "larger hopes and graver fears."

It might be urged against the poem that the elegiac meditations, which like the antislavery passages appear on three occasions, are excrescences too. That so far as I know they have not been thus regarded makes a direct defense unnecessary. But they may help us to see how intensely the poem is organized. Though upon two occasions they come just before the antislavery lines (a juxtaposition that has its point), we have even less right to dismiss them as clichés of nineteenth-century emotion. The central intent of the poem is not to memorialize a way of life (whether agrarian or domestic) that has been lost to an urban world, but rather to memorialize life that is always lost to death. As he concludes the scene of the laying of the fire, the poet exuberantly exclaims:

> Blow high, blow low, not all its snow
> Could quench our hearth-fire's ruddy glow.

This couplet he then follows with an apostrophaic lament, "O Time and Change! . . . The voices of that hearth are still," with its conclusion

> That Life is ever lord of Death,
> And Love can never lose its own!

Of these lines the whole poem constitutes a thoughtful, deeply felt, and beautifully modulated expression. If they sound a bit orotund, that effect does not mar the poem as a whole with its "homespun stuff" and "low rhythm." As the epigraph reads, the "Good Spirits, which be Angels of Light, are augmented not only by the Divine light of the Sun, but also by our common VVood Fire." In the cold of a New England winter and in the dark of death, Whittier's wood fire gives illumination and comfort.

Thirty years ago in one of its many apologies for the American muse, the *Cambridge History of American Literature* said what it could for our poet: "But no American who lived in the shadow of slavery and internecine strife, none who grew to manhood in the generation succeeding those epic days, would dream of measuring his love and veneration for Whittier by the scale of absolute art." Even for those upon whose lives the Civil War did not touch, this defense has pertinence. We should continue to think of Whittier as an important man in history and as a noble man in his own right. But we should also remember him as sometimes a poet by a most exacting scale.

BIRCHBROOK MILL

A noteless stream, the Birchbrook runs
  Beneath its leaning trees;
That low, soft ripple is its own,
  That dull roar is the sea's.

Of human signs it sees alone
  The distant church spire's tip,
And, ghost-like, on a blank of gray,
  The white sail of a ship.

No more a toiler at the wheel,
  It wanders at its will;   10
Nor dam nor pond is left to tell
  Where once was Birchbrook mill.

The timbers of that mill have fed
  Long since a farmer's fires;
His doorsteps are the stones that ground
  The harvest of his sires.

Man trespassed here; but Nature lost
  No right of her domain;
She waited, and she brought the old
  Wild beauty back again.   20

By day the sunlight through the leaves
  Falls on its moist, green sod,
And wakes the violet bloom of spring
  And autumn's golden-rod.

Its birches whisper to the wind,
  The swallow dips her wings
In the cool spray, and on its banks
  The gray song-sparrow sings.

But from it, when the dark night falls,
  The school-girl shrinks with dread;   30
The farmer, home-bound from his fields,
  Goes by with quickened tread.

They dare not pause to hear the grind
 Of shadowy stone on stone;
The plashing of a water-wheel
 Where wheel there now is none.

Has not a cry of pain been heard
 Above the clattering mill?
The pawing of an unseen horse,
 Who waits his mistress still?   40

Yet never to the listener's eye
 Has sight confirmed the sound;
A wavering birch line marks alone
 The vacant pasture ground.

No ghostly arms fling up to heaven
 The agony of prayer;
No spectral steed impatient shakes
 His white mane on the air.

The meaning of that common dread
 No tongue has fitly told;   50
The secret of the dark surmise
 The brook and birches hold.

What nameless horror of the past
 Broods here forevermore?
What ghost his unforgiven sin
 Is grinding o'er and o'er?

Does, then, immortal memory play
 The actor's tragic part,
Rehearsals of a mortal life
 And unveiled human heart?   60

God's pity spare a guilty soul
 That drama of its ill,
And let the scenic curtain fall
 On Birchbrook's haunted mill!

THE PENNSYLVANIA PILGRIM

Hail to posterity!
Hail, future men of Germanopolis!
　　Let the young generations yet to be
　　Look kindly upon this.
Think how your fathers left their native land,—
　　Dear German-land! O sacred hearths and homes!—
　　And, where the wild beast roams,
　　　　In patience planned
New forest-homes beyond the mighty sea,
　　There undisturbed and free　　　　　　　　　　10
To live as brothers of one family.
　　What pains and cares befell,
　　　　What trials and what fears,
Remember, and wherein we have done well
　　Follow our footsteps, men of coming years!
　　Where we have failed to do
　　　　Aright, or wisely live,
Be warned by us, the better way pursue,
And, knowing we were human, even as you,
　　　　Pity us and forgive!　　　　　　　　　　20
　　Farewell, Posterity!
　　Farewell, dear Germany!
　　Forevermore farewell!

PRELUDE

I sing the Pilgrim of a softer clime
　　And milder speech than those brave men's who brought
To the ice and iron of our winter time
　　A will as firm, a creed as stern, and wrought
　　With one mailed hand, and with the other fought.
Simply, as fits my theme, in homely rhyme
　　I sing the blue-eyed German Spener taught,　　　30
Through whose veiled, mystic faith the Inward Light,
　　Steady and still, an easy brightness, shone,
Transfiguring all things in its radiance white.
The garland which his meekness never sought
　　I bring him; over fields of harvest sown

With seeds of blessing, now to ripeness grown,
I bid the sower pass before the reapers' sight.

———

Never in tenderer quiet lapsed the day
From Pennsylvania's vales of spring away,
Where, forest-walled, the scattered hamlets lay   40

Along the wedded rivers. One long bar
Of purple cloud, on which the evening star
Shone like a jewel on a scimitar,

Held the sky's golden gateway. Through the deep
Hush of the woods a murmur seemed to creep,
The Schuylkill whispering in a voice of sleep.

All else was still. The oxen from their ploughs
Rested at last, and from their long day's browse
Came the dun files of Krisheim's home-bound cows.

And the young city, round whose virgin zone   50
The rivers like two mighty arms were thrown,
Marked by the smoke of evening fires alone,

Lay in the distance, lovely even then
With its fair women and its stately men
Gracing the forest court of William Penn,

Urban yet sylvan; in its rough-hewn frames
Of oak and pine the dryads held their claims,
And lent its streets their pleasant woodland names.

Anna Pastorius down the leafy lane
Looked city-ward, then stooped to prune again   60
Her vines and simples, with a sigh of pain.

For fast the streaks of ruddy sunset paled
In the oak clearing, and, as daylight failed,
Slow, overhead, the dusky night-birds sailed.

Again she looked: between green walls of shade,
With low-bent head as if with sorrow weighed,
Daniel Pastorius slowly came and said,

"God's peace be with thee, Anna!" Then he stood
Silent before her, wrestling with the mood
Of one who sees the evil and not good.   70

"What is it, my Pastorius?" As she spoke,
A slow, faint smile across his features broke,
Sadder than tears. "Dear heart," he said, "our folk

"Are even as others. Yea, our goodliest Friends
Are frail; our elders have their selfish ends,
And few dare trust the Lord to make amends

"For duty's loss. So even our feeble word
For the dumb slaves the startled meeting heard
As if a stone its quiet waters stirred;

"And, as the clerk ceased reading, there began   80
A ripple of dissent which downward ran
In widening circles, as from man to man.

"Somewhat was said of running before sent,
Of tender fear that some their guide outwent,
Troublers of Israel. I was scarce intent

"On hearing, for behind the reverend row
Of gallery Friends, in dumb and piteous show,
I saw, methought, dark faces full of woe.

"And, in the spirit, I was taken where
They toiled and suffered; I was made aware   90
Of shame and wrath and anguish and despair!

"And while the meeting smothered our poor plea
With cautious phrase, a Voice there seemed to be,
'As ye have done to these ye do to me!'

"So it all passed; and the old tithe went on
Of anise, mint, and cumin, till the sun
Set, leaving still the weightier work undone.

"Help, for the good man faileth! Who is strong,
If these be weak? Who shall rebuke the wrong,
If these consent? How long, O Lord! how long!"   100

He ceased; and, bound in spirit with the bound,
With folded arms, and eyes that sought the ground,
Walked musingly his little garden round.

About him, beaded with the falling dew,
Rare plants of power and herbs of healing grew,
Such as Van Helmont and Agrippa knew.

For, by the lore of Gorlitz' gentle sage,
With the mild mystics of his dreamy age
He read the herbal signs of nature's page,

As once he heard in sweet Von Merlau's bowers   110
Fair as herself, in boyhood's happy hours,
The pious Spener read his creed in flowers.

"The dear Lord give us patience!" said his wife,
Touching with finger-tip an aloe, rife
With leaves sharp-pointed like an Aztec knife

Or Carib spear, a gift to William Penn
From the rare gardens of John Evelyn,
Brought from the Spanish Main by merchantmen.

"See this strange plant its steady purpose hold,
And, year by year, its patient leaves unfold,   120
Till the young eyes that watched it first are old.

"But some time, thou hast told me, there shall come
A sudden beauty, brightness, and perfume;
The century-moulded bud shall burst in bloom.

"So may the seed which hath been sown to-day
Grow with the years, and, after long delay,
Break into bloom, and God's eternal Yea

"Answer at last the patient prayers of them
Who now, by faith alone, behold its stem
Crowned with the flowers of Freedom's diadem.   130

"Meanwhile, to feel and suffer, work and wait,
Remains for us. The wrong indeed is great,
But love and patience conquer soon or late."

"Well hast thou said, my Anna!" Tenderer
Than youth's caress upon the head of her
Pastorius laid his hand. "Shall we demur

"Because the vision tarrieth? In an hour
We dream not of, the slow-grown bud may flower,
And what was sown in weakness rise in power!"

Then through the vine-draped door whose legend read, 140
"Procul este profani!" Anna led
To where their child upon his little bed

Looked up and smiled. "Dear heart," she said, "if we
Must bearers of a heavy burden be,
Our boy, God willing, yet the day shall see

"When from the gallery to the farthest seat,
Slave and slave-owner shall no longer meet,
But all sit equal at the Master's feet."

On the stone hearth the blazing walnut block
Set the low walls a-glimmer, showed the cock   150
Rebuking Peter on the Van Wyck clock,

Shone on old tomes of law and physic, side
By side with Fox and Behmen, played at hide
And seek with Anna, amidst her household pride

Of flaxen webs, and on the table, bare
Of costly cloth or silver cup, but where,
Tasting the fat shads of the Delaware,

The courtly Penn had praised the good-wife's cheer,
And quoted Horace o'er her home-brewed beer,
Till even grave Pastorius smiled to hear.   160

In such a home, beside the Schuylkill's wave,
He dwelt in peace with God and man, and gave
Food to the poor and shelter to the slave.

For all too soon the New World's scandal shamed
The righteous code by Penn and Sidney framed,
And men withheld the human rights they claimed.

And slowly wealth and station sanction lent,
And hardened avarice, on its gains intent,
Stifled the inward whisper of dissent.

Yet all the while the burden rested sore   170
On tender hearts. At last Pastorius bore
Their warning message to the Church's door

In God's name; and the leaven of the word
Wrought ever after in the souls who heard,
And a dead conscience in its grave-clothes stirred

To troubled life, and urged the vain excuse
Of Hebrew custom, patriarchal use,
Good in itself if evil in abuse.

Gravely Pastorius listened, not the less
Discerning through the decent fig-leaf dress   180
Of the poor plea its shame of selfishness.

One Scripture rule, at least, was unforgot;
He hid the outcast, and bewrayed him not;
And, when his prey the human hunter sought,

He scrupled not, while Anna's wise delay
And proffered cheer prolonged the master's stay,
To speed the black guest safely on his way.

Yet who shall guess his bitter grief who lends
His life to some great cause, and finds his friends
Shame or betray it for their private ends?   190

How felt the Master when his chosen strove
In childish folly for their seats above;
And that fond mother, blinded by her love,

Besought him that her sons, beside his throne,
Might sit on either hand? Amidst his own
A stranger oft, companionless and lone,

God's priest and prophet stands. The martyr's pain
Is not alone from scourge and cell and chain;
Sharper the pang when, shouting in his train,

His weak disciples by their lives deny   200
The loud hosannas of their daily cry,
And make their echo of his truth a lie.

His forest home no hermit's cell he found,
Guests, motley-minded, drew his hearth around,
And held armed truce upon its neutral ground.

There Indian chiefs with battle-bows unstrung,
Strong, hero-limbed, like those whom Homer sung,
Pastorius fancied, when the world was young,

Came with their tawny women, lithe and tall,
Like bronzes in his friend Von Rodeck's hall,   210
Comely, if black, and not unpleasing all.

There hungry folk in homespun drab and gray
Drew round his board on Monthly Meeting day,
Genial, half merry in their friendly way,

Or, haply, pilgrims from the Fatherland,
Weak, timid, homesick, slow to understand
The New World's promise, sought his helping hand.

Or painful Kelpius from his hermit den
By Wissahickon, maddest of good men,
Dreamed o'er the Chiliast dreams of Petersen.   220

Deep in the woods, where the small river slid
Snake-like in shade, the Helmstadt Mystic hid,
Weird as a wizard, over arts forbid,

Reading the books of Daniel and of John,
And Behmen's Morning-Redness, through the Stone
Of Wisdom, vouchsafed to his eyes alone,

Whereby he read what man ne'er read before,
And saw the visions man shall see no more,
Till the great angel, striding sea and shore,

Shall bid all flesh await, on land or ships,   230
The warning trump of the Apocalypse,
Shattering the heavens before the dread eclipse.

Or meek-eyed Mennonist his bearded chin
Leaned o'er the gate; or Ranter, pure within,
Aired his perfection in a world of sin.

Or, talking of old home scenes, Op der Graaf
Teased the low back-log with his shodden staff,
Till the red embers broke into a laugh

And dance of flame, as if they fain would cheer
The rugged face, half tender, half austere,   240
Touched with the pathos of a homesick tear!

Or Sluyter, saintly familist, whose word
As law the Brethren of the Manor heard,
Announced the speedy terrors of the Lord,

And turned, like Lot at Sodom, from his race,
Above a wrecked world with complacent face
Riding secure upon his plank of grace!

Haply, from Finland's birchen groves exiled,
Manly in thought, in simple ways a child,
His white hair floating round his visage mild,   250

The Swedish pastor sought the Quaker's door,
Pleased from his neighbor's lips to hear once more
His long-disused and half-forgotten lore.

For both could baffle Babel's lingual curse,
And speak in Bion's Doric, and rehearse
Cleanthes' hymn or Virgil's sounding verse.

And oft Pastorius and the meek old man
Argued as Quaker and as Lutheran,
Ending in Christian love, as they began.

With lettered Lloyd on pleasant morns he strayed   260
Where Sommerhausen over vales of shade
Looked miles away, by every flower delayed,

Or song of bird, happy and free with one
Who loved, like him, to let his memory run
Over old fields of learning, and to sun

Himself in Plato's wise philosophies,
And dream with Philo over mysteries
Whereof the dreamer never finds the keys;

To touch all themes of thought, nor weakly stop
For doubt of truth, but let the buckets drop   270
Deep down and bring the hidden waters up.

For there was freedom in that wakening time
Of tender souls; to differ was not crime;
The varying bells made up the perfect chime.

On lips unlike was laid the altar's coal,
The white, clear light, tradition-colored, stole
Through the stained oriel of each human soul.

Gathered from many sects, the Quaker brought
His old beliefs, adjusting to the thought
That moved his soul the creed his fathers taught.   280

One faith alone, so broad that all mankind
Within themselves its secret witness find,
The soul's communion with the Eternal Mind,

The Spirit's law, the Inward Rule and Guide,
Scholar and peasant, lord and serf, allied,
The polished Penn and Cromwell's Ironside.

As still in Hemskerck's Quaker Meeting, face
By face in Flemish detail, we may trace
How loose-mouthed boor and fine ancestral grace

Sat in close contrast,—the clipt-headed churl,   290
Broad market-dame, and simple serving-girl
By skirt of silk and periwig in curl!

For soul touched soul; the spiritual treasure-trove
Made all men equal, none could rise above
Nor sink below that level of God's love.

So, with his rustic neighbors sitting down,
The homespun frock beside the scholar's gown,
Pastorius to the manners of the town

Added the freedom of the woods, and sought
The bookless wisdom by experience taught, 300
And learned to love his new-found home, while not

Forgetful of the old; the seasons went
Their rounds, and somewhat to his spirit lent
Of their own calm and measureless content.

Glad even to tears, he heard the robin sing
His song of welcome to the Western spring,
And bluebird borrowing from the sky his wing.

And when the miracle of autumn came,
And all the woods with many-colored flame
Of splendor, making summer's greenness tame, 310

Burned, unconsumed, a voice without a sound
Spake to him from each kindled bush around,
And made the strange, new landscape holy ground!

And when the bitter north-wind, keen and swift,
Swept the white street and piled the door-yard drift,
He exercised, as Friends might say, his gift

Of verse, Dutch, English, Latin, like the hash
Of corn and beans in Indian succotash;
Dull, doubtless, but with here and there a flash

Of wit and fine conceit,—the good man's play 320
Of quiet fancies, meet to while away
The slow hours measuring off an idle day.

At evening, while his wife put on her look
Of love's endurance, from its niche he took
The written pages of his ponderous book,

And read, in half the languages of man,
His "Rusca Apium," which with bees began,
And through the gamut of creation ran.

Or, now and then, the missive of some friend
In gray Altorf or storied Nürnberg penned 330
Dropped in upon him like a guest to spend

The night beneath his roof-tree. Mystical
The fair Von Merlau spake as waters fall
And voices sound in dreams, and yet withal

Human and sweet, as if each far, low tone,
Over the roses of her gardens blown
Brought the warm sense of beauty all her own.

Wise Spener questioned what his friend could trace
Of spiritual influx or of saving grace
In the wild natures of the Indian race.   340

And learned Schurmberg, fain, at times, to look
From Talmud, Koran, Veds, and Pentateuch,
Sought out his pupil in his far-off nook,

To query with him of climatic change,
Of bird, beast, reptile, in his forest range,
Of flowers and fruits and simples new and strange.

And thus the Old and New World reached their hands
Across the water, and the friendly lands
Talked with each other from their severed strands.

Pastorius answered all: while seed and root   350
Sent from his new home grew to flower and fruit
Along the Rhine and at the Spessart's foot;

And, in return, the flowers his boyhood knew
Smiled at his door, the same in form and hue,
And on his vines the Rhenish clusters grew.

No idler he; whoever else might shirk,
He set his hand to every honest work,—
Farmer and teacher, court and meeting clerk.

Still on the town seal his device is found,
Grapes, flax, and thread-spool on a trefoil ground,   360
With "Vinum, Linum et Textrinum" wound.

One house sufficed for gospel and for law,
Where Paul and Grotius, Scripture text and saw,
Assured the good, and held the rest in awe.

Whatever legal maze he wandered through,
He kept the Sermon on the Mount in view,
And justice always into mercy grew.

No whipping-post he needed, stocks, nor jail,
Nor ducking-stool; the orchard-thief grew pale
At his rebuke, the vixen ceased to rail,   370

The usurer's grasp released the forfeit land;
The slanderer faltered at the witness-stand,
And all men took his counsel for command.

Was it caressing air, the brooding love
Of tenderer skies than German land knew of,
Green calm below, blue quietness above,

Still flow of water, deep repose of wood
That, with a sense of loving Fatherhood
And childlike trust in the Eternal Good,

Softened all hearts, and dulled the edge of hate,   380
Hushed strife, and taught impatient zeal to wait
The slow assurance of the better state?

Who knows what goadings in their sterner way
O'er jagged ice, relieved by granite gray,
Blew round the men of Massachusetts Bay?

What hate of heresy the east-wind woke?
What hints of pitiless power and terror spoke
In waves that on their iron coast-line broke?

Be it as it may: within the Land of Penn
The sectary yielded to the citizen,   390
And peaceful dwelt the many-creeded men.

Peace brooded over all. No trumpet stung
The air to madness, and no steeple flung
Alarums down from bells at midnight rung.

The land slept well. The Indian from his face
Washed all his war-paint off, and in the place
Of battle-marches sped the peaceful chase,

Or wrought for wages at the white man's side,—
Giving to kindness what his native pride
And lazy freedom to all else denied.　　　　　　400

And well the curious scholar loved the old
Traditions that his swarthy neighbors told
By wigwam-fires when nights were growing cold,

Discerned the fact round which their fancy drew
Its dreams, and held their childish faith more true
To God and man than half the creeds he knew.

The desert blossomed round him; wheat-fields rolled
Beneath the warm wind waves of green and gold;
The planted ear returned its hundred-fold.

Great clusters ripened in a warmer sun　　　　　410
Than that which by the Rhine stream shines upon
The purpling hillsides with low vines o'errun.

About each rustic porch the humming-bird
Tried with light bill, that scarce a petal stirred,
The Old World flowers to virgin soil transferred;

And the first-fruits of pear and apple, bending
The young boughs down, their gold and russet blending,
Made glad his heart, familiar odors lending

To the fresh fragrance of the birch and pine,
Life-everlasting, bay, and eglantine,　　　　　　420
And all the subtle scents the woods combine.

Fair First-Day mornings, steeped in summer calm,
Warm, tender, restful, sweet with woodland balm,
Came to him, like some mother-hallowed psalm

To the tired grinder at the noisy wheel
Of labor, winding off from memory's reel
A golden thread of music. With no peal

Of bells to call them to the house of praise,
The scattered settlers through green forest-ways
Walked meeting-ward. In reverent amaze　　　　430

The Indian trapper saw them, from the dim
Shade of the alders on the rivulet's rim,
Seek the Great Spirit's house to talk with Him.

There, through the gathered stillness multiplied
And made intense by sympathy, outside
The sparrows sang, and the gold-robin cried,

A-swing upon his elm. A faint perfume
Breathed through the open windows of the room
From locust-trees, heavy with clustered bloom.

Thither, perchance, sore-tried confessors came, 440
Whose fervor jail nor pillory could tame,
Proud of the cropped ears meant to be their shame,

Men who had eaten slavery's bitter bread
In Indian isles; pale women who had bled
Under the hangman's lash, and bravely said

God's message through their prison's iron bars;
And gray old soldier-converts, seamed with scars
From every stricken field of England's wars.

Lowly before the Unseen Presence knelt
Each waiting heart, till haply some one felt 450
On his moved lips the seal of silence melt

Or, without spoken words, low breathings stole
Of a diviner life from soul to soul,
Baptizing in one tender thought the whole.

When shaken hands announced the meeting o'er,
The friendly group still lingered at the door,
Greeting, inquiring, sharing all the store

Of weekly tidings. Meanwhile youth and maid
Down the green vistas of the woodland strayed,
Whispered and smiled and oft their feet delayed. 460

Did the boy's whistle answer back the thrushes?
Did light girl laughter ripple through the bushes,
As brooks make merry over roots and rushes?

Unvexed the sweet air seemed. Without a wound
The ear of silence heard, and every sound
Its place in nature's fine accordance found.

And solemn meeting, summer sky and wood,
Old kindly faces, youth and maidenhood
Seemed, like God's new creation, very good!

And, greeting all with quiet smile and word,   470
Pastorius went his way. The unscared bird
Sang at his side; scarcely the squirrel stirred

At his hushed footstep on the mossy sod;
And, wheresoe'er the good man looked or trod,
He felt the peace of nature and of God.

His social life wore no ascetic form,
He loved all beauty, without fear of harm,
And in his veins his Teuton blood ran warm.

Strict to himself, of other men no spy,
He made his own no circuit-judge to try   480
The freer conscience of his neighbors by.

With love rebuking, by his life alone,
Gracious and sweet, the better way was shown,
The joy of one, who, seeking not his own,

And faithful to all scruples, finds at last
The thorns and shards of duty overpast,
And daily life, beyond his hope's forecast,

Pleasant and beautiful with sight and sound
And flowers upspringing in its narrow round,
And all his days with quiet gladness crowned.   490

He sang not; but if sometimes tempted strong,
He hummed what seemed like Altorf's Burschen-song,
His good wife smiled and did not count it wrong.

For well he loved his boyhood's brother-band;
His Memory, while he trod the New World's strand,
A double ganger walked the Fatherland!

If, when on frosty Christmas eves the light
Shone on his quiet hearth, he missed the sight
Of Yule-log, Tree, and Christ-child all in white;

And closed his eyes, and listened to the sweet
Old wait-songs sounding down his native street,
And watched again the dancers' mingling feet;

Yet not the less, when once the vision passed,
He held the plain and sober maxims fast
Of the dear Friends with whom his lot was cast.

Still all attuned to nature's melodies
He loved the bird's song in his dooryard trees,
And the low hum of home-returning bees;

The blossomed flax, the tulip-trees in bloom
Down the long street, the beauty and perfume
Of apple-boughs, the mingling light and gloom

Of Sommerhausen's woodlands, woven through
With sun-threads; and the music the wind drew,
Mournful and sweet, from leaves it overblew.

And evermore, beneath this outward sense,
And through the common sequence of events,
He felt the guiding hand of Providence

Reach out of space. A Voice spake in his ear,
And lo! all other voices far and near
Died at that whisper, full of meanings clear.

The Light of Life shone round him; one by one
The wandering lights, that all-misleading run,
Went out like candles paling in the sun.

That Light he followed, step by step, where'er
It led, as in the vision of the seer
The wheels moved as the spirit in the clear

And terrible crystal moved, with all their eyes
Watching the living splendor sink or rise,
Its will their will, knowing no otherwise.

500

510

520

Within himself he found the law of right,   530
He walked by faith and not the letter's sight,
And read his Bible by the Inward Light.

And if sometimes the slaves of form and rule,
Frozen in their creeds like fish in winter's pool,
Tried the large tolerance of his liberal school,

His door was free to men of every name,
He welcomed all the seeking souls who came,
And no man's faith he made a cause of blame.

But best he loved in leisure hours to see
His own dear Friends sit by him knee to knee,   540
In social converse, genial, frank, and free.

There sometimes silence (it were hard to tell
Who owned it first) upon the circle fell,
Hushed Anna's busy wheel, and laid its spell

On the black boy who grimaced by the hearth,
To solemnize his shining face of mirth;
Only the old clock ticked amidst the dearth

Of sound; nor eye was raised nor hand was stirred
In that soul-sabbath, till at last some word
Of tender counsel or low prayer was heard.   550

Then guests, who lingered but farewell to say
And take love's message, went their homeward way;
So passed in peace the guileless Quaker's day.

His was the Christian's unsung Age of Gold,
A truer idyl than the bards have told
Of Arno's banks or Arcady of old.

Where still the Friends their place of burial keep,
And century-rooted mosses o'er it creep,
The Nürnberg scholar and his helpmeet sleep.

And Anna's aloe? if it flowered at last   560
In Bartram's garden, did John Woolman cast
A glance upon it as he meekly passed?

And did a secret sympathy possess
That tender soul, and for the slave's redress
Lend hope, strength, patience? It were vain to guess.

Nay, were the plant itself but mythical,
Set in the fresco of tradition's wall
Like Jotham's bramble, mattereth not at all.

Enough to know that, through the winter's frost
And summer's heat, no seed of truth is lost,   570
And every duty pays at last its cost.

For, ere Pastorius left the sun and air,
God sent the answer to his life-long prayer;
The child was born beside the Delaware,

Who, in the power a holy purpose lends,
Guided his people unto nobler ends,
And left them worthier of the name of Friends.

And lo! the fulness of the time has come,
And over all the exile's Western home,
From sea to sea the flowers of freedom bloom!   580

And joy-bells ring, and silver trumpets blow;
But not for thee, Pastorius! Even so
The world forgets, but the wise angels know.

ICHABOD

So fallen! so lost! the light withdrawn
    Which once he wore!
The glory from his gray hairs gone
    Forevermore!

Revile him not, the Tempter hath
    A snare for all;
And pitying tears, not scorn and wrath,
    Befit his fall!

Oh, dumb be passion's stormy rage,
    When he who might   10
Have lighted up and led his age,
    Falls back in night.

Scorn! would the angels laugh, to mark
    A bright soul driven,
Fiend-goaded, down the endless dark,
    From hope and heaven!

Let not the land once proud of him
    Insult him now,
Nor brand with deeper shame his dim,
    Dishonored brow.   20

But let its humbled sons, instead,
    From sea to lake,
A long lament, as for the dead,
    In sadness make.

Of all we loved and honored, naught
    Save power remains;
A fallen angel's pride of thought,
    Still strong in chains.

All else is gone; from those great eyes
    The soul has fled: 30
When faith is lost, when honor dies,
    The man is dead!

Then, pay the reverence of old days
    To his dead fame;
Walk backward, with averted gaze,
    And hide the shame!

SKIPPER IRESON'S RIDE

Of all the rides since the birth of time,
Told in story or sung in rhyme,—
On Apuleius's Golden Ass,
Or one-eyed Calender's horse of brass,

Witch astride of a human back,
Islam's prophet on Al-Borák,—
The strangest ride that ever was sped
Was Ireson's, out from Marblehead!
  Old Floyd Ireson, for his hard heart,
    Tarred and feathered and carried in a cart   10
      By the women of Marblehead!

Body of turkey, head of owl,
Wings a-droop like a rained-on fowl,
Feathered and ruffled in every part,
Skipper Ireson stood in the cart.
Scores of women, old and young,
Strong of muscle, and glib of tongue,
Pushed and pulled up the rocky lane,
Shouting and singing the shrill refrain:
  "Here's Flud Oirson, fur his horrd horrt,   20
    Torr'd an' futherr'd an' corr'd in a corrt
      By the women o' Morble'ead!"

Wrinkled scolds with hands on hips,
Girls in bloom of cheek and lips,
Wild-eyed, free-limbed, such as chase
Bacchus round some antique vase,
Brief of skirt, with ankles bare,
Loose of kerchief and loose of hair,
With conch-shells blowing and fish-horns' twang,
Over and over the Mænads sang: 30
  "Here's Flud Oirson, fur his horrd horrt,
    Torr'd an' futherr'd an' corr'd in a corrt
      By the women o' Morble'ead!"

Small pity for him!—He sailed away
From a leaking ship in Chaleur Bay,—
Sailed away from a sinking wreck,
With his own town's-people on her deck!
"Lay by! lay by!" they called to him.
Back he answered, "Sink or swim!
Brag of your catch of fish again!"   40
And off he sailed through the fog and rain!
  Old Floyd Ireson, for his hard heart,
    Tarred and feathered and carried in a cart
      By the women of Marblehead!

Fathoms deep in dark Chaleur
That wreck shall lie forevermore.
Mother and sister, wife and maid,
Looked from the rocks of Marblehead
Over the moaning and rainy sea,—
Looked for the coming that might not be!   *50*
What did the winds and the sea-birds say
Of the cruel captain who sailed away?—
    Old Floyd Ireson, for his hard heart,
    Tarred and feathered and carried in a cart
    By the women of Marblehead!

Through the street, on either side,
Up flew windows, doors swung wide;
Sharp-tongued spinsters, old wives gray,
Treble lent the fish-horn's bray.
Sea-worn grandsires, cripple-bound,   *60*
Hulks of old sailors run aground,
Shook head, and fist, and hat, and cane,
And cracked with curses the hoarse refrain:
    "Here's Flud Oirson, fur his horrd horrt,
    Torr'd an' futherr'd an' corr'd in a corrt
    By the women o' Morble'ead!"

Sweetly along the Salem road
Bloom of orchard and lilac showed.
Little the wicked skipper knew
Of the fields so green and the sky so blue.   *70*
Riding there in his sorry trim,
Like an Indian idol glum and grim,
Scarcely he seemed the sound to hear
Of voices shouting, far and near:
    "Here's Flud Oirson, fur his horrd horrt,
    Torr'd an' futherr'd an' corr'd in a corrt
    By the women o' Morble'ead!"

"Hear me, neighbors!" at last he cried,—
"What to me is this noisy ride?
What is the shame that clothes the skin   *80*
To the nameless horror that lives within?
Waking or sleeping, I see a wreck,
And hear a cry from a reeling deck!

Hate me and curse me,—I only dread
The hand of God and the face of the dead!"
  Said old Floyd Ireson, for his hard heart,
  Tarred and feathered and carried in a cart
    By the women of Marblehead!

Then the wife of the skipper lost at sea
Said, "God has touched him! why should we!"   90
Said an old wife mourning her only son,
"Cut the rogue's tether and let him run!"
So with soft relentings and rude excuse,
Half scorn, half pity, they cut him loose,
And gave him a cloak to hide him in,
And left him alone with his shame and sin.
  Poor Floyd Ireson, for his hard heart,
  Tarred and feathered and carried in a cart
    By the women of Marblehead!

MAUD MULLER

Maud Muller on a summer's day
Raked the meadow sweet with hay.

Beneath her torn hat glowed the wealth
Of simple beauty and rustic health.

Singing, she wrought, and her merry glee
The mock-bird echoed from his tree.

But when she glanced to the far-off town,
White from its hill-slope looking down,

The sweet song died, and a vague unrest
And a nameless longing filled her breast,—   10

A wish that she hardly dared to own,
For something better than she had known.

The Judge rode slowly down the lane,
Smoothing his horse's chestnut mane.

He drew his bridle in the shade
Of the apple-trees, to greet the maid,

And asked a draught from the spring that flowed
Through the meadow across the road.

She stooped where the cool spring bubbled up,
And filled for him her small tin cup,   20

And blushed as she gave it, looking down
On her feet so bare, and her tattered gown.

"Thanks!" said the Judge; "a sweeter draught
From a fairer hand was never quaffed."

He spoke of the grass and flowers and trees,
Of the singing birds and the humming bees;

Then talked of the haying, and wondered whether
The cloud in the west would bring foul weather.

And Maud forgot her brier-torn gown,
And her graceful ankles bare and brown;   30

And listened, while a pleased surprise
Looked from her long-lashed hazel eyes.

At last, like one who for delay
Seeks a vain excuse, he rode away.

Maud Muller looked and sighed: "Ah me!
That I the Judge's bride might be!

"He would dress me up in silks so fine,
And praise and toast me at his wine.

"My father should wear a broadcloth coat;
My brother should sail a painted boat.   40

"I'd dress my mother so grand and gay,
And the baby should have a new toy each day.

"And I'd feed the hungry and clothe the poor,
And all should bless me who left our door."

The Judge looked back as he climbed the hill,
And saw Maud Muller standing still.

"A form more fair, a face more sweet,
Ne'er hath it been my lot to meet.

"And her modest answer and graceful air
Show her wise and good as she is fair. 50

"Would she were mine, and I to-day,
Like her, a harvester of hay;

"No doubtful balance of rights and wrongs,
Nor weary lawyers with endless tongues,

"But low of cattle and song of birds,
And health and quiet and loving words."

But he thought of his sisters, proud and cold,
And his mother, vain of her rank and gold.

So, closing his heart, the Judge rode on,
And Maud was left in the field alone. 60

But the lawyers smiled that afternoon,
When he hummed in court an old love-tune;

And the young girl mused beside the well
Till the rain on the unraked clover fell.

He wedded a wife of richest dower,
Who lived for fashion, as he for power.

Yet oft, in his marble hearth's bright glow,
He watched a picture come and go;

And sweet Maud Muller's hazel eyes
Looked out in their innocent surprise. 70

Oft, when the wine in his glass was red,
He longed for the wayside well instead;

And closed his eyes on his garnished rooms
To dream of meadows and clover-blooms.

And the proud man sighed, with a secret pain,
"Ah, that I were free again!

"Free as when I rode that day,
Where the barefoot maiden raked her hay."

She wedded a man unlearned and poor,
And many children played round her door. 80

But care and sorrow, and childbirth pain,
Left their traces on heart and brain.

And oft, when the summer sun shone hot
On the new-mown hay in the meadow lot,

And she heard the little spring brook fall
Over the roadside, through the wall,

In the shade of the apple-tree again
She saw a rider draw his rein;

And, gazing down with timid grace,
She felt his pleased eyes read her face. 90

Sometimes her narrow kitchen walls
Stretched away into stately halls;

The weary wheel to a spinnet turned,
The tallow candle an astral burned,

And for him who sat by the chimney lug,
Dozing and grumbling o'er pipe and mug,

A manly form at her side she saw,
And joy was duty and love was law.

Then she took up her burden of life again,
Saying only, "It might have been."   100

Alas for maiden, alas for Judge,
For rich repiner and household drudge!

God pity them both! and pity us all,
Who vainly the dreams of youth recall.

For of all sad words of tongue or pen,
The saddest are these: "It might have been!"

Ah, well! for us all some sweet hope lies
Deeply buried from human eyes;

And, in the hereafter, angels may
Roll the stone from its grave away!   110

BARBARA FRIETCHIE

Up from the meadows rich with corn,
Clear in the cool September morn,

The clustered spires of Frederick stand
Green-walled by the hills of Maryland.

Round about them orchards sweep,
Apple and peach tree fruited deep,

Fair as the garden of the Lord
To the eyes of the famished rebel horde,

On that pleasant morn of the early fall
When Lee marched over the mountain-wall;   10

Over the mountains winding down,
Horse and foot, into Frederick town.

Forty flags with their silver stars,
Forty flags with their crimson bars,

Flapped in the morning wind: the sun
Of noon looked down, and saw not one.

Up rose old Barbara Frietchie then,
Bowed with her fourscore years and ten;

Bravest of all in Frederick town,
She took up the flag the men hauled down; 20

In her attic window the staff she set,
To show that one heart was loyal yet.

Up the street came the rebel tread,
Stonewall Jackson riding ahead.

Under his slouched hat left and right
He glanced; the old flag met his sight.

"Halt!"—the dust-brown ranks stood fast.
"Fire!"—out blazed the rifle-blast.

It shivered the window, pane and sash;
It rent the banner with seam and gash. 30

Quick, as it fell, from the broken staff
Dame Barbara snatched the silken scarf.

She leaned far out on the window-sill,
And shook it forth with a royal will.

"Shoot, if you must, this old gray head,
But spare your country's flag," she said.

A shade of sadness, a blush of shame,
Over the face of the leader came;

The nobler nature within him stirred
To life at that woman's deed and word; 40

"Who touches a hair of yon gray head
Dies like a dog! March on!" he said.

All day long through Frederick street
Sounded the tread of marching feet:

All day long that free flag tost
Over the heads of the rebel host.

Ever its torn folds rose and fell
On the loyal winds that loved it well,

And through the hill-gaps sunset light
Shone over it with a warm good-night.   50

Barbara Frietchie's work is o'er,
And the Rebel rides on his raids no more.

Honor to her! and let a tear
Fall, for her sake, on Stonewall's bier.

Over Barbara Frietchie's grave,
Flag of Freedom and Union, wave!

Peace and order and beauty draw
Round thy symbol of light and law;

And ever the stars above look down
On thy stars below in Frederick town!   60

SNOW–BOUND

A WINTER IDYL

"As the Spirit of Darkness be stronger in the dark, so Good Spirits, which be Angels of Light, are augmented not only by the Divine light of the Sun, but also by our common VVood Fire: and as the Celestial Fire drives away dark spirits, so also this our Fire of VVood doth the same."—Cor. Agrippa, *Occult Philosophy*, Book I. ch. v.

"Announced by all the trumpets of the sky,
Arrives the snow, and, driving o'er the fields,
Seems nowhere to alight: the whited air
Hides hills and woods, the river and the heaven,
And veils the farm-house at the garden's end.

The sled and traveller stopped, the courier's feet
Delayed, all friends shut out, the housemates sit
Around the radiant fireplace, enclosed
In a tumultuous privacy of Storm."

              EMERSON, *The Snow Storm.*

The sun that brief December day
Rose cheerless over hills of gray,
And, darkly circled, gave at noon
A sadder light than waning moon.
Slow tracing down the thickening sky
Its mute and ominous prophecy,
A portent seeming less than threat,
It sank from sight before it set.
A chill no coat, however stout,
Of homespun stuff could quite shut out,   10
A hard, dull bitterness of cold,
That checked, mid-vein, the circling race
Of life-blood in the sharpened face,
The coming of the snow-storm told.
The wind blew east; we heard the roar
Of Ocean on his wintry shore,
And felt the strong pulse throbbing there
Beat with low rhythm our inland air.

Meanwhile we did our nightly chores,
Brought in the wood from out of doors,   20
Littered the stalls, and from the mows
Raked down the herd's-grass for the cows:
Heard the horse whinnying for his corn;
And, sharply clashing horn on horn,
Impatient down the stanchion rows
The cattle shake their walnut bows;
While, peering from his early perch
Upon the scaffold's pole of birch,
The cock his crested helmet bent
And down his querulous challenge sent.   30

Unwarmed by any sunset light
The gray day darkened into night,
A night made hoary with the swarm
And whirl-dance of the blinding storm,

As zigzag, wavering to and fro,
Crossed and recrossed the wingèd snow:
And ere the early bedtime came
The white drift piled the window-frame,
And through the glass the clothes-line posts
Looked in like tall and sheeted ghosts.   40

So all night long the storm roared on:
The morning broke without a sun;
In tiny spherule traced with lines
Of Nature's geometric signs,
In starry flake, and pellicle,
All day the hoary meteor fell;
And, when the second morning shone,
We looked upon a world unknown,
On nothing we could call our own.
Around the glistening wonder bent   50
The blue walls of the firmament,
No cloud above, no earth below,—
A universe of sky and snow!
The old familiar sights of ours
Took marvellous shapes; strange domes and towers
Rose up where sty or corn-crib stood,
Or garden-wall, or belt of wood;
A smooth white mound the brush-pile showed,
A fenceless drift what once was road;
The bridle-post an old man sat   60
With loose-flung coat and high cocked hat;
The well-curb had a Chinese roof;
And even the long sweep, high aloof,
In its slant splendor, seemed to tell
Of Pisa's leaning miracle.

A prompt, decisive man, no breath
Our father wasted: "Boys, a path!"
Well pleased (for when did farmer boy
Count such a summons less than joy?)
Our buskins on our feet we drew;   70
With mittened hands, and caps drawn low,
To guard our necks and ears from snow,
We cut the solid whiteness through.
And, where the drift was deepest, made

A tunnel walled and overlaid
With dazzling crystal: we had read
Of rare Aladdin's wondrous cave,
And to our own his name we gave,
With many a wish the luck were ours
To test his lamp's supernal powers.   80
We reached the barn with merry din,
And roused the prisoned brutes within.
The old horse thrust his long head out,
And grave with wonder gazed about;
The cock his lusty greeting said,
And forth his speckled harem led;
The oxen lashed their tails, and hooked,
And mild reproach of hunger looked;
The hornèd patriarch of the sheep,
Like Egypt's Amun roused from sleep,   90
Shook his sage head with gesture mute,
And emphasized with stamp of foot.

All day the gusty north-wind bore
The loosening drift its breath before;
Low circling round its southern zone,
The sun through dazzling snow-mist shone.
No church-bell lent its Christian tone
To the savage air, no social smoke
Curled over woods of snow-hung oak.
A solitude made more intense   100
By dreary-voicèd elements,
The shrieking of the mindless wind,
The moaning tree-boughs swaying blind,
And on the glass the unmeaning beat
Of ghostly finger-tips of sleet.
Beyond the circle of our hearth
No welcome sound of toil or mirth
Unbound the spell, and testified
Of human life and thought outside.
We minded that the sharpest ear   110
The buried brooklet could not hear.
The music of whose liquid lip
Had been to us companionship,
And, in our lonely life, had grown
To have an almost human tone.

As night drew on, and, from the crest
Of wooded knolls that ridged the west,
The sun, a snow-blown traveller, sank
From sight beneath the smothering bank,
We piled, with care, our nightly stack   120
Of wood against the chimney-back,—
The oaken log, green, huge, and thick,
And on its top the stout back-stick;
The knotty forestick laid apart,
And filled between with curious art
The ragged brush; then, hovering near,
We watched the first red blaze appear,
Heard the sharp crackle, caught the gleam
On whitewashed wall and sagging beam,
Until the old, rude-furnished room   130
Burst, flower-like, into rosy bloom;
While radiant with a mimic flame
Outside the sparkling drift became,
And through the bare-boughed lilac-tree
Our own warm hearth seemed blazing free.
The crane and pendent trammels showed,
The Turk's heads on the andirons glowed;
While childish fancy, prompt to tell
The meaning of the miracle,
Whispered the old rhyme: "*Under the tree,*   140
When fire outdoors burns merrily,
There the witches are making tea."
The moon above the eastern wood
Shone at its full; the hill-range stood
Transfigured in the silver flood,
Its blown snows flashing cold and keen,
Dead white, save where some sharp ravine
Took shadow, or the sombre green
Of hemlocks turned to pitchy black
Against the whiteness at their back.   150
For such a world and such a night
Most fitting that unwarming light,
Which only seemed where'er it fell
To make the coldness visible.

Shut in from all the world without,
We sat the clean-winged hearth about,

Content to let the north-wind roar
In baffled rage at pane and door,
While the red logs before us beat
The frost-line back with tropic heat;   160
And ever, when a louder blast
Shook beam and rafter as it passed,
The merrier up its roaring draught
The great throat of the chimney laughed;
The house-dog on his paws outspread
Laid to the fire his drowsy head,
The cat's dark silhouette on the wall
A couchant tiger's seemed to fall;
And, for the winter fireside meet,
Between the andirons' straddling feet,   170
The mug of cider simmered slow,
The apples sputtered in a row,
And, close at hand, the basket stood
With nuts from brown October's wood.

What matter how the night behaved?
What matter how the north-wind raved?
Blow high, blow low, not all its snow
Could quench our hearth-fire's ruddy glow.
O Time and Change!—with hair as gray
As was my sire's that winter day,   180
How strange it seems, with so much gone
Of life and love, to still live on!
Ah, brother! only I and thou
Are left of all that circle now,—
The dear home faces whereupon
That fitful firelight paled and shone.
Henceforward, listen as we will,
The voices of that hearth are still;
Look where we may, the wide earth o'er,
Those lighted faces smile no more.   190
We tread the paths their feet have worn,
    We sit beneath their orchard trees,
    We hear, like them, the hum of bees
And rustle of the bladed corn;
We turn the pages that they read,
    Their written words we linger o'er.
But in the sun they cast no shade,

No voice is heard, no sign is made,
   No step is on the conscious floor!
Yet Love will dream, and Faith will trust   200
(Since He who knows our need is just),
That somehow, somewhere, meet we must.
Alas for him who never sees
The stars shine through his cypress-trees!
Who, hopeless, lays his dead away,
Nor looks to see the breaking day
Across the mournful marbles play!
Who hath not learned, in hours of faith,
   The truth to flesh and sense unknown,
That Life is ever lord of Death,   210
   And Love can never lose its own!

We sped the time with stories old,
Wrought puzzles out, and riddles told,
Or stammered from our school-book lore
"The Chief of Gambia's golden shore."
How often since, when all the land
Was clay in Slavery's shaping hand,
As if a far-blown trumpet stirred
The languorous sin-sick air, I heard:
"Does not the voice of reason cry,   220
   Claim the first right which Nature gave,
From the red scourge of bondage fly,
   Nor deign to live a burdened slave!"
Our father rode again his ride
On Memphremagog's wooded side;
Sat down again to moose and samp
In trapper's hut and Indian camp;
Lived o'er the old idyllic ease
Beneath St. François' hemlock-trees;
Again for him the moonlight shone   230
On Norman cap and bodiced zone;
Again he heard the violin play
Which led the village dance away,
And mingled in its merry whirl
The grandam and the laughing girl.
Or, nearer home, our steps he led
Where Salisbury's level marshes spread
   Mile-wide as flies the laden bee;

Where merry mowers, hale and strong,
Swept, scythe on scythe, their swaths along   240
     The low green prairies of the sea.
We shared the fishing off Boar's Head,
     And round the rocky Isles of Shoals
     The hake-broil on the drift-wood coals;
The chowder on the sand-beach made,
Dipped by the hungry, steaming hot,
With spoons of clam-shell from the pot.
We heard the tales of witchcraft old,
And dream and sign and marvel told
To sleepy listeners as they lay   250
Stretched idly on the salted hay,
Adrift along the winding shores,
When favoring breezes deigned to blow
The square sail of the gundelow
And idle lay the useless oars.

Our mother, while she turned her wheel
Or run the new-knit stocking-heel,
Told how the Indian hordes came down
At midnight on Cocheco town,
And how her own great-uncle bore   260
His cruel scalp-mark to fourscore.
Recalling, in her fitting phrase,
     So rich and picturesque and free
     (The common unrhymed poetry
Of simple life and country ways),
The story of her early days,—
She made us welcome to her home;
Old hearths grew wide to give us room;
We stole with her a frightened look
At the gray wizard's conjuring-book,   270
The fame whereof went far and wide
Through all the simple country side;
We heard the hawks at twilight play,
The boat-horn on Piscataqua,
The loon's weird laughter far away;
We fished her little trout-brook, knew
What flowers in wood and meadow grew,
What sunny hillsides autumn-brown
She climbed to shake the ripe nuts down,

Saw where in sheltered cove and bay   *280*
The ducks' black squadron anchored lay,
And heard the wild-geese calling loud
Beneath the gray November cloud.
Then, haply, with a look more grave,
And soberer tone, some tale she gave
From painful Sewel's ancient tome,
Beloved in every Quaker home,
Of faith fire-winged by martyrdom,
Or Chalkley's Journal, old and quaint,—
Gentlest of skippers, rare sea-saint!—   *290*
Who, when the dreary calms prevailed,
And water-butt and bread-cask failed,
And cruel, hungry eyes pursued
His portly presence, mad for food,
With dark hints muttered under breath
Of casting lots for life or death,
Offered, if Heaven withheld supplies,
To be himself the sacrifice.
Then, suddenly, as if to save
The good man from his living grave,   *300*
A ripple on the water grew,
A school of porpoise flashed in view.
"Take, eat," he said, "and be content;
These fishes in my stead are sent
By Him who gave the tangled ram
To spare the child of Abraham."

Our uncle, innocent of books,
Was rich in lore of fields and brooks,
The ancient teachers never dumb
Of Nature's unhoused lyceum.   *310*
In moons and tides and weather wise,
He read the clouds as prophecies,
And foul or fair could well divine,
By many an occult hint and sign,
Holding the cunning-warded keys
To all the woodcraft mysteries;
Himself to Nature's heart so near
That all her voices in his ear
Of beast or bird had meanings clear,
Like Apollonius of old,   *320*

Who knew the tales the sparrows told,
Or Hermes, who interpreted
What the sage cranes of Nilus said;
A simple, guileless, childlike man,
Content to live where life began;
Strong only on his native grounds,
The little world of sights and sounds
Whose girdle was the parish bounds,
Whereof his fondly partial pride
The common features magnified,   330
As Surrey hills to mountains grew
In White of Selborne's loving view,—
He told how teal and loon he shot,
And how the eagle's eggs he got,
The feats on pond and river done,
The prodigies of rod and gun;
Till, warming with the tales he told,
Forgotten was the outside cold,
The bitter wind unheeded blew,
From ripening corn the pigeons flew,   340
The partridge drummed i' the wood, the mink
Went fishing down the river-brink.
In fields with bean or clover gay,
The woodchuck, like a hermit gray,
    Peered from the doorway of his cell;
The muskrat plied the mason's trade,
And tier by tier his mud-walls laid;
And from the shagbark overhead
    The grizzled squirrel dropped his shell.

Next, the dear aunt, whose smile of cheer   350
And voice in dreams I see and hear,—
The sweetest woman ever Fate
Perverse denied a household mate,
Who, lonely, homeless, not the less
Found peace in love's unselfishness,
And welcome wheresoe'er she went,
A calm and gracious element,
Whose presence seemed the sweet income
And womanly atmosphere of home,—
Called up her girlhood memories,   360
The huskings and the apple-bees,

The sleigh-rides and the summer sails,
Weaving through all the poor details
And homespun warp of circumstance
A golden woof-thread of romance.
For well she kept her genial mood
And simple faith of maidenhood;
Before her still a cloud-land lay,
The mirage loomed across her way;
The morning dew, that dries so soon   370
With others, glistened at her noon;
Through years of toil and soil and care,
From glossy tress to thin gray hair,
All unprofaned she held apart
The virgin fancies of the heart.
Be shame to him of woman born
Who hath for such but thought of scorn.

There, too, our elder sister plied
Her evening task the stand beside;
A full, rich nature, free to trust,   380
Truthful and almost sternly just,
Impulsive, earnest, prompt to act,
And make her generous thought a fact,
Keeping with many a light disguise
The secret of self-sacrifice.
O heart sore-tried! thou hast the best
That Heaven itself could give thee,—rest,
Rest from all bitter thoughts and things!
    How many a poor one's blessing went
    With thee beneath the low green tent   390
Whose curtain never outward swings!

As one who held herself a part
Of all she saw, and let her heart
    Against the household bosom lean,
Upon the motley-braided mat
Our youngest and our dearest sat,
Lifting her large, sweet, asking eyes,
    Now bathed in the unfading green
And holy peace of Paradise.
Oh, looking from some heavenly hill,   400
    Or from the shade of saintly palms,
    Or silver reach of river calms,

Do those large eyes behold me still?
With me one little year ago :—
The chill weight of the winter snow
   For months upon her grave has lain;
And now, when summer south-winds blow
   And brier and harebell bloom again,
I tread the pleasant paths we trod,
I see the violet-sprinkled sod   410
Whereon she leaned, too frail and weak
The hillside flowers she loved to seek,
Yet following me where'er I went
With dark eyes full of love's content.
The birds are glad; the brier-rose fills
The air with sweetness; all the hills
Stretch green to June's unclouded sky;
But still I wait with ear and eye
For something gone which should be nigh,
A loss in all familiar things,   420
In flower that blooms, and bird that sings.
And yet, dear heart! remembering thee,
   Am I not richer than of old?
Safe in thy immortality,
     What change can reach the wealth I hold?
     What chance can mar the pearl and gold
Thy love hath left in trust with me?
And while in life's late afternoon,
   Where cool and long the shadows grow,
I walk to meet the night that soon   430
   Shall shape and shadow overflow,
I cannot feel that thou art far,
Since near at need the angels are;
And when the sunset gates unbar,
   Shall I not see thee waiting stand,
And, white against the evening star,
   The welcome of thy beckoning hand?

Brisk wielder of the birch and rule,
The master of the district school
Held at the fire his favored place,   440
Its warm glow lit a laughing face
Fresh-hued and fair, where scarce appeared
The uncertain prophecy of beard.

He teased the mitten-blinded cat,
Played cross-pins on my uncle's hat,
Sang songs, and told us what befalls
In classic Dartmouth's college halls.
Born the wild Northern hills among,
From whence his yeoman father wrung
By patient toil subsistence scant,   *450*
Not competence and yet not want,
He early gained the power to pay
His cheerful, self-reliant way;
Could doff at ease his scholar's gown
To peddle wares from town to town;
Or through the long vacation's reach
In lonely lowland districts teach,
Where all the droll experience found
At stranger hearths in boarding round,
The moonlit skater's keen delight,   *460*
The sleigh-drive through the frosty night,
The rustic party, with its rough
Accompaniment of blind-man's-buff,
And whirling-plate, and forfeits paid,
His winter task a pastime made.
Happy the snow-locked homes wherein
He tuned his merry violin,
Or played the athlete in the barn,
Or held the good dame's winding-yarn,
Or mirth-provoking versions told   *470*
Of classic legends rare and old,
Wherein the scenes of Greece and Rome
Had all the commonplace of home,
And little seemed at best the odds
'Twixt Yankee pedlers and old gods;
Where Pindus-born Arachthus took
The guise of any grist-mill brook,
And dread Olympus at his will
Became a huckleberry hill.

A careless boy that night he seemed;   *480*
  But at his desk he had the look
And air of one who wisely schemed,
  And hostage from the future took
  In trainèd thought and lore of book.

Large-brained, clear-eyed, of such as he
Shall Freedom's young apostles be,
Who, following in War's bloody trail,
Shall every lingering wrong assail;
All chains from limb and spirit strike,
Uplift the black and white alike;　　　490
Scatter before their swift advance
The darkness and the ignorance,
The pride, the lust, the squalid sloth,
Which nurtured Treason's monstrous growth,
Made murder pastime, and the hell
Of prison-torture possible;
The cruel lie of caste refute,
Old forms remould, and substitute
For Slavery's lash the freeman's will,
For blind routine, wise-handed skill;　　　500
A school-house plant on every hill,
Stretching in radiate nerve-lines thence
The quick wires of intelligence;
Till North and South together brought
Shall own the same electric thought,
In peace a common flag salute,
And, side by side in labor's free
And unresentful rivalry,
Harvest the fields wherein they fought.

Another guest that winter night　　　510
Flashed back from lustrous eyes the light.
Unmarked by time, and yet not young,
The honeyed music of her tongue
And words of meekness scarcely told
A nature passionate and bold,
Strong, self-concentred, spurning guide,
Its milder features dwarfed beside
Her unbent will's majestic pride.
She sat among us, at the best,
A not unfeared, half-welcome guest,　　　520
Rebuking with her cultured phrase
Our homeliness of words and ways.
A certain pard-like, treacherous grace
Swayed the lithe limbs and dropped the lash,
Lent the white teeth their dazzling flash;

And under low brows, black with night,
Rayed out at times a dangerous light;
The sharp heat-lightnings of her face
Presaging ill to him whom Fate
Condemned to share her love or hate.   530
A woman tropical, intense
In thought and act, in soul and sense,
She blended in a like degree
The vixen and the devotee,
Revealing with each freak or feint
The temper of Petruchio's Kate,
The raptures of Siena's saint.
Her tapering hand and rounded wrist
Had facile power to form a fist;
The warm, dark languish of her eyes   540
Was never safe from wrath's surprise.
Brows saintly calm and lips devout
Knew every change of scowl and pout;
And the sweet voice had notes more high
And shrill for social battle-cry.

Since then what old cathedral town
Has missed her pilgrim staff and gown,
What convent-gate has held its lock
Against the challenge of her knock!
Through Smyrna's plague-hushed thoroughfares,   550
Up sea-set Malta's rocky stairs,
Gray olive slopes of hills that hem
Thy tombs and shrines, Jerusalem,
Or startling on her desert throne
The crazy Queen of Lebanon
With claims fantastic as her own,
Her tireless feet have held their way;
And still, unrestful, bowed, and gray,
She watches under Eastern skies,
    With hope each day renewed and fresh,   560
    The Lord's quick coming in the flesh,
Whereof she dreams and prophesies!

Where'er her troubled path may be,
    The Lord's sweet pity with her go!
The outward wayward life we see,
    The hidden springs we may not know.

Nor is it given us to discern
    What threads the fatal sisters spun,
    Through what ancestral years has run
The sorrow with the woman born,   570
What forged her cruel chain of moods,
What set her feet in solitudes,
    And held the love within her mute,
What mingled madness in the blood,
    A life-long discord and annoy,
    Water of tears with oil of joy,
And hid within the folded bud
    Perversities of flower and fruit.
It is not ours to separate
The tangled skein of will and fate,   580
To show what metes and bounds should stand
Upon the soul's debatable land,
And between choice and Providence
Divide the circle of events;
But He who knows our frame is just,
Merciful and compassionate,
And full of sweet assurances
And hope for all the language is,
That He remembereth we are dust!

At last the great logs, crumbling low,   590
Sent out a dull and duller glow,
The bull's-eye watch that hung in view,
Ticking its weary circuit through,
Pointed with mutely warning sign
Its black hand to the hour of nine.
That sign the pleasant circle broke:
My uncle ceased his pipe to smoke,
Knocked from its bowl the refuse gray
And laid it tenderly away;
Then roused himself to safely cover   600
The dull red brands with ashes over.
And while, with care, our mother laid
The work aside, her steps she stayed
One moment, seeking to express
Her grateful sense of happiness
For food and shelter, warmth and health,
And love's contentment more than wealth,

With simple wishes (not the weak,
Vain prayers which no fulfilment seek,
But such as warm the generous heart,   610
O'er-prompt to do with Heaven its part)
That none might lack, that bitter night,
For bread and clothing, warmth and light.

Within our beds awhile we heard
The wind that round the gables roared,
With now and then a ruder shock,
Which made our very bedsteads rock.
We heard the loosened clapboards tost,
The board-nails snapping in the frost;
And on us, through the unplastered wall,   620
Felt the light sifted snow-flakes fall.
But sleep stole on, as sleep will do
When hearts are light and life is new;
Faint and more faint the murmurs grew,
Till in the summer-land of dreams
They softened to the sound of streams,
Low stir of leaves, and dip of oars,
And lapsing waves on quiet shores.

Next morn we wakened with the shout
    Of merry voices high and clear;   630
    And saw the teamsters drawing near
To break the drifted highways out.
Down the long hillside treading slow
We saw the half-buried oxen go,
Shaking the snow from heads uptost,
Their straining nostrils white with frost.
Before our door the straggling train
Drew up, an added team to gain.
The elders threshed their hands a-cold,
    Passed, with the cider-mug, their jokes   640
    From lip to lip; the younger folks
Down the loose snow-banks, wrestling rolled,
Then toiled again the cavalcade
    O'er windy hill, through clogged ravine,
    And woodland paths that wound between
Low drooping pine-boughs winter-weighed.
From every barn a team afoot,

At every house a new recruit,
Where, drawn by Nature's subtlest law,
Haply the watchful young men saw   *650*
Sweet doorway pictures of the curls
And curious eyes of merry girls,
Lifting their hands in mock defence
Against the snow-ball's compliments,
And reading in each missive tost
The charm with Eden never lost.

We heard once more the sleigh-bells' sound;
    And, following where the teamsters led,
The wise old Doctor went his round,
Just pausing at our door to say,   *660*
In the brief autocratic way
Of one who, prompt at Duty's call
Was free to urge her claim on all,
    That some poor neighbor sick abed
At night our mother's aid would need.
For, one in generous thought and deed
    What mattered in the sufferer's sight
    The Quaker matron's inward light,
The Doctor's mail of Calvin's creed?
All hearts confess the saints elect   *670*
    Who, twain in faith, in love agree,
And melt not in an acid sect
    The Christian pearl of charity!

So days went on: a week had passed
Since the great world was heard from last.
The Almanac we studied o'er,
Read and reread our little store
Of books and pamphlets, scarce a score;
One harmless novel, mostly hid
From younger eyes, a book forbid,   *680*
And poetry (or good or bad,
A single book was all we had),
Where Ellwood's meek, drab-skirted Muse,
    A stranger to the heathen Nine,
    Sang, with a somewhat nasal whine,
The wars of David and the Jews.
At last the floundering carrier bore

The village paper to our door.
Lo! broadening outward as we read,
To warmer zones the horizon spread;   690
In panoramic length unrolled
We saw the marvels that it told.
Before us passed the painted Creeks,
    And daft McGregor on his raids
    In Costa Rica's everglades.
And up Taygetos winding slow
Rode Ypsilanti's Mainote Greeks,
A Turk's head at each saddle-bow!
Welcome to us its week-old news,
Its corner for the rustic Muse,   700
    Its monthly gauge of snow and rain,
Its record, mingling in a breath
The wedding bell and dirge of death:
Jest, anecdote, and love-lorn tale,
The latest culprit sent to jail;
Its hue and cry of stolen and lost,
Its vendue sales and goods at cost,
    And traffic calling loud for gain.
We felt the stir of hall and street,
The pulse of life that round us beat;   710
The chill embargo of the snow
Was melted in the genial glow;
Wide swung again our ice-locked door,
And all the world was ours once more!

Clasp, Angel of the backward look
    And folded wings of ashen gray
    And voice of echoes far away,
The brazen covers of thy book;
The weird palimpsest old and vast,
Wherein thou hid'st the spectral past;   720
Where, closely mingling, pale and glow
The characters of joy and woe;
The monographs of outlived years,
Or smile-illumed or dim with tears,
    Green hills of life that slope to death,
And haunts of home, whose vistaed trees
Shade off to mournful cypresses,
    With the white amaranths underneath.

Even while I look, I can but heed
   The restless sands' incessant fall,   730
Importunate hours that hours succeed
Each clamorous with its own sharp need,
   And duty keeping pace with all.
Shut down and clasp the heavy lids;
I hear again the voice that bids
The dreamer leave his dream midway
For larger hopes and graver fears:
Life greatens in these later years,
The century's aloe flowers to-day!

Yet, haply, in some lull of life,   740
Some Truce of God which breaks its strife,
The worldling's eyes shall gather dew,
   Dreaming in throngful city ways
Of winter joys his boyhood knew;
And dear and early friends—the few
Who yet remain—shall pause to view
   These Flemish pictures of old days;
Sit with me by the homestead hearth
And stretch the hands of memory forth
   To warm them at the wood-fire's blaze!   750
And thanks untraced to lips unknown
Shall greet me like the odors blown
From unseen meadows newly mown,
Or lilies floating in some pond,
Wood-fringed, the wayside gaze beyond;
The traveller owns the grateful sense
Of sweetness near, he knows not whence,
And, pausing, takes with forehead bare
The benediction of the air.

Holmes

A superficially good case for Oliver Wendell Holmes as a metaphysical poet could be made from critical dicta upon him. "Instead of ideality," a nineteenth-century writer says, "he gives us conceits that are often apt, often graceful, and often, it must be added, pushed too far." At about the same time Leslie Stephen wrote that *The Chambered Nautilus* did not quite touch him as it should because it seemed too "ingenious." In 1931 a critic complained, "His fancy was too fertile; images rushed in upon him in overwhelming numbers."

Some of Holmes' own remarks may likewise appear to warrant his classification as a metaphysical. Among miscellaneous literary notes at the back of one of his casebooks in the 1840's is the entry: "Attempting to write poetry like Herbert's or Donne's." What Holmes said on imagery also shows him close to some of the metaphysical techniques. "To fix the image all unveiled and warm" had been set as the highest poetic purpose in his Metrical Essay of 1836. In the preface of his collected poems of the same year, he had defended extravagance and hyperbole: ". . . a metrical arabesque of a storm or a summer, if its images, though hyperbolical, are conceivable, and consistent with each other, is a perfectly healthy and natural exercise of the imagination, and not, as some might think, a voluntary degradation of its office." Though one will not find either unveiled or far-fetched images abounding in the poetry, one does meet them on nearly every page of the prose. Donne's famous comparison of the lovers with the legs of a compass certainly creates an analogy of no more shocking disparates than does Holmes' comparison of the poet and the goose: "A poet, like the goose, sails without visible landmarks to unexplored regions of truth, which philosophy has yet to lay down on its atlas. The philosopher gets his tracks by observation; the poet trusts to his inner sense, and makes the straighter and swifter line."

It will be rightly answered that no matter what the disparity of lovers and compasses or poets and geese, Donne makes an analogy on many levels with a subtlety that Holmes lacks. Such a distinction was appropriately recognized by S. I. Hayakawa when he first pointed out metaphysical affinities in Holmes. But Holmes does have genuine elements of metaphysical technique, which as this essay will suggest we have not recognized enough.

Perhaps *The Two Streams* (p. 115) shows as well as any poem Holmes' achievement and shortcoming in this mode. As I have written elsewhere at greater length, the poem results from a perceptive line of poetic inquiry that began when Holmes found the image of the separating waters at the Continental Divide "running loose in my mind, without a halter" and that ended only when he finally worked out his "lesson for the day" in *The Professor at the Breakfast-Table.* Holmes picked up the image from a setting in the Andes, but there the waters could run only to the Atlantic or Pacific. Dissatisfied with that either-or choice, he transferred his scene to the Canadian Rockies, where the eastward stream first flows toward the Atlantic and is then diverted to the Arctic. But the effect of the change does not emerge in the earlier part of the poem:

> Yon stream, whose sources run
> Turned by a pebble's edge,
> Is Athabasca, rolling toward the sun
> Through the cleft mountain-ledge.

Thus in the second stanza of the poem, the Athabasca is rolling toward the sun, which both of itself and in context with the third stanza suggests an eastward course to the Atlantic. Such is the impression which the reader holds as he continues through the fourth stanza and begins the fifth:

> So from the heights of Will
> Life's parting stream descends,
> And, as a moment turns its slender rill,
> Each widening torrent bends,—

> From the same cradle's side,
> From the same mother's knee,—

If he responds conventionally to the poet's language, he tentatively identifies the eastward direction of "life's parting stream" with the better course. It is "toward the sun" and has not *strayed* "to evening's ocean." But out of this complacent reading of Holmes' "illustration of the will" he is suddenly shocked:

> One to long darkness and the frozen tide,
> One to the Peaceful Sea!

The values are reversed. The westward stream has passed through "the tangled braid Of foam-flecked Oregon" to the serenity of the Pacific; and the Athabasca has changed from sunlight to cold night.

Holmes has given his poem a sense of perverse complexity which we might expect from an admirer of metaphysical poetry. Yet he has not written with all, or even the essential, qualities of Donne. The analogy between the Continental Divide and a decision (whether from a free or predetermined will) was far from unsuspected in Holmes' day, as a contemporary charge of plagiarism makes plain. The epithets (for the wall, "rocky"; for the rill, twice "slender") are, though exact, conventional; and the tone is declamatory. Nature remains disparate from man, as the materials are didacticized by the heavy-handed "*So* from the heights of Will" in the final stanzas. Though the verses have complexity, it is that of poetic wit rather than poetic imagination. On this subject Holmes had observed: "[Wit] throws a single ray, separated from the rest,—red, yellow, blue, or any intermediate shade,—upon an object; never white light; that is the province of wisdom . . . Poetry uses the rainbow tints for special effects, but always keeps its essential object in the purest white light of truth." The threefold distinction about wit, wisdom, and poetry that Holmes makes here has pertinence.

Though Holmes is not a metaphysical poet, and even if many will qualify his metaphysical aspect more than has been done here, there can be little doubt that Holmes agrees with the neometaphysicals of our day in his impatient regard for romanticism. Partly his disdain was that of the writer of humorous verse for sentimental excess. Early in his career he wrote the ballad of *The Spectre Pig* as a riposte against the "spectre horse" of the senior Dana's *Buccaneer*. In *The Autocrat* papers he had his fun with melodrama:

> When the poor hero flounders in despair,
> Some dear lost uncle turns up millionaire,
> Clasps the young scapegrace with paternal joy,
> Sobs on his neck, "*My boy!* MY BOY!! MY BOY!!!"

A half-dozen years later the amusing *Sea Dialogue* disposed of poetic rapture, inflated vocabulary, and patronage of the working classes in a half-hundred sparkling lines. At other times, with so much occasional verse that called for popular sentiments, Holmes himself slipped into sentimentality more easily than these attacks on it would suggest. But as in his familiar verse he holds pathos in check with humor, in his occasional poems he often redeems sentimentality from excess. The consciously bathetic ending of one of his class poems ("*Hic jacet* Joe. *Hic jacet* Bill.") is a case in point. In his tribute to the wealthy philanthropist George Peabody he begins:

> Bankrupt! our pockets inside out!
> Empty of words to speak his praises!

And with this extravagantly modest opening provides ballast for the ballooning praise that follows.

But Holmes goes well beyond disdain of the maudlin in his attacks on romanticism. His Phi Beta Kappa poem of 1843 shows him at his most outspoken against the transcendentalists:

> . . . their "many-sided" man,—
> A weak eclectic, groping vague and dim,
> Whose every angle is a half-starved whim,
> Blind as a mole and curious as a lynx,
> Who rides a beetle, which he calls a "Sphinx."
>
> Deluded infants! will they ever know
> Some doubts must darken o'er the world below,
> Though all the Platos of the nursery trail
> Their "clouds of glory" at the go-cart's tail?

As Eleanor M. Tilton, his most recent and best biographer, has said, "At the moments when his contemporaries were discovering Wordsworth and Emerson, Holmes was dissecting cadavers, thumping tuberculous chests, reading physiology, and writing prescriptions." But one still feels that whatever Holmes' activities during the period of romantic-transcendental ferment, his nature would never have permitted him to become more than a sympathetic observer.

Upon two notable occasions Holmes did become such a sympathetic observer. In the early 1850's he delivered a series of lectures at the Lowell Institute on the British romantic poets. He did not like what he had said well enough to publish it, and the collection of newspaper reports by a later scholar makes plain that the approach was a combination of biography and quotation revealing Holmes largely out of touch with his subjects. Apparently unwilling to attack directly, he implied reservations. As the biographer of Emerson, however, Holmes is more happy in his role of observer. Reservations also appeared in this book, which Holmes —rather to the surprise of his contemporaries—undertook in the years immediately following Emerson's death. But the work is not so unsatisfactory as the traditional animosity of Holmes to transcendentalism prepared its early and later readers to believe. It does not pretend to present Emerson definitively, but only in so far as he was useful and valid to men of Holmes' own cast of mind. Since the book gave much pleasure to Henry Adams, it at least need not cause all the rest of us extreme unhappiness.

Though it gave him pleasure, Adams wanted more, and of a sort that Holmes would have been unwilling to offer: an incisive chapter on Emerson's limitations. In asking for this he wrote, "I fear that Emerson, with all his immortal longings and oneness with nature, could not have returned such a compliment [as your book] in kind." But in his journals Emerson, now no longer alive to return it, had anticipated the compliment from Holmes. There he wrote from time to time: "Holmes came out late in life, with a strong sustained growth for two or three years, like old pear trees which have done nothing for ten years, and at last begin and grow great." "Holmes's poem was a bright sparkle . . ." "Wendell Holmes hits right . . . by his instinct at obeying a just perception of what *is* important, instead of feeling about how he shall get some verses together on the subject." "Really catholic, more catholic than Lowell." "A sharp taste for a fact, instead of a blur of a word." A romantic, Emerson saw the admirable quality in Holmes, just as Holmes—neoclassical, empiric, a self-confessed Philistine—saw it in Emerson. Emerson has left no extensive impression of Holmes' poetry as Holmes did in his chapter on Emerson's poetry in the biography, and when he put down most of these passages in the journal he was thinking of the man and his prose. Yet the poetry he had somewhat in mind too: the sharp taste for fact, the just perception, the catholicity are present in the verses as surely though not as generously as in the prose. And in so far as Holmes' poetry had metaphysical traits, Emerson would have seen in it something common with his own.

We find the sharp taste for fact in many of our poet's images. These are not quite what Emerson called for in his essay on the poet: logrolling, stumps and their politics, fisheries, the northern trade, the southern planting, the western clearing. Holmes is not the national, but the provincial poet. A descendant of Anne Bradstreet, a reader of Cotton Mather, he displays a New England homeliness, a Puritan familiarity with household detail. It is a pity that he could not have known the Colonial poet Edward Taylor (also a physician), with his spinning wheels, bowling alleys, coaches, and sugar cakes. Seldom achieving—or seeking—a grandiosity of conception, when Holmes looks for it he does not search among grandiose materials. Even his two best serious poems, *The Living Temple* and *The Chambered Nautilus*, are based upon materials becoming to a naturalist.

A good contrast with contemporary treatment of a poetic image is provided by *The Ship of State*, a "sentiment" that Holmes read at a Fourth of July celebration in 1877. Using a stock image that Longfellow had made famous thirty years before and that countless orators had drawn upon, he candidly examines particulars:

> But still she rocks a little, it is true,
> And there *are* passengers whose faces white
> Show they don't feel as happy as they might;

> Yet on the whole her crew are quite content,
> Since its wild fury the typhoon has spent,
> And willing, if her pilot thinks it best,
> To head a little nearer south by west.

This is more pawky than poetical, though the end of the poem with its generalities in relation to the earlier details shows modest achievement. Rather close in mood are the witty but sophomoric successes of such earlier poems as *Evening: By a Tailor*.

> Day has put on his jacket, and around
> His burning bosom buttoned it with stars.

Yet all this shows a metaphorical liveliness, and there are examples with more finish, as the youthful visions that are "Gone, like tenants that quit without warning, Down the back entry of time" and the genre pictures of *My Aunt* and *Dorothy Q.* An interesting poem, and one that seems generally overlooked, is *The Peau de Chagrin of State Stret* (p. 115). The title glances back at Balzac's novel with its word play on *chagrin* as shagreen and grief. Holmes writes his poem about bonds and coupons, with a nicely handled extension into human mortality. In the first stanza the allusion is open:

> While the eight per cent it gives
> And the rate at which one lives
> Correspond!

The last stanza more subtly centers in the ironic use of "investment" as a financial transaction and as clothing or integument.

The homely muse of our poet (a "verbicide" that he perhaps would have liked) intimately relates with his character. Outside of literature he dealt with things in the same spirit, whether the hand-stereoscope that he invented or the cadavers that he neatly dissected. "It is a sin for a puny little fellow like me to mutilate one of your six-foot men as if he were a sheep,—but *vive la science!*" When he looked around him, we find healthy skepticism in his estimate and self-awareness in his relationships. Indians? "The story of one red ant is the story of all red ants." Committees? "I hate being officially and necessarily in the presence of men most of whom, either from excessive zeal in the good cause or from constitutional obtuseness, are incapable of being *bored* . . ." Reform? "How easy it would be to join a party and be popular! . . . Please not to mourn over me then, as one that is lost to truth." These expressions will still offend pious liberalism, for they have an edge as cutting now as when they were first milled. Nor would Holmes insist on the permanence of their value, for he shrewdly saw that his opinions, radical as they might seem in his own day, would sometime appear "too timid and conservative for intelligent readers, if they are still read by any."

This modest doubt of his future reputation also encompasses his whole literary work. In the *Epilogue to the Breakfast-Table Series*, writing about a visit to a bookstore as of 1972, he promises in an enthusiastic outburst to rebind his cheap purchase of his work but "Read you—perhaps—some other time." Such self-depreciation does not signify the gnawing self-doubt that so many critics have found, but a common-sense regard for the clouded future of literary immortality. Here it creates a fresh verse in delightful counterpoint of the *monumentum aere perennius* motif, just as in *Contentment* one has a fine specific against the traditional boast of spiritual contentment that spurns the shows of the world. Writing from the text of Goldsmith's "Man wants but little here below," Holmes lists his negligible demands in food, money, horses, and jewels. "One good-sized diamond in a pin,—Some, *not so large*, in rings . . ." Elsewhere he had quipped:

> Man wants but little drink below,
> But wants that little strong.

While all this might come to no more than an urbane philistinism, in Holmes it produces a sense of image that in craftsmanship and exactitude is worth prizing. We have seen that against the critical demands of his time Holmes defended hyperbolical images as "a perfectly healthy and natural exercise of the imagination." Thus he recognized the power of the "material imagery" of Toplady's hymn *Rock of Ages, Cleft for Me*: "The imagination wants help, and if it cannot get it in pictures, statues, crucifixes, etc., it will find it in words." Unfortunately Holmes did not generally allow himself the freedom in poetry that he did in prose. The passage in *The Autocrat* in which poetry is described in terms of meerschaum pipes makes one of many which seems to me as satisfying as literary art has achieved:

I mean to say that a genuine poem is capable of absorbing an indefinite amount of the essence of our own humanity,—its tenderness, its heroism, its regrets, its aspirations, so as to be gradually stained through with a divine secondary color derived from ourselves. So you see it must take time to bring the sentiment of a poem into harmony with our nature, by staining ourselves through every thought and image our being can penetrate.

Too often the images of the poems are more trite than this, and less vivid. But even though they are so often used—Holmes perhaps felt that the

aging process worked as validly with the image as with the total poem
—they are used with force.

One of the best of the serious poems, *The Living Temple* (p. 116),
demonstrates his ability to write within conventional imagery and yet
explore it with freshness. The major image of the poem, that of the body
as temple, derives clearly from the scriptural text, "Know ye not that your
body is the temple of the Holy Ghost . . .?" But the reference, as de-
veloped, is to a Greco-Roman temple (a direction that the body-and-build-
ing analogies made by several classical writers may have suggested), and
the details describe a temple grove as distinguished from the building alone.

A duality of concept results which keeps the poem from being merely,
as some have described it, "a vigorous frontal attack on Puritanism, which
regarded the flesh with fear and contempt as the vessel of corruption."
The last stanza makes a sharp qualification of this interpretation, for
when the body and the temple fall into decay, the prayer is for ever-
lasting incorruptibility:

> When wasting age and wearying strife
> Have sapped the leaning walls of life,
> When darkness gathers over all,
> And the last tottering pillars fall,
> Take the poor dust thy mercy warms,
> And mold it into heavenly forms!

Though not consistently pressing his image throughout all the poem,
Holmes always remains aware of it. The several departures as in the
"slave" of line 17 and the "reins" of line 29 keep in touch with the classi-
cal culture that is centered on the temple and grove in such words as
"soft air," "caves," "fountains," "walls," and "pillars."

> The smooth, soft air with pulse-like waves
> Flows murmuring through its hidden caves,
> Whose streams of brightening purple rush,
> Fired with a new and livelier blush,
> While all their burden of decay,
> The ebbing current steals away,
> And red with Nature's flame they start
> From the warm fountains of the heart.

With the word "mysterious" in the next to the last stanza one reaches
the inner shrine of the temple—the holy of holies. It is possibly not too
searching to remember also that the once pagan temples were rebuilt by
early Christians for their own religious rites.

The duality of Christian-pagan concepts should not obscure the duality of basic images. Though the title is *The Living Temple,* for his professional friends the author called it "The Anatomist's Hymn." It is that indeed, so much so that one critic has found fault with its "unintentional surrealistic effects" and many readers—who otherwise scorn the nineteenth century's unwillingness to be physiologically frank—are a little uneasy with the descriptions of the bloodstream, eye, and brain. Except that Holmes would not have known the word "surrealistic," it is surely wrong to dismiss as unintentional the poet's use of the substratum of the traditional body-as-temple in a poem which then draws upon the unexploited details of his anatomical knowledge.

The Living Temple also reminds us of the freshness that we find in Holmes' treatment of nature as a type of man. Since here nature is that of man's body, its use as a store of moral knowledge is not so distinct. But the treatment is still close to that of *The Chambered Nautilus* and *The Deacon's Masterpiece.* Unlike his contemporaries, Holmes did not use natural picturesqueness for the basis of analogy. With them he believed that "the universe swam in an ocean of similitudes and analogies," but usually he did not take his ocean on faith. After investigating the background of *The Chambered Nautilus,* Nelson F. Adkins has wisely seen it as "the direct result of the teaching of the eighteenth-century deists." "From such a belief," he goes on to say, "it is only a step to an allied conception that not only nature as a whole but each and every particle making up the physical universe may teach spiritual and moral truths." The tendency of Holmes' poetical contemporaries was to remain within the general analogical practice and to forget that the eighteenth century was often specifically scientific in its treatment. Also, as much as they absorbed romantic intuitionalism, nature was treated with yearning more than with perception. Except for Thoreau, they were content to be suffused in nature. But Holmes, who kept close to the days when Newton was among the poets, carried a tape to measure the girth of trees. The rational, objective, and calculating Holmes may thus seem at a disadvantage as a poet; yet in such poems as *The Living Temple* these very qualities serve him well. Because of them he achieves concreteness, and out of his shrewdness emerges vivid truth. He had been called a Philistine, and retorted that it was after all

> A stubborn race, that, spurning foreign law,
> Was much belabored with an ass's jaw.

The couplet, with its balance and surprise, reminds us of Holmes' thorough permeation by neoclassical tradition. Though he had metaphysical techniques and though neoclassical poetry coming between the metaphysicals and romantics had qualities of both, the essential Holmes certainly lies within the tradition of the eighteenth century. As a New Englander, a first generation post-Colonial who would have absorbed elements of the Ramian aesthetic without probably knowing Ramus directly, Holmes stood still closer to the metaphysicals than did the Augustans. Yet also as a New Englander of the early nineteenth century he had been brought up on the neoclassical authors. His favorite reading, he says in his autobiographical notes, was Pope's Homer. "To the present time the grand couplets ring in my ears and stimulate my imagination, in spite of their formal symmetry."

His common sense has its obvious connection with the enlightenment, and more particularly in his attitude toward art he exhibits an eighteenth-century standard. Literature is social, communicable, and though not at the apex of human activity has a secure place. Holmes did not make a religion of it, as did the romantics. In this he stands close to most of his American contemporaries, who absorbed only some of the full romantic influence; but even from them he stands a little apart, for he was almost impervious to it.

The distinction gives an advantage to Holmes, whose relation to art shows less insecurity, for example, than appears in Whittier. In the *Prologue* to the *Songs in Many Keys*, published early in the Civil War, there is a dismissal of poetry that could be urged as containing the quality of Whittier's abjectness. Yet even here Holmes does not so much depreciate poetic activity as place it. When asked whether he took more satisfaction from having written his essay on puerperal fever, with its immediate result in the saving of lives, or from having written *The Chambered Nautilus*, Holmes began his reply with what seems as absolute a rightness as could be demanded: "I think I will not answer the question you put me." But happily for defining his artistic position he risked going beyond this negative wisdom.

I had a savage pleasure, I confess, in handling those two professors . . . But in writing the poem I was filled with a better feeling—the highest state of mental exaltation and the most crystalline clairvoyance, as it seemed to me, that had ever been granted to me—I mean that lucid vision of one's thought, and all forms of expression which will be at once precise and musical, which is the poet's special gift, however large or small in amount or value. There is a more selfish pleasure to be had out of the poem—perhaps a nobler satisfaction from the life-saving labor.

We may wish that he had not used the words "nobler" and "more selfish," but Holmes has discriminated well between an artistic and a humanitarian value. With his apparently contradictory "savage-nobler" and "better-selfish" he also has set off writing as composition from writing as achievement. Holmes knew the limitations of utilitarianism, as his witty lines in *The Coming Era* demonstrate; but he wisely mediated between art and life in a way that the romantics, with their sometimes hysterical fear of science and technology, could not.

For those of us who believe that there is a real but not an absolute division between light and serious poetry, he shows less perception in estimating occasional verse and his practice of it. In *A Rhymed Lesson* he protests that

> While my gay stanza pleased the banquet's lords,
> The soul within was tuned to deeper chords!

And this excuse seems to mark his main justification. Thus we get only a biographical rationalization for a self-imposed literary task. But in recognizing a difference and in implying a common ground, Holmes comes out better. Asked by a correspondent in 1875 for comment upon his own poems, he made the divisions of earlier, serious, lighter, and mixed. Disregarding the lack of classificatory logic in the first heading, we can follow Holmes in the distinction between his second and third headings and in the recognition of a more inclusive genre in the fourth. In one of his class poems he made the plea that a light poet might "do a fellow good After a scolding from Carlyle or Ruskin."

Trouble in justifying himself as an occasional poet may be further deduced from his frequent insistence upon the amount of work that it takes. Poetry is "a cold-blooded, haggard, anxious, worrying hunt after rhymes which can be made serviceable, after images which will be effective, after phrases which are sonorous." But though he shows this attitude more usually with light verse, we should also connect it, as John P. Pritchard does, with Horace's insistence upon the labor of the file. When Holmes dealt with the composition of serious poems, however, he was more apt to emphasize inspiration. But to make this a link between Holmes and romanticism, as some have done, is shortsighted. Even Horace gave recognition to inward prompting, and Pope did not deny "a grace beyond the reach of art."

The confessional nature of Holmes' writing has also been adduced as a sign of partial alliance with the romantics. Yet Holmes, who knew James Boswell as the author of *The Life of Samuel Johnson* rather than as a diarist, was a Boswell writing out himself, and not a Rousseau. If a man of sensibility, he was one of public sensibility. "But this I know, that I am like so many others of my fellow-creatures, that when I smile, I feel as if they must; when I cry, I think their eyes fill; and it always seems to me that when I am most truly myself I come nearest to them . . ." His confessions, as Harry Hayden Clark has remarked, were not the heart-outpourings of the romantic, but the social wisdom of the breakfast table.

Holmes' reference to his *Dorothy Q.* shows that intuitively his private thoughts were public property, though the remark has an ironic tinge. "I was surprised," he said in *The Poet at the Breakfast-Table*, "to find how many other people had portraits of their great-grandmothers or other progenitors, about which they felt as I did about mine, and for whom I had spoken, thinking I was speaking for myself only. And so I am not afraid to talk very freely with you, my precious reader or listener."

Commonly cited as showing the neoclassical tradition in Holmes are the heroic couplets in his *Poem* of 1883,

> Nor let the rhymester of the hour deride
> The straight-backed measure with its stately stride,

and accompanying mention of Dryden, Pope, Goldsmith, Byron, and Campbell. Perhaps more convincing evidence as to how thoroughly Holmes operated in the older tradition appears in his poem on Shelley with which he concluded his seventh lecture on the English poets. Writing on the man who to his audience was the personification of romantic excess, Holmes uses a traditional elegiac form that closes with a stanza addressed to the passing stranger. The poem further abounds in neoclassical epithets and images:

> Slow from the shore the sullen waves retire;
> His form a nobler element shall claim;
> Nature baptized him in ethereal fire,
> And Death shall crown him with a wreath of flame.

How fully at one Holmes was with the tradition is also shown by the ability to mock at it. Numerous examples are scattered throughout his poems, as of the theatre crowd that "smooths its caudal plumage as it sits." *Aestivation: An Unpublished Poem, by My Late Latin Tutor* provides a full-scale burlesque:

> Me wretched! Let me curr to quercine shades!
> Effund your albid hausts, lactiferous maids!

This witty awareness of the language of the eighteenth century is perceptively recognized by Alexander C. Kern as setting the tone of *The Chambered Nautilus* (p. 117). Pointing out that the ship of pearl is really pearl, the irised ceiling is iridescent, the lustrous crypt has luster, he finds "a kind of serious parody of the abstract style in which the diction has real as well as habitual connotation." Since recent studies have made it plain that neoclassical language at its best sought this link between the universal and particular, I should not want to go so far as to declare

Holmes' method here parody even of a serious sort. But whatever the poet's intention, it is altogether just to recognize his delicate handling of language in a poem that in many other respects shows a remarkable co-ordination of poetic abilities.

This favorite poem of Holmes (though he wrote it himself, he added) will indeed, if read within its tradition, still do its author great credit. The rather obvious display of rhythmic effectiveness, the exclamatory style, and the too patently contrived dramatic situation will keep us from perfect sympathy, even as they do in our reading of Dryden's *Alexander's Feast*. At the same time, there is enough in the poem to carry appreciation of it beyond such drawbacks.

As with any poem that approaches greatness, the essential effect of the work does not belong to a period or genre. Neoclassical in language and science, as has been said, the poem also exhibits metaphysical aspects in its dexterous handling of image as well as in the presence of counter-suggestion. Two pairs of contradictory values are developed throughout the poem, and each member of each pair is exhibited in carefully controlled relation to the other. The first line, "This is the ship of pearl, which, poets feign," introduces poetic fancy, which is expounded throughout the whole stanza:

> This is the ship of pearl, which, poets feign,
> Sails the unshadowed main,—
> The venturous bark that flings
> On the sweet summer wind its purpled wings
> In gulfs enchanted, where the Siren sings,
> And coral reefs lie bare,
> Where the cold sea-maids rise to sun their streaming hair.

Though not mocking the preciosity of a feigned classical myth, Holmes has the wit to draw a picturesque scene out of the materials of which the ship of pearl in the second and "scientific" stanza is wrecked:

> Its webs of living gauze no more unfurl;
> Wrecked is the ship of pearl!
> And every chambered cell,
> Where its dim dreaming life was wont to dwell,
> As the frail tenant shaped his growing shell,
> Before thee lies revealed,—
> Its irised ceiling rent, its sunless crypt unsealed!

This destruction he had anticipated in his opening stanza with the Siren, who perhaps enchants the reader as much as she is fabled to enchant sailors. In the fourth stanza the poet finally differentiates between myth and science—

> From thy dead lips a clearer note is born
> Than ever Triton blew from wreathèd horn!—

and thus resolves his first antithesis.

In the meanwhile the "scientific" stanza has not only set up opposition to the stanza of poetic fancy, but it has introduced the death of the nautilus: "Wrecked is the ship of pearl!" This pessimistic view has its antithesis in the optimism of the third stanza, with the sense of growth and progress as the nautilus annually leaves "the past year's dwelling for the new." We are now prepared for the "heavenly message," named in the fourth stanza and specified in the fifth:

> Build thee more stately mansions, O my soul,
>   As the swift seasons roll!
>   Leave thy low-vaulted past!
> Let each new temple, nobler than the last,
> Shut thee from heaven with a dome more vast,
>   Till thou at length art free,
> Leaving thine outgrown shell by life's unresting sea!

Against the second stanza, whose shift from dwelling to crypt finds a counterpart in the fifth stanza's change from mansions to temple, we may not limit the ethic of the poem to an easy philosophy of personal growth, but must regard it as expressing a triumph ultimate in death. In the fifth stanza the temples "*Shut* thee from heaven with a dome more vast" until the soul is free, and presumably the same rending of the ceiling, the same unsealing of the crypt produce this liberation. The message is thus rendered less buoyantly and more complexly than many critics have thought. Using the vocabulary of eighteenth-century diction and the rationalism of its scientific deism, Holmes has brought unique modulations partly absorbed from contemporary optimism (as links with passages in Emerson's *Compensation* and *The Problem* show), but more interestingly indebted to the dark New England heritage of his Calvinistic forebears.

Much of Holmes' appeal to the modern reader may be precisely in his not having the bland poise of enlightenment. Just because he "never formulated his beliefs," as his biographer Morse tells us, he has a universality that we should not overlook. A Calvinist become Unitarian who sweepingly denounced the old orthodoxies, he knew that he could never get wholly away from his earlier creed. "We are all tattooed in our cradles with the beliefs of our tribe . . ." A scientific deist, his imagination fed itself "upon the old litanies, so often warmed by the human breath," and his hymn beginning "O Love Divine, that stooped to share," though nonsectarian in its intent, is thoroughly at home in the evangelical hymnals where it may be found. The namer and defender of a Brahmin Boston, his thinking moved irregularly in the cultural inhibitions of his milieu.

These dualities should not be so much construed as resulting in uncertainty as in allowing Holmes a flexibility of understanding and a rich comprehension of life. Not himself a creative thinker, his questing mind led him to a position that shows remarkable links with twentieth-century developments in anthropology and psychology. Connection with Freud has been urged in the republication of his fiction as *The Psychiatric Novels of Oliver Wendell Holmes*. Though the claims of its editor, a former president of the American Psychoanalytic Association, have been questioned, they have not been disposed of. Overgenerous as they seem and heightened by the personal enthusiasm of a discoverer, they at least reveal Holmes as alert to psychological problems of basic importance.

"I go for man, sir, for woman, sir," Holmes had said in his *Breakfast-Table* series. Though he barred many areas of human experience to literature and attacked such writers as Zola and Whitman, he did not close these areas to the physician. Thus, in spite of his dismay at what realism was doing to polite letters and in spite of his closing his poems and novels to overtly sexual experience, one feels that Holmes is no genteel denier of life. His professional frankness in medical circles does not warrant this estimate so much, however, as the vigorous acceptance of life that one finds in such poems—superficially dainty though they may be—as *My Aunt* and *Dorothy Q.* Again, Holmes is not one sided, for his awareness of generation, birth, and youth is balanced by the acceptance of old age and death. Written in his early twenties, *The Last Leaf* provides a true promise of Holmes' long, well-rounded life. With a comprehensive acceptance of humanity, with an intellectual liveliness exploring widely in the thought of his time, and with an inbred awareness of emotional and philosophical positions disparate from his own, Holmes fulfills Emerson's judgment as "really catholic," a truly representative man.

These qualities are largely present in the poetry. They are seldom fully and perhaps never supremely there. Holmes' poems are nearly always lively, but most of them are an occasional pleasure—even as they are occasional verses—and not abiding. It is an error, however, to dismiss Holmes' poetry as thin, or vapid, or lacking in tension. The author of *The Chambered Nautilus* is neither a pretty moralizer nor a careless craftsman.

A glance at two final poems may help to establish the qualities of our poet by re-emphasizing certain matters in applying them to material not previously touched upon in this essay. The first is well known and light— a poem generally accepted as successful but for all that rather too complacently regarded. Barrett Wendell's reading of *The Deacon's Masterpiece* (p. 118) in 1900 as an attack on Calvanism has perhaps given the poem a special appeal for us, though at the same time it has diverted readers from a full literary consideration of the work. Whether Wendell is right or not, there is enough evidence for his theory to make it at least worth being aware of. *The Autocrat* contains many hits at orthodoxy, and the remark introducing the poem as "a rhymed problem" may lend itself to interpretation as an open hint. Though no suspicion of the poem as a Calvinistic gloss was expressed in Holmes' lifetime, perhaps realization was too widespread to need comment. Certainly a passage written less than a year later uses the central word of the poem with direct reference to Jonathan Edwards:

The commentary of the laymen on the preaching and practising of Jonathan Edwards was, that, after twenty-three years of endurance, they turned him out by a vote of twenty to one, and passed a resolve that he should never preach for them again. A man's logical and analytical adjustments are of little consequence, compared to his primary relations with Nature and truth; and people have sense enough to find it out in the long run; they know what "logic" is worth.

Had Holmes caused the shay to be built in 1754 (the date of Edwards' *Freedom of the Will*) instead of 1755, the major direction of the satire would have been clinched. Still it has been pointed out that the poem appeared in the centennial of Edwards' death. More significant perhaps, the Lisbon earthquake of 1755 received its literary importance from Voltaire's *Candide*, where Pangloss's celebrated comment that "All this is for the best" is followed by remarks on original sin and free will. "It was on the terrible Earthquake-day That the Deacon finished the one-hoss shay."

I cannot therefore discount Wendell's reading as completely as does Holmes' most recent biographer. But she is right in urging that the poem applies to any dogma inflexibly held, the system "of the homeopathist Hahnemann, for instance," or one might add a system of literary criticism. The author himself seems to have adumbrated the medical reference in a letter to Theodore Parker that Miss Tilton cites. And in a preface to the 1892 edition of the poem we find Holmes cheerfully announcing a "practical lesson." Since experience shows that mechanisms usually break first at the same point, "The workman should see to it that this part should never give way; then find the next most vulnerable place, and so on, until he arrives logically at the perfect result attained by the deacon."

The most sensible conclusion is that the story does function as a pertinent comment on Calvinism, homeopathy, and even manufacturing. In so far as each direction is hinted by Holmes he shows a breadth assuring that the poem like "a tree and truth" will outlive its own hundred years. But the general truths should not keep us from seeing the particular truths: the firm grounding in the character of the deacon and his successors, the homely attention to the details of the shay, and the inevitability of the narrative.

> But the Deacon swore (as Deacons do,
> With an "I dew vum," or an "I tell *yeou*")
> He would build one shay to beat the taown
> 'N' the keounty 'n' all the kentry raoun';
> It should be so built that it *could n'* break daoun . . .

> Thoroughbrace bison-skin, thick and wide;
> Boot, top, dasher, from tough old hide
> Found in the pit when the tanner died.
> That was the way he "put her through."
> "There!" said the Deacon, "naow she'll dew!"

Finally there is Holmes' refusal to specify the immediate direction of his comment: "Logic is logic. That's all I say." The reference is not only to the logic of a tightly constructed system but as well to that of a well-made shay and poem.

The second of the two final poems that display Holmes' virtuosity is not as well known as the first. It should be, for it assures us clearly of the challenge of Holmes' thought and the dexterity of its structure, even though after presenting the poem for a celebration at the Harvard Club of New York Holmes claimed that he had no inkling the ideas would be attacked. *Two Sonnets: Harvard* (p. 121) depends on the two mottoes of the college. One, "Christo et ecclesiæ," was adopted, Holmes thought, about 1700 under Increase Mather as a sign of orthodox reaffirmation. The other, "Veritas," of the original college seal had been discarded by Mather and— after a rather more complex history than Holmes notes—re-established popularly in 1874 by its inscription on Memorial Hall. Since 1885, seven years after the sonnets, both mottoes have appeared on the great seal of the university.

Unlike *The Deacon's Masterpiece* these sonnets have a serious nature and do not draw upon everyday material. But as with the earlier poem they are full of wit and (through use of Biblical imagery) solidly based upon concrete things, and as with *The Two Streams* and *The Chambered Nautilus* they show a rich complexity of thought. Two main images occur.

The first, belonging to the "Christo et Ecclesiæ" sonnet, likens Harvard and its overseers to Solomon's temple and its priests:

> Christ and the Church. *Their* church, whose narrow door
> Shut out the many, who if over bold
> Like hunted wolves were driven from the fold . . .

Its particular reference is to Araunah the Jebusite who sold his threshing floor to David for the altar site on Mt. Moriah. The second image, in the "Veritas" sonnet, follows the retrogressive chronology of the order of the mottoes and goes to an older Hebrew legend, that of the Garden of Eden. In 1643, the poet says, Harvard's scholars were not afraid

> Lest the fair fruit that wrought the woe of man
> By far Euphrates—where our sire began
> His search for truth, and, seeking, was betrayed—
> Might work new treason in their forest shade,
> Doubling the curse that brought life's shortened span.

Around these images Holmes weaves a gorgeous web of close-spun poetry and in the introduction of minor images reinforces their significance. Thus "chosen flock" of the first line contrasts with "hunted wolves" of the eleventh line. The address to Harvard as "nurse of the future" is a natural extension of Eve's part in Adam's sin. But a third specific Hebrew legend also makes an appearance—that of Joshua and his conquest of the city Jericho when the priests marched around it and blew upon their trumpets. This legend first comes to us as a part of the "Christo et Ecclesiæ" sonnet, where the temple mocks "The ram's-horn summons of the windy foes Who stand like Joshua's army" and wait to see it toppling. Here identification at first seems careless, for we should expect God's chosen people to be the attackers, even as the Israelites. But Holmes, who had once praised the Philistines as a stubborn race, ironically changes the expected values to make orthodox Harvard the besieged Canaanites. In the second sonnet he returns to the legend in its expected terms, since "by faith the walls of Jericho fell down," with orthodoxy attacking secular truth.

> Cast thy brave truth on every warring blast!
> Stretch thy white hand to that forbidden bough,
> And let thine earliest symbol be thy last!

Fruitfully and daringly using Old Testament materials, Holmes joins them with blasphemous dexterity. Yet in them he retains both their sectarian meaning and the larger catholicity of their truth in his time and ours.

THE TWO STREAMS

Behold the rocky wall
That down its sloping sides
Pours the swift rain-drops, blending, as they fall,
In rushing river-tides!

Yon stream, whose sources run
Turned by a pebble's edge,
Is Athabasca, rolling toward the sun
Through the cleft mountain-ledge.

The slender rill had strayed,
But for the slanting stone,   10
To evening's ocean, with the tangled braid
Of foam-flecked Oregon.

So from the heights of Will
Life's parting stream descends,
And, as a moment turns its slender rill,
Each widening torrent bends,—

From the same cradle's side,
From the same mother's knee,—
One to long darkness and the frozen tide,
One to the Peaceful Sea!   20

THE PEAU DE CHAGRIN OF STATE STREET

How beauteous is the bond
In the manifold array
Of its promises to pay,
While the eight per cent it gives
And the rate at which one lives
    Correspond!

But at last the bough is bare
Where the coupons one by one
Through their ripening days have run,
And the bond, a beggar now,   10
Seeks investment anyhow,
    Anywhere!

THE LIVING TEMPLE

Not in the world of light alone,
Where God has built his blazing throne,
Nor yet alone in earth below,
With belted seas that come and go,
And endless isles of sunlit green,
Is all thy Maker's glory seen:
Look in upon thy wondrous frame,—
Eternal wisdom still the same!

The smooth, soft air with pulse-like waves
Flows murmuring through its hidden caves,   10
Whose streams of brightening purple rush,
Fired with a new and livelier blush,
While all their burden of decay
The ebbing current steals away,
And red with Nature's flame they start
From the warm fountains of the heart.

No rest that throbbing slave may ask,
Forever quivering o'er his task,
While far and wide a crimson jet
Leaps forth to fill the woven net   20
Which in unnumbered crossing tides
The flood of burning life divides,
Then, kindling each decaying part,
Creeps back to find the throbbing heart.

But warmed with that unchanging flame
Behold the outward moving frame,
Its living marbles jointed strong
With glistening band and silvery thong,
And linked to reason's guiding reins
By myriad rings in trembling chains,   30
Each graven with the threaded zone
Which claims it as the master's own.

See how yon beam of seeming white
Is braided out of seven-hued light,
Yet in those lucid globes no ray
By any chance shall break astray.

Hark how the rolling surge of sound,
Arches and spirals circling round,
Wakes the hushed spirit through thine ear
With music it is heaven to hear. 40

Then mark the cloven sphere that holds
All thought in its mysterious folds;
That feels sensation's faintest thrill,
And flashes forth the sovereign will;
Think on the stormy world that dwells
Locked in its dim and clustering cells!
The lightning gleams of power it sheds
Along its hollow glassy threads!

O Father! grant thy love divine
To make these mystic temples thine! 50
When wasting age and wearying strife
Have sapped the leaning walls of life,
When darkness gathers over all,
And the last tottering pillars fall,
Take the poor dust thy mercy warms,
And mould it into heavenly forms!

THE CHAMBERED NAUTILUS

This is the ship of pearl, which, poets feign,
Sails the unshadowed main,—
The venturous bark that flings
On the sweet summer wind its purpled wings
In gulfs enchanted, where the Siren sings,
And coral reefs lie bare,
Where the cold sea-maids rise to sun their streaming hair.

Its webs of living gauze no more unfurl;
Wrecked is the ship of pearl!
And every chambered cell,
Where its dim dreaming life was wont to dwell,
As the frail tenant shaped his growing shell, 10
Before thee lies revealed,—
Its irised ceiling rent, its sunless crypt unsealed!

Year after year beheld the silent toil
    That spread his lustrous coil;
      Still, as the spiral grew,
He left the past year's dwelling for the new,
Stole with soft step its shining archway through,
      Built up its idle door,   20
Stretched in his last-found home, and knew the old no more.

Thanks for the heavenly message brought by thee,
    Child of the wandering sea,
      Cast from her lap, forlorn!
From thy dead lips a clearer note is born
Than ever Triton blew from wreathèd horn!
      While on mine ear it rings,
Through the deep caves of thought I hear a voice that sings:—

Build thee more stately mansions, O my soul,
    As the swift seasons roll!   30
      Leave thy low-vaulted past!
Let each new temple, nobler than the last,
Shut thee from heaven with a dome more vast,
      Till thou at length art free,
Leaving thine outgrown shell by life's unresting sea!

THE DEACON'S MASTERPIECE

OR, THE WONDERFUL "ONE-HOSS SHAY"

A LOGICAL STORY

Have you heard of the wonderful one-hoss shay,
That was built in such a logical way
It ran a hundred years to a day,
And then, of a sudden, it—ah, but stay,
I'll tell you what happened without delay,
Scaring the parson into fits,
Frightening people out of their wits,—
Have you ever heard of that, I say?

Seventeen hundred and fifty-five.
Georgius Secundus was then alive,—   10
Snuffy old drone from the German hive.

That was the year when Lisbon-town
Saw the earth open and gulp her down,
And Braddock's army was done so brown,
Left without a scalp to its crown.
It was on the terrible Earthquake-day
That the Deacon finished the one-hoss shay.

Now in building of chaises, I tell you what,
There is always *somewhere* a weakest spot,—
In hub, tire, felloe, in spring or thill,   20
In panel, or crossbar, or floor, or sill,
In screw, bolt, thoroughbrace,—lurking still,
Find it somewhere you must and will,—
Above or below, or within or without,—
And that's the reason, beyond a doubt,
That a chaise *breaks down*, but does n't *wear out*.

But the Deacon swore (as Deacons do,
With an "I dew vum," or an "I tell *yeou*")
He would build one shay to beat the taown
'N' the keounty 'n' all the kentry raoun';   30
It should be so built that it *could n'* break daown:
"Fur," said the Deacon, " 't 's mighty plain
Thut the weakes' place mus' stan' the strain;
'N' the way t' fix it, uz I maintain,
              Is only jest
T' make that place uz strong uz the rest."

So the Deacon inquired of the village folk
Where he could find the strongest oak,
That could n't be split nor bent nor broke,—
That was for spokes and floor and sills;   40
He sent for lancewood to make the thills;
The crossbars were ash, from the straightest trees,
The panels of white-wood, that cuts like cheese,
But lasts like iron for things like these;
The hubs of logs from the "Settler's ellum,"—
Last of its timber,—they could n't sell 'em,
Never an axe had seen their chips,
And the wedges flew from between their lips,
Their blunt ends frizzled like celery-tips;
Step and prop-iron, bolt and screw,   50

Spring, tire, axle, and linchpin too,
Steel of the finest, bright and blue;
Thoroughbrace bison-skin, thick and wide;
Boot, top, dasher, from tough old hide
Found in the pit when the tanner died.
That was the way he "put her through."
"There!" said the Deacon, "naow she 'll dew!"

Do! I tell you, I rather guess
She was a wonder, and nothing less!
Colts grew horses, beards turned gray,   60
Deacon and deaconess dropped away,
Children and grandchildren—where were they?
But there stood the stout old one-hoss shay
As fresh as on Lisbon-earthquake-day!

EIGHTEEN HUNDRED;—it came and found
The Deacon's masterpiece strong and sound.
Eighteen hundred increased by ten;—
"Hahnsum kerridge" they called it then.
Eighteen hundred and twenty came;—
Running as usual; much the same.   70
Thirty and forty at last arrive,
And then come fifty, and FIFTY-FIVE.

Little of all we value here
Wakes on the morn of its hundredth year
Without both feeling and looking queer.
In fact, there's nothing that keeps its youth,
So far as I know, but a tree and truth.
(This is a moral that runs at large;
Take it.—You 're welcome.—No extra charge.)

FIRST OF NOVEMBER,—the Earthquake-day,—   80
There are traces of age in the one-hoss shay,
A general flavor of mild decay,
But nothing local, as one may say.
There could n't be,—for the Deacon's art
Had made it so like in every part
That there was n't a chance for one to start.
For the wheels were just as strong as the thills,
And the floor was just as strong as the sills,
And the panels just as strong as the floor,

And the whipple-tree neither less nor more,⠀⠀⠀⠀⠀*90*
And the back crossbar as strong as the fore,
And spring and axle and hub *encore*.
And yet, *as a whole*, it is past a doubt
In another hour it will be *worn out*!

First of November, 'Fifty-five!
This morning the parson takes a drive.
Now, small boys, get out of the way!
Here comes the wonderful one-hoss shay,
Drawn by a rat-tailed, ewe-necked bay.
"Huddup!" said the parson.—Off went they.⠀⠀⠀⠀⠀*100*
The parson was working his Sunday's text,—
Had got to *fifthly*, and stopped perplexed
At what the—Moses—was coming next.
All at once the horse stood still,
Close by the meet'n'-house on the hill.
First a shiver, and then a thrill,
Then something decidedly like a spill,—
And the parson was sitting upon a rock,
At half past nine by the meet'n'-house clock,—
Just the hour of the Earthquake shock!⠀⠀⠀⠀⠀*110*
What do you think the parson found,
When he got up and stared around?
The poor old chaise in a heap or mound,
As if it had been to the mill and ground!
You see, of course, if you're not a dunce,
How it went to pieces all at once,—
All at once, and nothing first,—
Just as bubbles do when they burst.

End of the wonderful one-hoss shay.
Logic is logic. That's all I say.⠀⠀⠀⠀⠀*120*

TWO SONNETS: HARVARD

"CHRISTO ET ECCLESIÆ." 1700

To God's anointed and his chosen flock:
⠀⠀So ran the phrase the black-robed conclave chose
⠀⠀To guard the sacred cloisters that arose

Like David's altar on Moriah's rock.
Unshaken still those ancient arches mock
    The ram's-horn summons of the windy foes
    Who stand like Joshua's army while it blows
And wait to see them toppling with the shock.
Christ and the Church. *Their* church, whose narrow door
    Shut out the many, who if over bold   10
    Like hunted wolves were driven from the fold,
Bruised with the flails these godly zealots bore,
    Mindful that Israel's altar stood of old
Where echoed once Araunah's threshing-floor.

1643 "VERITAS." 1878

TRUTH: So the frontlet's older legend ran,
    On the brief record's opening page displayed;
    Not yet those clear-eyed scholars were afraid
Lest the fair fruit that wrought the woe of man
By far Euphrates—where our sire began
    His search for truth, and, seeking, was betrayed—
    Might work new treason in their forest shade,
Doubling the curse that brought life's shortened span.
Nurse of the future, daughter of the past,
    That stern phylactery best becomes thee now: 10
    Lift to the morning star thy marble brow!
Cast thy brave truth on every warring blast!
    Stretch thy white hand to that forbidden bough,
And let thine earliest symbol be thy last!

Lowell

IN CONTRAST with the public's complete acceptance of his contemporaries, Lowell's place as a schoolroom poet was scarcely warranted by the actual use of his poetry. "I am the first poet," he once boldly prophesied, "who has endeavored to express the American Idea, and I shall be popular by and by." But in the older anthologies we must look for the "American Idea" in the adventures of Sir Launfal, who, far from being native, does not even deserve accreditation as a British envoy to the culture of the United States. And though for the main exhibits of his poetry recent anthologies have shifted to *The Biglow Papers* and *A Fable for Critics*, the connection with the "American Idea" in these topical verses concerned with native wars and authors seems slight at best. Besides as poetry they are admittedly sporting gestures—dialect, propaganda, and miscellany—all very well in their genre but seldom resulting in a "shock of recognition" or a permanent cultivation of response.

My guess is that Lowell received his place of schoolroom poet as a gesture to his general accomplishment in letters and to his association with Holmes and Longfellow. The sentimentalities and didacticisms in which he indulged were neither of the kind nor frequency to secure him a firm place in the schoolroom heart. The public may also have felt that here was a man who ought to be a good poet, even a better one than most of his contemporaries could hope to be. The sense of life and of the word revealed in critical papers, letters, and conversation point to poetry potentially great. But it seldom reached greatness and it failed to achieve a real audience in Lowell's time and ours.

Yet more than most, Lowell has suffered from misrepresentation in anthologies. Usually we find a couple of *Biglow Papers*, the parts of *A Fable for Critics* that characterize other authors appearing in the same volume, and a few shorter pieces in a conventional lyric mood. That is the general pattern, but individually several anthologists do better, though in a sporadic rather than consistent way. Thus George Whicher (1950) prints the Commemoration Ode, Jay B. Hubbell (1936, 1949) some of the late political satires, Harry Hayden Clark (1936) all the later odes and *The Cathedral*, and William Smith Clark (1948, in a book of Lowell selections) *The Cathedral* and *Fitz Adam's Story*. Within its fifteen pages—a generous allotment in the plan of the volumes—the fresh selection of Auden's and Pearson's *Poets of the English Language* (1950) includes *An Oriental Apologue*. Each of the poems noted stems from the same root that produced *The Biglow Papers* and *A Fable*, and they deserve their place. But none of the anthologists prints all of these pertinent poems, or even enough of them to represent their man justly. Instead (except for Auden and Pearson) they fill the page allotments with such inferior Lowellisms as *Hebe*, *Beaver Brook*, *Rhœcus*, and *The Petition*.

These anthologists do not include, I am happy to say, the poem *After the Burial*, which readers of the nineteenth century probably liked best after *The Vision of Sir Launfal*. Today more readers, at least in the university schoolroom, may know the poem than any other, for it appears in Brooks' and Warren's *Understanding Poetry*. One is relieved that these critics make no analysis of *After the Burial* and restrict themselves to a few questions only; but to find Lowell appearing with this poem in this book still disheartens, especially since in 1889 Lowell as president of the Modern Language Association had challenged sterile literary scholarship with ideals anticipating those of Brooks and his associates a half-century later. The questions of *Understanding Poetry* are more lenient, however, than they might be, for they cite two stanzas (3 and 11) as better than the rest of the poem and two stanzas (10 and 12) as especially poor. My own belief is that the first five stanzas are a vulgarly extended mocking of a cliché and the remaining ones are heterogeneous, with the whole dramatic situation of a querulousness ill-conceived for the occasion. It is also true, though, that in one of the stanzas that is particularly reproved, I find an aside ("But not all the preaching since Adam Has made Death other than Death") that as an epigram well bears its own weight

Lowell has written a worse poem on the death of a child, and it is either good luck that Brooks and Warren did not know *The Changeling* or courteous tact if knowing it they refrained from printing it. The poem is an even drossier mirror of low popular taste than *After the Burial*. But badly as Lowell did here, he has done better too. *Agassiz*, written in 1874 upon the death of the Harvard scientist, deserves Henry James' epithet "magnificent" and his calling it "the truest expression of [Lowell's] poetic nature" after the Commemoration Ode.

Agassiz (p. 141) has a quality of full-bodied talk, an educated man's mingling of the colloquial and formal, which seldom falls into prosiness and which still rings upon the ear. We need not wonder that James so unreservedly praised the poem, for in it James probably saw a masterly achievement in that same style which we find in his later fictions. Though except for Agassiz himself the poem offers no controlling image or sequence of images such as in James' novels, it has a passionately intelligent unfolding of a central theme.

That theme may be roughly stated as the need for an awareness of the past in the present, a consolation that in spite of the rather too pat idea of immortality appearing in the last section of the poem seems as hard won a solution as any in the great elegies. The poem starts by anticipating this theme. Using the telegraphed dispatch of Agassiz' death in contrast with the traditional announcement of death in pastoral elegy, Lowell suddenly compares the nature of its shock with a mythic past:

> Earth sentient seems again as when of old
> > The horny foot of Pan
> Stamped, and the conscious horror ran
> Beneath men's feet through all her fibres cold . . .

This intermingling of past and present marks the whole of the first section. Lowell discards the pastoral appeal to "mountains, woods, and streams, to help us mourn him." Instead he calls upon the "strong poets of a more unconscious day"—Jonson and Chapman—to help him organize the "simpler moods" that "befit our modern themes."

The next three sections center in a description of Agassiz, the second describing the scientist in his social character, the third as a member of the Saturday Club, and the fourth in his relation to New England. For a time Lowell seems to have left his central theme, but as we come to the stanzas on the Saturday Club we begin to realize that Lowell, in writing of it and especially of its members who are no longer alive, urges the living presence of the past. This he makes explicit in the fourth section as the memory of Agassiz returning home with Lowell after one of the dinners is invoked:

> Still can I hear his voice's shrilling might . . .
> Call Oken back, or Humboldt, or Lamarck,
> Or Cuvier's taller shade, and many more
> Whom he had seen, or knew from others' sight,
> And make them men to me as ne'er before . . .
> "Good night!" and, ere the distance grew too wide,
> "Good night!" again; and now with cheated ear
> I half hear his who mine shall never hear.

Speculating further in this fourth section about the impact of the "grim outcrop" of New England's "granite edge" upon Agassiz, Lowell comes to his two final sections. The first of these offers no consolation, but rather in contrast with the spiritual drive of New England witnessed in the preceding lines hymns pagan praise for life and laments at death.

> Truly this life is precious to the root,
> And good the feel of grass beneath the foot;
> To lie in buttercups and clover-bloom,
> > Tenants in common with the bees,
> And watch the white clouds drift through gulfs of trees,
> Is better than long waiting in the tomb . . .

Over against this materialism the sixth section offers a concept of immortality. Discarding the pagan possibilities of an "endless slumber" or a sleep in which dreamy consciousness accompanies the reabsorption of the body by nature, Lowell shares Agassiz' own hope:

> And he was sure to be
> Somehow, somewhere, imperishable as He,
> Not with His essence mystically combined,
> As some high spirits long, but whole and free,
> A perfected and conscious Agassiz.

Such an existence, Lowell also suggests, may be realized on the earthly plane as well, as scholars will "trace his features with an eye less dim Than ours whose sense familiar wont makes dumb." Here the poet enforces the central theme of his elegy by an adumbration of heavenly and earthly immortality that is in keeping with it. It is also a belief that, whatever we think of its snobbish implications, attracted Henry James in his admiration of the poem. A quarter of a century later James was to make full and systematic argument for the survival of consciousness beyond death when it had been adequately cultivated in life.

Yet in spite of an occasional achievement of this sort, which we neglect to our impoverishment, Lowell was a poor poet. To speculate upon the personal reasons behind this failure is for the psychologist rather than the literary critic. But neither Lowell nor the critics have abstained. Lowell himself had many excuses at hand: his early impulse toward reform, the deadening hand of academic routine, the fact that when the muse was invited, she did not appear. Critics have disdained these as rationalizations, but the main reason they generally give—indolence— seems to evade verification just as much. For though this indolence may be regarded as a disinclination to think rather than a disinclination to work, one can easily point to better poets who have done less thinking or raise the question with T. S. Eliot whether it is the business of a poet to do much thinking anyway. About all that seems profitable for literary criticism to observe is that Lowell, if he did not know the reason for his failure, recognized the fact itself. "I am perfectly conscious that I have not yet got the best of my poetry out of me," he wrote to his friend Briggs in 1850. Twenty-five years later he spoke of himself as "but third-rate compared with the masters." Earlier he had penned the epitaph which, though unused, he kept among his papers until his death:

> Here lies that part of J. R. L.
> That hampered him from doing well . . .

Putting aside the personal reasons, we find public ones present through-out the whole body of the verse. Most specifically we feel Lowell's habit of genteel romanticism (though this diminished with his growth, as Harry Hayden Clark has shown) and Lowell's inability to cultivate a particular kind of poetry with its obverse in a facile imitation of too many poets ("the chameleon of nineteenth-century literature," as Leon Howard has called him). What emerges from this situation is a general weakness that one feels every time one comes to considering a literary characteristic. The language falls into prosiness or archaism, the morality into tidy didacti-cism, the ironies into pettiness. Lowell can seldom take an image from the concrete to the universal without diluting its earthiness or muddying its ideal, and he regularly commits himself to formlessness.

Especially since they differentiate his work so largely from his ideals, these two final ineptitudes deserve fuller comment. Lowell edited one of the few nineteenth-century editions of Donne's poetry in 1855, which though in itself of no scholarly value led to the annotations that formed the basis of the Lowell-Norton edition of 1895, a work that Grierson over-generously declares has such merit that if he had known of its existence earlier he probably would not have undertaken his own definitive text. But if the acquaintance with Donne accounted for some of the "violent phrases" for which contemporaries sometimes upbraided Lowell, it does not inform the greater part of his imagery.

As for Lowell's lack of form, we are surprised at the failing in view of what he says in his prose. In his fine essay on the criticism, Norman Foerster makes it clear that Lowell prized unity—"Lowell's creed is almost the unwritten constitution of the republic of letters." But as Odell Shepard has written, echoing the uneasiness of most writers on the poetry, *The Vision of Sir Launfal* is "one of the worst constructed poems in English." By and large Lowell exhibits neither craftsmanship in form nor the more desirable concord of discordants that lets us think of him as a poet who created artistic designs of self-containment and permanence.

So curious is the structure of *The Vision* that it is well to examine it. Out of such examination comes the essential method of Lowell which, with but few exceptions, is present in all his poems of merit: the form and tone of the familiar verse essay, emphasizing the digressive and disparate, yet constantly working toward an ultimate unity of effect. In *The Vision* he did not achieve this goal, and certainly the sentimental reform of Sir Launfal cancels incidental merits of the poem. Yet in all its weakness the work has interest as a prestudy of later accomplishment.

Everyone feels the distortion. By line count the prelude to the first part is longer than the first part itself (95 lines to 78), and the prelude to the second part is more than half as long as what follows (66 lines to

108). Lowell recognized this odd apportioning, as his reference to the poem in a letter as "a sort of a story" and his apology for the plot in the preface "if I may give that name to anything so slight" suggest. The poem itself also makes clear that he looked upon it as an improvisation, for the opening stanza describes the organist who "first lets his fingers wander as they list" and then "nearer draws his theme first guessed by faint auroral flushes." Touching upon this key and that, the poet plays upon the theme of man's rebirth in the rebirth of nature.

Yet he does so by starts and jumps, and except for the exultant passage on June in the first prelude makes a creaking and even wretched performance. The banality of the revivifying power of June may be somewhat tempered by the use of winter, but if so, it results in only the slightest sense of resistance. To the extent that Lowell understood what his readers were after (he anticipated that the poem was "more likely to be popular than what I write generally") he had his method. He also had method in knowing he was *not* writing a self-sustaining narrative, but as yet he had not fully discovered his flair for the familiar verse essay. The choice of medieval matter treated in a serious fashion could indeed hardly lend itself to such success. Yet *The Vision of Sir Launfal* points the way.

In 1848, the same year that saw publication of *The Vision*, the two poems by which Lowell is at present recognized also appeared. Neither is of high poetical order, and the value we attach to both is for qualities which, though not antipoetical, are nonpoetical. We like *A Fable for Critics* because it makes shrewd judgments of mid-nineteenth-century American authors that have stood remarkably well in the critical developments of the past hundred years; and we like *The Biglow Papers*, of which the first part was published in 1848, because it contains incisive writing on the Mexican and Civil Wars.

These are incidental values. To only a slight degree can we speak of the works as poetical units, but somewhat more certainly we may regard them as experiments in the direction of familiar verse essays. *A Fable for Critics* is the better illustration, since from the first Lowell conceived it as a complete piece. Like *The Vision* it has rudiments of plot which the author treats with the same irresponsibility.

> I'd apologize here for my many digressions,
> Were it not that I'm certain to trip into fresh ones . . .

Toward the end of the work he runs a footnote:

> Turn back now to page—goodness only knows what,
> And take a fresh hold on the thread of my plot.

But unlike *The Vision* Lowell here presents his fable in a comic spirit, not asking the reader to receive—or even remember—the story in the same way that he is asked to respond to that of the serious piece.

Without some awareness of this background, a certain loss occurs in reading the individual judgments that make up each part. One should remember that they come from Phoebus Apollo himself and contrast with the pseudocritical judgments of the day. At the same time Apollo is a humanized god, with foibles to qualify his greatness—a god who watches a pastoral procession of shepherds with a newspaper reporter at his elbow. The setting allows for the mixture of gravity and scurrility that appears in Lowell's evaluations of his contemporaries. Their incisiveness lets them stand alone, and they have rightly become the valued small change of criticism as well as larger bills of credit that we can draw against. But though they stand alone, they still form parts of the larger whole in which Lowell is happily working toward a genre that gives free play to his talent.

As a whole *The Biglow Papers* also accords with the tradition of the familiar essay. Here I omit the word "verse," since the framework is contrived out of prose letters which present Hosea Biglow partly in his own person and partly through the auspices of his father and his pastor. But as with *The Vision of Sir Launfal*, if with different particulars, the framework succeeds but poorly in integrating the tale. Though we *can* read it as an extended fiction and in part do (several articles by Arthur Voss have best shown how), most of us have little sense of any enhancement of the individual pieces; the story of the ill-considered revision for the 1848 edition, told by Mr. Howard in his stimulating biography, goes a long way toward explaining our ultimate dissatisfaction.

Yet in one or two of the parts we again find Lowell operating in the direction which marks the best. *Sunthin' in the Pastoral Line*, from the second series, presents most ingratiatingly the sense of controlled improvisation. Starting out as an attack against the denationalization of nature by American poets ("Why, I'd give more for one live bobolink Than a square mile o' larks in printer's ink"), the poet describes spring in Massachusetts and then (with digressions, as that on modern education) presents a dream vision of the Pilgrim Father with his prophetic advice on the Civil War. All this coheres loosely by the demand for a realistic view of native life, whether of nature or politics, but it must be admitted that the links are weak both in appearance and in actuality. The poem does not have the sense of mastery in its form that we find in such a work as *Agassiz*.

Along with all the poems of *The Biglow Papers*, *Sunthin' in the Pastoral Line* also has another quality that Lowell never thoroughly practiced in his poetry but which he did use with distinction. That is native idiom, which receives its best expression in this series. One of the finest defenses anywhere by anyone is the introduction that Lowell wrote for the second series in 1862.

It had long seemed to me that the great vice of American writing and speaking was a studied want of simplicity, that we were in danger of coming to look on our mother-tongue as a dead language, to be sought in the grammar and dictionary rather than in the heart, and that our only chance of escape was by seeking it at its living sources among those who were, as Scottowe says of Major-General Gibbons, "divinely illiterate." . . . No language after it has faded into *diction*, none that cannot suck up the feeding juices secreted for it in the rich mother-earth of common folk, can bring forth a sound and lusty book. True vigor and heartiness of phrase do not pass from page to page, but from man to man, where the brain is kindled and the lips suppled by downright living interest and by passion in its very throe . . . There is death in the dictionary . . .

But in spite of this noble passage on the source of vigor in language, in *The Biglow Papers* Lowell used his language as rustic utterance more often to characterize Hosea than to give us a sense of "the natural stronghold of his homely dialect." In writing in the person of a provincial, Lowell acts the part of connoisseur rather than stylist. Like the French court, he is playing a game of shepherds and shepherdesses.

The distinction between Lowell's use of native language in *The Biglow Papers* and the full use he might have given to it in real poetry should not be made absolute. Henry James called these poems Lowell's "most literary production" and in so doing must have felt the force of language as one of its principal characteristics. Thackeray is said to have exclaimed, "Why a man who can delight the world with such creations as *Hosea Biglow* should insist upon writing second-rate serious verse I cannot see." In their creation of character and in their universalizing of a specific political problem, as well as in their sense of style, Lowell goes beyond the immediate into the literary. But he had the choice of writing more poetry of the school of native humor and perfecting his instrument there or of writing poems of formal literary pretension ("serious verse"). He took the latter way and most of it was second rate; yet it is probable that if he had developed the stylistic perception present in his dialect verse, his serious verse need not have been second rate at all.

When he followed a natural line of development from *The Biglow Papers* into the familiar verse essay written in colloquial style, there is no reason to disparage his accomplishment. In *The Nooning*, a poem which he began in 1849 and never finished, he may have worked in this direction, though the evidence is partial and not all the completed parts of this frame-poem accord with the possibility. Yet *Fitz Adam's Story*

(p. 155) seems central to the mature concept of *The Nooning* because after its appearance in a magazine its book publication was delayed more than twenty years with the probable hope of adding to it and rounding out the original project. If it is central, it shows what Lowell might have done in greater quantity and with more cultivation. Though one of Lowell's best, too few readers know it.

Upon completing it Lowell wrote, "It is very homely, but right from nature." The central story is about a deacon who goes to hell and tries to outsmart the devil. But this makes up only 200 of the 600 lines and reaches us through a series of obliquities. The story, though the deacon's, is told by an American expatriate, partly cynic and partly man of feeling. He had got it from an Uncle Reuben, who in turn seems to have heard it from the farmer involved in the action.

That handing on of the narrative suggests that Lowell is back in the familiar verse essay. Only now he has come into his own. We are not upset by the lack of structure as we are with *The Vision*; nor as with *A Fable* are we aware of an intention without being convinced of its realization. All 600 lines of *Fitz Adam's Story* are of New England, realized in a fashion more anticipatory of Robert Frost than even Whittier's *Snow-Bound*.

> Ah! there's a deal of sugar in the sun!
> Tap me in Indian summer, I should run
> A juice to make rock-candy of . . .

With its description of the expatriated narrator, his digressions on religion, authors, and scenery, his arrival at the village inn and characterization of its host and habitués, and finally with the long-delayed folk tale about the deacon, the story gives a rich evocation of many lives. From the multiplicity of its materials, it achieves a center. Lowell has found the complex spirit of his province, rooted in a religion made up of stern sincerity and hard hypocrisy, realized in the variety of its growths from Colonial days down to the latest pale branch—an Adam if not an Adams. "Yet still the New World spooked it in his veins, A ghost he could not lay with all his pains."

In finding this spirit and putting it into poetry, Lowell also found himself more fully than in any of his famous efforts of 1848. Lacking the breadth of these earlier poems, *Fitz Adam's Story* has greater depth; and if we could match it with a half-dozen other poems of the same kind (as Lowell probably intended we might by his plan for *The Nooning*), we could surely say that here was the poet for whom we had hoped. But we cannot. What we do find are other poems related to it in familiarity of style, and these serve to keep Lowell from complete disregard as a poet.

So far we have mostly been concerned with Lowell's failure in a great many of his poems and with his real but limited accomplishment in his two principal works, *A Fable for Critics* and *The Biglow Papers*. In our inquiry two poems have thrust themselves to the fore as superior to his failures and with advantages beyond those of the two best-known pieces. Of these, one, *Fitz Adam's Story*, belongs with the familiar verse essays and the other, *Agassiz*, with the odes. In these two genres I believe Lowell came closest to poetical greatness, and in our final consideration we shall turn to the work in these groups.

But first Lowell's lyrics, as a group entirely apart from these, and his miscellaneous satirical poems, as one closely related, will be worth a glance. If I find only two lyrics of Lowell worth preserving, it may seem somewhat rude to the poet. But it is better to give firm recognition to what deserves it than half-hearted assent to a number of poems that do not. What happened to a good many of Lowell's lyrics may be what Lowell recognized as occurring in *The Washers of the Shroud*. "I began it as a lyric, but it *would* be too aphoristic for that, and finally flatly refused to sing at any price."

Of the two lyrics one is early and one late. The former, *To the Dandelion* (p. 171), shows the same breaking away from lyric intensity that Lowell remarked more fully in *The Washers*. Though there may be difference of opinion at the point in which the break occurs, every reader will admit that somewhere it happens. Walter Blair writes that perhaps in the fourth stanza the imagery breaks, and others intent upon rooting out the didactic heresy have found it in the sixth with the words "Thou teachest." Both views have truth. Certainly the imagery shifts in the fourth stanza; in the fifth one wonders how the poet is going to solve his further difficulties; and in the sixth one concludes that he can be credited only with a valiant try.

In the first two stanzas we have a striking series of variations around the word "gold." They come with a strong surge of language:

> Dear common flower, that grow'st beside the way,
> Fringing the dusty road with harmless gold . . .

The children picking them are "high-hearted buccaneers" finding an "Eldorado," and the stanzas are heavy with opulence—"wealth," "Spanish prow," "largess," "value." "Thou art my tropics and mine Italy," Lowell begins the third stanza, extending his imagery a little unsteadily but still justifiably from that of the wealth-seeking conquistadors. He is back, however, with the "golden-cuirassed bee," and now introduces new colors in "the white lily's breezy tent" and "the dark green" from which the "yellow circles burst." In the fourth and fifth stanzas Lowell sings of his own childhood, playing largely against the whiteness but with undertones of the other new color—"deep shadows on the grass" and "dark old tree." The gold is transposed into the child's spiritual recognition of nature, whether of "one white cloud" moving like a "stray lamb" or of a robin singing like an angel "with news from heaven."

But now one is watching the images pile up and wondering what the poet will do with them all. His solution is to retire into aphorism. There is some order in the retreat as again, in the sixth and final stanza, we get a backward glance at the opulence ("How like a prodigal doth nature seem") and childhood innocence ("a child's undoubting wisdom"). But the poem has lost its hold.

In *Auspex* (p. 172), the later poem, Lowell has kept control and working in a shorter poem with fewer images has produced his finest lyric. It is one not without pun and irony, the word "auspex" carrying the meanings of a poet and an interpreter of omens who examines both the flight of birds and the organs of an animal for his soothsaying. "Lark" and "linnet," primarily European songbirds, take us back to Lowell's early call for an American nomenclature ("square mile o' larks in printer's ink"). By means of this wit the poignancy of the loss of song and life emerges strongly.

Using a figure more violent than picturesque, that of the heart as a nest, Lowell dramatically poises his lyric at the moment of change:

> Nest that *had* song-birds in it . . .
> Instead of lark or linnet,
> *Shall* whirl dead leaves and snow.

Briefly in the middle stanza he regrets that his poems had shown too much aspiration—"Had they been swallows only." But without carrying through the implications of this wish he breaks off in mourning the loss of any song (for "their," as I take it, may refer either to the songbirds or the swallows) :

> Woe's me, I shall be lonely
> When I can feel no longer
> The impatience of their wings!

At last he recognizes that the songbirds are gone—"A moment, sweet delusion, Like birds the brown leaves hover"—and the catastrophe is at hand. With this recognition the image broadens out from that of the heart as nest to the chaotic overwhelming of author and work:

> But it will not be long
> Before their wild confusion
> Fall wavering down to cover
> The poet and his song.

Should one read the poem biographically an additional poignancy emerges when we think of Lowell's erring self-estimate and the obliteration of his work in the last half century. But in its own right the lyric furnishes all the materials for heightened feeling and dispassionate art.

In several of his satirical pieces Lowell has left work that it is pleasant, if not compulsory, to be acquainted with. In length these may go from the two-line epigram on the political boss—

> Skilled to pull wire, he baffles Nature's hope,
> Who sure intended him to stretch a rope—

to *The Unhappy Lot of Mr. Knott*. The latter, an exuberantly silly story of nearly a thousand lines, has delicious sallies upon the mid-nineteenth-century Carpenter's Gothic and table rapping, and again makes us wish that Lowell had cultivated more fully a type in which he displays so much talent. To be sure he has left us other examples of this kind of thing— *An Oriental Apologue, Without and Within, Our Own*, and the *Fragment of a Pindarique Ode in the manner of the late divine Mr. Abraham Cowley*—but he scarcely respected what he had done. He did not include *Our Own* and the *Fragment* in his collected work. Of his diverting translation of the burlesque opera *Il Pesceballo*, now generally available in a collection edited by Thelma M. Smith, there was no printed recognition of his authorship until five years after his death. The well-known story of Lowell's muttering "*The Washers of the Shroud!*" and walking away when Emerson praised *The Biglow Papers* also underlines his misconception of his true literary flair.

For Lowell's real achievement, as this essay argues, was close to these satirical pieces and, in so far as those named antedate it, derived from them. We have already seen its origins in *A Fable* and *The Biglow Papers* and its full realization in *Fitz Adam's Story*. *The Cathedral* also was written in this genre of the familiar verse essay, and to it we may add *An Epistle to George William Curtis, A Familiar Epistle to a Friend*, and *Under the Willows*. That two are named epistles shows the closeness of all these poems to the verse epistle. Since a substantial part of Lowell's literary accomplishment may well be, as William Smith Clark thinks, his prose letters, the closeness of the two genres further justifies the naming of the familiar verse essays as Lowell's best in poetry.

All these poems have in common a similarity of structure and language. Upon the surface they appear as awkward in their ordering as many of Lowell's poems are in essence. In language they also may first seem to be less than satisfactory, for certainly they do not cultivate the native idiom to the extent that *The Biglow Papers* do. But these later poems draw together with a final sense of wholeness, and they exhibit

a learned-colloquial style, easy and efficient, that has little trace of the
archaic poetical. As Barrett Wendell says, " 'Literary' you feel this man
again and again; but by and by you begin to feel that, after all, this litera-
ture proceeds from an intensely human being with a peculiarly Yankee
nature." Lowell admitted the colloquial when it was of good blood, and
though we may think his standard of family too high, in these poems we
can enjoy the liberated result.

Beginning with the 1844 volume, Ferris Greenslet has found that
"whimsicality begins to sparkle through." These later poems go far
beyond, in that whimsicality *is* their texture. Consciously wayward in
structure and language, Lowell reveals a new kind of unity. The image
of the improvising organist of *The Vision* is succeeded by another in
A Familiar Epistle:

> Not drop by drop, with watchful skill,
> Gathered in Art's deliberate still,
> But life's insensible completeness
> Got as the ripe grape gets its sweetness,
> As if it had a way to fuse
> The golden sunlight into juice.

In *An Epistle to George William Curtis*, arbitrarily divided as the poem
is by a gap of thirteen years in composition, the differences between the
two men and the two sides of Lowell's nature are brought into a unity.
"Little I ask of Fate; will she refuse Some days of reconcilement with
the Muse?" the poet asks; and by the mastery of his form gives affirma-
tive answer. Artistic concord also emerges from *Under the Willows*, in
which Lowell achieves the same sense of poetic solidity. Not only in the
whole but in the parts he now displays finish. Even the metaphor shows
the control hitherto lacking, as the whaling image of *A Familiar Epistle*
or that of the Charles River in *Under the Willows*, with its sudden yet
meaningful shift:

> Blue toward the west, and bluer and more blue,
> Living and lustrous as a woman's eyes
> Look once and look no more, with southward curve
> Ran crinkling sunniness, like Helen's hair
> Glimpsed in Elysium, insubstantial gold . . .

Of these familiar verse essays, *The Cathedral* (p. 173) is known best
and deserves to be. Its title may be unfortunate in suggesting a kind of
monumental solidity; but though naming the poem first "A Day at
Chartres" and regretting he did not keep the name, Lowell was after all
persuaded to make the change and probably liked having the informality
held in check by the new title. Mr. Greenslet has remarked upon "a pithy

and noble grandiloquence" in Lowell's style at its very best, and though
in this poem Lowell's emphasis seems to have leaned toward Gothic
grotesque rather than Gothic majesty, it has both elements.

More than any other poem by Lowell, whether serious or comic in
intent, *The Cathedral* displays homely imagery. Partly it is of a sort
which belongs to any age: "This unthrift housekeeping that will not brook
A dish warmed-over at the feast of life," and "To-day's eternal truth
To-morrow proved Frail as frost-landscapes on a window-pane." But
more striking is Lowell's use of imagery from his own world:

>   . . . life's scenery,
> Where the same slide must double all its parts,
> Shoved in for Tarsus and hitched back for Tyre. . .
>
> That drony vacuum of compulsory prayer,
> Still pumping phrases for the Ineffable,
> Though all the valves of memory gasp and wheeze. . .
>
> Doubtless his church will be no hospital
> For superannuate forms and mumping shams,
> No parlor where men issue policies
> Of life-assurance on the Eternal Mind . . .

These are thrown against the traditional glory of Chartres (for admittedly
Lowell "Scarce saw the minster for the thoughts it stirred") in a fine
irony of effect. Yet the cathedral itself, "Imagination's very self in stone,"
still looms in the background as the poet tries to offer mediation between
"commonplace" and "miracle."

Philosophically Lowell does not do this to the satisfaction of many
of his readers, who may well find fault either with his conclusion or
argument or both. But *The Cathedral* remains poetry even after its beliefs
are discounted. The work has four main sections. In the first (lines
1–212), Lowell writes of his early impressions of nature, recognizing
man's self-deception: "These first sweet frauds upon our consciousness
That blend the sensual with its imaged world." In spite of this, the poet
defends the "incomes of experience," his visit to Chartres, his dinner at a
"pea-green inn," and his walk in the park. In the second part (lines
213–501) Lowell faces the cathedral and with it the problem of super-
natural faith. To such faith he is partly drawn, yet at best he can propose
a nostalgic religion ("seeing where God *has* been, trust in Him") or one
that "Will see God rather in the strenuous doubt, Than in the creed."
From this conclusion he turns (lines 502–732) to the impact of democracy
on religion. Western man is sufficient in his own strength, and Lowell

is attracted by "this brown-fisted rough," believing however that there will be a return to a modified tradition:

> . . . yet he, unconscious heir
> To the influence sweet of Athens and of Rome,
> And old Judæa's gift of secret fire,
> Spite of himself shall surely learn to know
> And worship some ideal of himself,
> Some divine thing, large-hearted, brotherly,
> Not nice in trifles, a soft creditor,
> Pleased with his world, and hating only cant.

How much humorous discernment Lowell shows in this passage is hard to judge. One is reminded of a recent description in *The New Yorker* of the religion of a New York restaurant owner and his friends: "As a rule, God is referred to in the society, with an easy familiarity, as the Big Fellow Upstairs, the Big Fellow, or the Big Guy." Even Lowell's liberal Christianity and linguistics would have ill prepared him for quite this expression, and I suspect he is shocked by his own lines, for he quickly makes substitution of this concept with one of "The Cross, bold type of shame to homage turned." In different and less overt terms he comes back, contrasting the building of Chartres with building "Gothic contract-shams, because Our deacons have discovered that it pays." For a sounder religious ideal Lowell announces, "I can wait." Then in full revulsion he denounces a demagogic ideal of freedom as contrasted with one related to "private virtue strong in self-restraint." Realizing the impasse, Lowell quits the cathedral in the final part (lines 733–813): "I walked forth saddened; for all thought is sad, And leaves a bitterish savor in the brain." But looking up, he sees a sparrow-hawk. Here is an answer to the "wondrous cure-all in equality," when nature "from the premise sparrow here below" draws "sure conclusion of the hawk above,"

> Pleased with the soft-billed songster, pleased no less
> With the fierce beak of natures aquiline.

In an "enduring Nature, force conservative" Lowell finds a solution of the early impressions of nature, one justified by a full view and not the deception of his earlier pantheism. Yet his evidence of God remains in his impression and not in creed. But the experience at Chartres has warned him that both creed and impression are delusive:

> I fear not Thy withdrawal; more I fear,
> Seeing, to know Thee not, hoodwinked with dreams
> Of signs and wonders, while, unnoticed, Thou,
> Walking Thy garden still, commun'st with men,
> Missed in the commonplace of miracle.

With these lines Lowell brings his long meditation into poetic focus. The commonplace of miracle, whether of childhood days or an adult experience at Chartres, can still be had. Though Lowell's conclusion lacks in sharpness or security, it has come through the materials of the poem and is more than sentimental affirmation.

The Cathedral edges toward the outer limits of the familiar verse essay, as we see when we compare it with the light gracefulness of *Fitz Adam's Story*. In his later odes Lowell, still close to this tradition, has definitely stepped beyond the bounds. In a sense they represent an advance, since they move in the direction of a deeply felt and profound poetry; and such they might have been had Lowell not given them an increasingly severe formality. In the order of their writing they mark a regression as each strays farther from the center of Lowell's essential poetic accomplishment. The *Ode Recited at the Harvard Commemoration* (1865) as most closely akin to the familiar verse essay is best; *Agassiz* (1874) is not much inferior; but with the *Three Memorial Poems* of 1875 and 1876 we are apt to feel that the severity of Lowell's effort has pressed out the whimsicality of his talent.

In speaking of the Commemoration Ode (p. 193) in this way, I am aware of speaking against the influential critical voices of our day. In his *American Renaissance* F. O. Matthiessen remarked that "a confusion between what was really felt and the desire to move an audience vitiated Lowell's 'Commemoration Ode,' and left a stain of factitious rhetoric as unmistakable as tobacco-juice for a token of the age's general failure to distinguish between the nature of the two arts [rhetoric and poetry]." Possibly taken to task for these strong terms, nine years later he repeated his judgment as sternly (if less picturesquely) in the introduction to *The Oxford Book of American Verse*.

It is hard to argue against the charge that a poem is rhetoric rather than poetry—or for that matter to establish it. Though commonly used as exclusive opposites (if a poem is not poetry, it is rhetoric—or sentiment, when we follow Yeats' threefold distinction), the terms overlap. If what Matthiessen means is what William Van O'Connor has complained about—that through ornamentation Lowell "expected to elevate the basically prosaic teaching"—we have something more to work on. But even so, difficulties arise in discriminating between moral observation appropriate to poetry and teaching that is "basically prosaic."

In the ode Lowell deals with a subject surely proper for poetry. He mediates betwen absolutes and particulars; and though he uses the occasion of the Civil War, he consciously avoids making the poem either immediately historical or political. In the opening section he sets as the first instance of the conflict between absolutes and particulars that between song and deeds; then he moves in the next four sections to another antagonistic pairing, war and truth. But as he has made song and deed concrete with the ode itself and the lives of the Harvard soldiers, so he makes war the recent Civil War and truth the "Veritas" of Harvard's seal.

> They followed her and found her
> Where all may hope to find,
> Not in the ashes of the burnt-out mind,
> But beautiful, with danger's sweetness round her.

Only in a life embodying such truth by deed of warfare can permanence be found, and as the first example of such embodiment the poet pays tribute to Lincoln in the central (yet digressive) section of the poem. After this passage on Lincoln, that "New birth of our new soil, the first American," we turn to another pair of opposites, death and the ideal of goodness. Again in their meeting, the death for a cause, Lowell finds permanence, but not now of the individual man as Lincoln, but of American manhood. Beginning with the tenth section and extending through the twelfth and final section, we have a passage balancing the early one on Lincoln, and like it serving both as digression and climax. These deaths have redeemed the nation, producing many first Americans in Lincoln's image:

> 'T is no Man we celebrate,
> By his country's victories great,
> A hero half, and half the whim of Fate,
> But the pith and marrow of a Nation
> Drawing force from all her men . . .

In this also is the merit of the poet, who keeps "measure with his people" by singing of their deeds and leading them in their new dedication.

This then is the subject and something of the method. Although we may smile at Lowell's optimistic hope in the aftermath of the Civil War (later on he recognized fully the evils of the period), we should not put the poem aside as rhetoric or sentiment. It is true that frequently we run into the same carelessness in imagery that we have found elsewhere in Lowell's poetry, such as in the conglomeration of sunshine, stars, clay, and fountains of lines 97–100 that Mr. O'Connor has quite rightly suspected. But the poem is consistently oriented upon its basic images. And while we must count the blemishes, they do not obliterate the beauty that it has.

A closer glance at one of these sections may reassure us. We can properly choose the fourth, in which the sunshine, stars, clay, and fountain "image" occurs. It has three main movements, in which the hopeless flux of life and the hoped-for permanence are discriminated. In lines 66 to 74 (the first nine lines of the section), life is presented as a meaningless fluid, from the beginning in 66 ("Our slender life runs rippling by") to the ending in 73–74 ("Than such as flows and ebbs with Fortune's fickle moon?"). The second passage looks at life directly in terms of a false search for wealth (compare the earlier word "fortune"). We behave as puppets with "our little hour of strut and rave, With all our pasteboard passions and desires." Though it may be objected here that Lowell has us both as actors and bankers, even that combination might be defended, since Lowell brings the two activities together:

> But stay! no age was e'er degenerate
> Unless men held it at too cheap a rate
> For in our likeness still we shape our fate.

From lines 91 to 107 Lowell shifts to figures concerned essentially with light; as already remarked, he also slips into clay and fountains and into tears and seed as well. But in the last three lines—

> A light across the sea,
> Which haunts the soul and will not let it be,
> Still beaconing from the heights of undegenerate years—

he has brought together his two enveloping images of fluidity and light, while with the word "undegenerate" he looks back at the middle section.

Here we should take Lowell for what he is, at heart a writer of the familiar verse essay, rather than making him conform to arbitrary expectations. The section is flexible, digressive, improvised; but beneath the haphazardness is a unity that produces pleasure out of the disparateness of material. There is also further aesthetic satisfaction in the sudden exploration of the material in colloquial terms, though rather less here and in the odes generally than we have in *The Cathedral*.

These closing pages are not written with the hope of making the reader forget the enormously disheartening effect that Lowell's verses as a whole produce. What I believe is that Lowell had a real genius for a certain kind of poem. When he remained within that kind or did not depart from it widely, he wrote poetry that still serves its purpose and offers sweetness. But that poetry is so small in bulk that we are close to not having it, as he indeed was perilously close to not producing it.

As the godfather of the child whom we have come to know as the novelist Virginia Woolf, Lowell wrote some *Verses Intended to Go with a Posset Dish*. They are tender, playful, and fit, even if unforeseeing how fully his goddaughter would later deserve them. But it is unfortunate that a godfather of Lowell could not have sent these verses to the poet himself to act as a charm. Filling the posset cup with wishes that the child may inherit all life's graciousness, Lowell ends:

> Thus, then, the cup is duly filled;
> Walk steady, dear, lest all be spilled.

As an artist, our poet did not walk steady; and though he did not spill all from his cup, he spilled much.

AGASSIZ

> Come
> Dicesti *egli ebbe?* non viv' egli ancora?
> Non fiere gli occhi suoi lo dolce lome?[1]

I

1.

The electric nerve, whose instantaneous thrill
Makes next-door gossips of the antipodes,
Confutes poor Hope's last fallacy of ease,—
The distance that divided her from ill:
Earth sentient seems again as when of old
   The horny foot of Pan
Stamped, and the conscious horror ran
Beneath men's feet through all her fibres cold:
Space's blue walls are mined; we feel the throe
From underground of our night-mantled foe: *10*
   The flame-winged feet
Of Trade's new Mercury, that dry-shod run
Through briny abysses dreamless of the sun,
  Are mercilessly fleet,
  And at a bound annihilate
Ocean's prerogative of short reprieve;
   Surely ill news might wait,
And man be patient of delay to grieve:
   Letters have sympathies
  And tell-tale faces that reveal,   *20*
   To senses finer than the eyes,
Their errand's purport ere we break the seal;

---

[1] *Inferno*, x, 67–69.

They wind a sorrow round with circumstance
To stay its feet, nor all unwarned displace
The veil that darkened from our sidelong glance
        The inexorable face:
        But now Fate stuns as with a mace;
The savage of the skies, that men have caught
        And some scant use of language taught,
            Tells only what he must,—   30
The steel-cold fact in one laconic thrust.

2.

So thought I, as, with vague, mechanic eyes,
I scanned the festering news we half despise
        Yet scramble for no less,
And read of public scandal, private fraud,
Crime flaunting scot-free while the mob applaud,
Office made vile to bribe unworthiness,
        And all the unwholesome mess
The Land of Honest Abraham serves of late
        To teach the Old World how to wait,   40
            When suddenly,
As happens if the brain, from overweight
        Of blood, infect the eye,
Three tiny words grew lurid as I read,
And reeled commingling: *Agassiz is dead.*
As when, beneath the street's familiar jar,
An earthquake's alien omen rumbles far,
Men listen and forebode, I hung my head,
        And strove the present to recall,
As if the blow that stunned were yet to fall.   50

3.

    Uprooted is our mountain oak,
That promised long security of shade
And brooding-place for many a wingèd thought;
    Not by Time's softly cadenced stroke
With pauses of relenting pity stayed,
But ere a root seemed sapt, a bough decayed,
From sudden ambush by the whirlwind caught
And in his broad maturity betrayed!

4.

Well might I, as of old, appeal to you,
    O mountains, woods, and streams,   60
To help us mourn him, for ye loved him too;
    But simpler moods befit our modern themes,
And no less perfect birth of nature can,
Though they yearn tow'rd him, sympathize with man,
Save as dumb fellow-prisoners through a wall;
    Answer ye rather to my call,
Strong poets of a more unconscious day,
When Nature spake nor sought nice reasons why,
Too much for softer arts forgotten since
That teach our forthright tongue to lisp and mince,   70
And drown in music the heart's bitter cry!
Lead me some steps in your directer way,
Teach me those words that strike a solid root
        Within the ears of men;
Ye chiefly, virile both to think and feel,
Deep-chested Chapman and firm-footed Ben,
For he was masculine from head to heel.
Nay, let himself stand undiminished by
With those clear parts of him that will not die.
Himself from out the recent dark I claim   80
To hear, and, if I flatter him, to blame;
To show himself, as still I seem to see,
A mortal, built upon the antique plan,
Brimful of lusty blood as ever ran,
And taking life as simply as a tree!
To claim my foiled good-by let him appear,
Large-limbed and human as I saw him near,
Loosed from the stiffening uniform of fame:
And let me treat him largely: I should fear,
(If with too prying lens I chanced to err,   90
Mistaking catalogue for character),
His wise forefinger raised in smiling blame.
Nor would I scant him with judicial breath
And turn mere critic in an epitaph;
I choose the wheat, incurious of the chaff
That swells fame living, chokes it after death,
And would but memorize the shining half
Of his large nature that was turned to me:

Fain had I joined with those that honored him
With eyes that darkened because his were dim,   100
And now been silent: but it might not be.

II

1.

In some the genius is a thing apart,
    A pillared hermit of the brain,
Hoarding with incommunicable art
        Its intellectual gain;
        Man's web of circumstance and fate
        They from their perch of self observe,
Indifferent as the figures on a slate
        Are to the planet's sun-swung curve
        Whose bright returns they calculate;   110
        Their nice adjustment, part to part,
Were shaken from its serviceable mood
By unpremeditated stirs of heart
    Or jar of human neighborhood:
Some find their natural selves, and only then,
In furloughs of divine escape from men,
    And when, by that brief ecstasy left bare
        Driven by some instinct of desire,
They wander worldward, 't is to blink and stare,
Like wild things of the wood about a fire,   120
Dazed by the social glow they cannot share;
        His nature brooked no lonely lair,
But basked and bourgeoned in copartnery,
Companionship, and open-windowed glee:
        He knew, for he had tried,
        Those speculative heights that lure
The unpractised foot, impatient of a guide,
        Tow'rd ether too attenuately pure
For sweet unconscious breath, though dear to pride,
        But better loved the foothold sure   130
Of paths that wind by old abodes of men
Who hope at last the churchyard's peace secure,
And follow time-worn rules, that them suffice,
Learned from their sires, traditionally wise,
Careful of honest custom's how and when;
His mind, too brave to look on Truth askance,

No more those habitudes of faith could share,
But, tinged with sweetness of the old Swiss manse,
Lingered around them still and fain would spare.
Patient to spy a sullen egg for weeks,   140
The enigma of creation to surprise,
His truer instinct sought the life that speaks
Without a mystery from kindly eyes;
In no self-spun cocoon of prudence wound,
He by the touch of men was best inspired,
And caught his native greatness at rebound
From generosities itself had fired;
Then how the heat through every fibre ran,
Felt in the gathering presence of the man,
While the apt word and gesture came unbid!   150
Virtues and faults it to one metal wrought,
  Fined all his blood to thought,
And ran the molten man in all he said or did.
All Tully's rules and all Quintilian's too
He by the light of listening faces knew,
And his rapt audience all unconscious lent
Their own roused force to make him eloquent;
Persuasion fondled in his look and tone;
Our speech (with strangers prudish) he could bring
To find new charm in accents not her own;   160
Her coy constraints and icy hindrances
Melted upon his lips to natural ease,
As a brook's fetters swell the dance of spring.
Nor yet all sweetness: not in vain he wore,
Nor in the sheath of ceremony, controlled
By velvet courtesy or caution cold,
That sword of honest anger prized of old,
  But, with two-handed wrath,
If baseness or pretension crossed his path,
  Struck once nor needed to strike more.   170

2.

  His magic was not far to seek,—
He was so human! Whether strong or weak,
Far from his kind he neither sank nor soared,
But sate an equal guest at every board:
No beggar ever felt him condescend,

No prince presume; for still himself he bare
At manhood's simple level, and where'er
He met a stranger, there he left a friend.
How large an aspect! nobly unsevere,
With freshness round him of Olympian cheer,   180
Like visits of those earthly gods he came;
His look, wherever its good-fortune fell,
Doubled the feast without a miracle,
And on the hearthstone danced a happier flame;
Philemon's crabbed vintage grew benign;
Amphitryon's gold-juice humanized to wine.

III

1.

The garrulous memories
Gather again from all their far-flown nooks,
Singly at first, and then by twos and threes,
Then in a throng innumerable, as the rooks   190
Thicken their twilight files
Tow'rd Tintern's gray repose of roofless aisles:
Once more I see him at the table's head
When Saturday her monthly banquet spread
To scholars, poets, wits,
All choice, some famous, loving things, not names,
And so without a twinge at others' fames;
Such company as wisest moods befits,
Yet with no pedant blindness to the worth
Of undeliberate mirth,   200
Natures benignly mixed of air and earth,
Now with the stars and now with equal zest
Tracing the eccentric orbit of a jest.

2.

I see in vision the warm-lighted hall,
The living and the dead I see again,
And but my chair is empty; 'mid them all
'T is I that seem the dead: they all remain
Immortal, changeless creatures of the brain:
Wellnigh I doubt which world is real most,
Of sense or spirit, to the truly sane;   210

In this abstraction it were light to deem
Myself the figment of some stronger dream;
They are the real things, and I the ghost
That glide unhindered through the solid door,
Vainly for recognition seek from chair to chair,
And strive to speak and am but futile air,
As truly most of us are little more.

3.

Him most I see whom we most dearly miss,
    The latest parted thence,
His features poised in genial armistice   220
And armed neutrality of self-defence
Beneath the forehead's walled pre-eminence,
While Tyro, plucking facts with careless reach,
Settles off-hand our human how and whence;
The long-trained veteran scarcely wincing hears
The infallible strategy of volunteers
Making through Nature's walls its easy breach,
And seems to learn where he alone could teach.
Ample and ruddy, the board's end he fills
As he our fireside were, our light and heat,   230
Centre where minds diverse and various skills
Find their warm nook and stretch unhampered feet;
I see the firm benignity of face,
Wide-smiling champaign, without tameness sweet,
The mass Teutonic toned to Gallic grace,
The eyes whose sunshine runs before the lips
While Holmes's rockets curve their long ellipse,
    And burst in seeds of fire that burst again
    To drop in scintillating rain.

4.

There too the face half-rustic, half-divine,   240
Self-poised, sagacious, freaked with humor fine,
Of him who taught us not to mow and mope
About our fancied selves, but seek our scope
In Nature's world and Man's, nor fade to hollow trope,
Content with our New World and timely bold
To challenge the o'ermastery of the Old;
Listening with eyes averse I see him sit

Pricked with the cider of the Judge's wit
(Ripe-hearted homebrew, fresh and fresh again),
While the wise nose's firm-built aquiline   250
     Curves sharper to restrain
The merriment whose most unruly moods
Pass not the dumb laugh learned in listening woods
     Of silence-shedding pine:
Hard by is he whose art's consoling spell
Hath given both worlds a whiff of asphodel,
His look still vernal 'mid the wintry ring
Of petals that remember, not foretell,
The paler primrose of a second spring.

5.

And more there are: but other forms arise   260
And seen as clear, albeit with dimmer eyes:
First he from sympathy still held apart
By shrinking over-eagerness of heart,
Cloud charged with searching fire, whose shadow's sweep
Heightened mean things with sense of brooding ill,
And steeped in doom familiar field and hill,—
New England's poet, soul reserved and deep,
November nature with a name of May,
Whom high o'er Concord plains we laid to sleep,
While the orchards mocked us in their white array   270
And building robins wondered at our tears,
Snatched in his prime, the shape august
That should have stood unbent 'neath fourscore years,
The noble head, the eyes of furtive trust,
     All gone to speechless dust.
     And he our passing guest,
Shy nature, too, and stung with life's unrest,
Whom we too briefly had but could not hold,
Who brought ripe Oxford's culture to our board,
     The Past's incalculable hoard,   280
Mellowed by scutcheoned panes in cloisters old,
Seclusions ivy-hushed, and pavements sweet
With immemorial lisp of musing feet;
Young head time-tonsured smoother than a friar's,
Boy face, but grave with answerless desires,
Poet in all that poets have of best,

But foiled with riddles dark and cloudy aims,
    Who now hath found sure rest,
Not by still Isis or historic Thames,
Nor by the Charles he tried to love with me,   *290*
But, not misplaced, by Arno's hallowed brim,
Nor scorned by Santa Croce's neighboring fames,
    Haply not mindless, wheresoe'er he be,
Of violets that to-day I scattered over him;
    He, too, is there,
After the good centurion fitly named,
Whom learning dulled not, nor convention tamed,
Shaking with burly mirth his hyacinthine hair,
Our hearty Grecian of Homeric ways,
Still found the surer friend where least he hoped the praise.
    300

6.

    Yea truly, as the sallowing years
Fall from us faster, like frost-loosened leaves
Pushed by the misty touch of shortening days,
    And that unwakened winter nears,
'T is the void chair our surest guest receives,
'T is lips long cold that give the warmest kiss,
'T is the lost voice comes oftenest to our ears;
We count our rosary by the beads we miss:
    To me, at least, it seemeth so,
An exile in the land once found divine,   *310*
    While my starved fire burns low,
And homeless winds at the loose casement whine
Shrill ditties of the snow-roofed Apennine.

IV

1.

Now forth into the darkness all are gone,
But memory, still unsated, follows on,
Retracing step by step our homeward walk,
With many a laugh among our serious talk,
    Across the bridge where, on the dimpling tide,
The long red streamers from the windows glide,
    Or the dim western moon   *320*
Rocks her skiff's image on the broad lagoon,
And Boston shows a soft Venetian side

In that Arcadian light when roof and tree,
Hard prose by daylight, dream in Italy;
Or haply in the sky's cold chambers wide
Shivered the winter stars, while all below,
As if an end were come of human ill,
The world was wrapt in innocence of snow
And the cast-iron bay was blind and still;
These were our poetry; in him perhaps   330
Science had barred the gate that lets in dream,
And he would rather count the perch and bream
Than with the current's idle fancy lapse;
And yet he had the poet's open eye
That takes a frank delight in all it sees,
Nor was earth voiceless, nor the mystic sky,
To him the life-long friend of fields and trees:
Then came the prose of the suburban street,
Its silence deepened by our echoing feet,
And converse such as rambling hazard finds;   340
Then he who many cities knew and many minds,
And men once world-noised, now mere Ossian forms
Of misty memory, bade them live anew
As when they shared earth's manifold delight,
In shape, in gait, in voice, in gesture true,
And, with an accent heightening as he warms,
Would stop forgetful of the shortening night,
Drop my confining arm, and pour profuse
Much worldly wisdom kept for others' use,
Not for his own, for he was rash and free,   350
His purse or knowledge all men's, like the sea.
Still can I hear his voice's shrilling might
(With pauses broken, while the fitful spark
He blew more hotly rounded on the dark
To hint his features with a Rembrandt light)
Call Oken back, or Humboldt, or Lamarck,
Or Cuvier's taller shade, and many more
Whom he had seen, or knew from others' sight,
And make them men to me as ne'er before:
Not seldom, as the undeadened fibre stirred   360
Of noble friendships knit beyond the sea,
German or French thrust by the lagging word,
For a good leash of mother-tongues had he.
At last, arrived at where our paths divide,

"Good night!" and, ere the distance grew too wide,
"Good night!" again; and now with cheated ear
I half hear his who mine shall never hear.

2.

Sometimes it seemed as if New England air
For his large lungs too parsimonious were,
As if those empty rooms of dogma drear   370
Where the ghost shivers of a faith austere
   Counting the horns o'er of the Beast,
Still scaring those whose faith in it is least,
As if those snaps o' th' moral atmosphere
That sharpen all the needles of the East,
   Had been to him like death,
Accustomed to draw Europe's freer breath
     In a more stable element;
Nay, even our landscape, half the year morose,
Our practical horizon grimly pent,   380
Our air, sincere of ceremonious haze,
Forcing hard outlines mercilessly close,
Our social monotone of level days,
   Might make our best seem banishment;
     But it was nothing so;
   Haply his instinct might divine,
Beneath our drift of puritanic snow,
   The marvel sensitive and fine
Of sanguinaria over-rash to blow
And trust its shyness to an air malign;   390
Well might he prize truth's warranty and pledge
In the grim outcrop of our granite edge,
Or Hebrew fervor flashing forth at need
In the gaunt sons of Calvin's iron breed,
As prompt to give as skilled to win and keep;
But, though such intuitions might not cheer,
   Yet life was good to him, and, there or here,
With that sufficing joy, the day was never cheap;
   Thereto his mind was its own ample sphere,
And, like those buildings great that through the year   400
Carry one temperature, his nature large
Made its own climate, nor could any marge
Traced by convention stay him from his bent:
He had a habitude of mountain air;

He brought wide outlook where he went,
　　And could on sunny uplands dwell
Of prospect sweeter than the pastures fair
　　High-hung of viny Neufchâtel;
　　　　Nor, surely, did he miss
　　　　Some pale, imaginary bliss　　　　　　410
Of earlier sights whose inner landscape still was Swiss.

v

1.

I cannot think he wished so soon to die
With all his senses full of eager heat,
And rosy years that stood expectant by
To buckle the winged sandals on their feet,
He that was friends with Earth, and all her sweet
Took with both hands unsparingly:
Truly this life is precious to the root,
And good the feel of grass beneath the foot;
To lie in buttercups and clover-bloom,　　　　420
　　Tenants in common with the bees,
And watch the white clouds drift through gulfs of trees,
Is better than long waiting in the tomb;
Only once more to feel the coming spring
As the birds feel it, when it bids them sing,
　　Only once more to see the moon
Through leaf-fringed abbey-arches of the elms
　　Curve her mild sickle in the West
Sweet with the breath of hay-cocks, were a boon
Worth any promise of soothsayer realms　　　　430
Or casual hope of being elsewhere blest;
　　To take December by the beard
And crush the creaking snow with springy foot,
While overhead the North's dumb streamers shoot,
Till Winter fawn upon the cheek endeared,
　　Then the long evening-ends
　　Lingered by cosy chimney-nooks,
With high companionship of books
　　Or slippered talk of friends
　　And sweet habitual looks,　　　　　　440
Is better than to stop the ears with dust:
Too soon the spectre comes to say, "Thou must!"

2.

When toil-crooked hands are crost upon the breast,
    They comfort us with sense of rest;
They must be glad to lie forever still;
    Their work is ended with their day;
Another fills their room; 't is the World's ancient way,
    Whether for good or ill;
But the deft spinners of the brain,
Who love each added day and find it gain,   450
    Them overtakes the doom
To snap the half-grown flower upon the loom
(Trophy that was to be of lifelong pain),
The thread no other skill can ever knit again.
    'T was so with him, for he was glad to live,
'T was doubly so, for he left work begun;
Could not this eagerness of Fate forgive
    Till all the allotted flax were spun?
It matters not; for, go at night or noon,
A friend, whene'er he dies, has died too soon,   460
And, once we hear the hopeless *He is dead*,
So far as flesh hath knowledge, all is said.

VI

1.

I seem to see the black procession go:
That crawling prose of death too well I know,
The vulgar paraphrase of glorious woe;
I see it wind through that unsightly grove,
Once beautiful, but long defaced
With granite permanence of cockney taste
And all those grim disfigurements we love:
There, then, we leave him: Him? such costly waste 470
Nature rebels at: and it is not true
Of those most precious parts of him we knew:
    Could we be conscious but as dreamers be,
'T were sweet to leave this shifting life of tents
Sunk in the changeless calm of Deity;
Nay, to be mingled with the elements,
The fellow-servants of creative powers,
Partaker in the solemn year's events,
To share the work of busy-fingered hours,

To be night's silent almoner of dew,   480
To rise again in plants and breathe and grow,
To stream as tides the ocean caverns through,
Or with the rapture of great winds to blow
About earth's shaken coignes, were not a fate
     To leave us all-disconsolate;
Even endless slumber in the sweetening sod
     Of charitable earth
That takes out all our mortal stains,
And makes us cleanlier neighbors of the clod,
     Methinks were better worth   490
Than the poor fruit of most men's wakeful pains,
     The heart's insatiable ache:
     But such was not his faith,
     Nor mine: it may be he had trod
Outside the plain old path of *God thus spake*,
     But God to him was very God
     And not a visionary wraith
     Skulking in murky corners of the mind,
     And he was sure to be
Somehow, somewhere, imperishable as He,   500
Not with His essence mystically combined,
As some high spirits long, but whole and free,
     A perfected and conscious Agassiz.
And such I figure him: the wise of old
Welcome and own him of their peaceful fold,
     Not truly with the guild enrolled
     Of him who seeking inward guessed
     Diviner riddles than the rest,
     And groping in the darks of thought
     Touched the Great Hand and knew it not;   510
     Rather he shares the daily light,
     From reason's charier fountains won,
Of his great chief, the slow-paced Stagyrite,
And Cuvier clasps once more his long-lost son.

2.

The shape erect is prone: forever stilled
The winning tongue; the forehead's high-piled heap,
A cairn which every science helped to build,
Unvalued will its golden secrets keep:

He knows at last if Life or Death be best:
Wherever he be flown, whatever vest   520
The being hath put on which lately here
So many-friended was, so full of cheer
To make men feel the Seeker's noble zest,
We have not lost him all; he is not gone
To the dumb herd of them that wholly die;
The beauty of his better self lives on
In minds he touched with fire, in many an eye
He trained to Truth's exact severity;
He was a Teacher: why be grieved for him
Whose living word still stimulates the air?   530
In endless file shall loving scholars come
The glow of his transmitted touch to share,
And trace his features with an eye less dim
Than ours whose sense familiar wont makes dumb.

FITZ ADAM'S STORY

The next whose fortune 't was a tale to tell
Was one whom men, before they thought, loved well,
And after thinking wondered why they did,
For half he seemed to let them, half forbid,
And wrapped him so in humors, sheath on sheath,
'T was hard to guess the mellow soul beneath;
But, once divined, you took him to your heart,
While he appeared to bear with you as part
Of life's impertinence, and once a year
Betrayed his true self by a smile or tear,   10
Or rather something sweetly shy and loath,
Withdrawn ere fully shown, and mixed of both.
A cynic? Not precisely: one who thrust
Against a heart too prone to love and trust,
Who so despised false sentiment he knew
Scarce in himself to part the false and true,
And strove to hide, by roughening o'er the skin,
Those cobweb nerves he could not dull within.
Gentle by birth, but of a stem decayed,
He shunned life's rivalries and hated trade;   20

On a small patrimony and larger pride,
He lived uneaseful on the Other Side
(So he called Europe), only coming West
To give his Old-World appetite new zest;
Yet still the New World spooked it in his veins,
A ghost he could not lay with all his pains;
For never Pilgrims' offshoot scapes control
Of those old instincts that have shaped his soul.
A radical in thought, he puffed away
With shrewd contempt the dust of usage gray,   30
Yet loathed democracy as one who saw,
In what he longed to love, some vulgar flaw,
And, shocked through all his delicate reserves,
Remained a Tory by his taste and nerves,
His fancy's thrall, he drew all ergoes thence,
And thought himself the type of common sense;
Misliking women, not from cross or whim,
But that his mother shared too much in him,
And he half felt that what in them was grace
Made the unlucky weakness of his race.   40
What powers he had he hardly cared to know,
But sauntered through the world as through a show;
A critic fine in his haphazard way,
A sort of mild La Bruyère on half-pay.
For comic weaknesses he had an eye
Keen as an acid for an alkali,
Yet you could feel, through his sardonic tone,
He loved them all, unless they were his own.
You might have called him, with his humorous twist,
A kind of human entomologist;   50
As these bring home, from every walk they take,
Their hat-crowns stuck with bugs of curious make,
So he filled all the lining of his head
With characters impaled and ticketed,
And had a cabinet behind his eyes
For all they caught of mortal oddities.
He might have been a poet—many worse—
But that he had, or feigned, contempt of verse;
Called it tattooing language, and held rhymes
The young world's lullaby of ruder times.   60
Bitter in words, too indolent for gall,
He satirized himself the first of all,

In men and their affairs could find no law,
And was the ill logic that he thought he saw.

   Scratching a match to light his pipe anew,
With eyes half shut some musing whiffs he drew
And thus began: "I give you all my word,
I think this mock-Decameron absurd;
Boccaccio's garden! how bring that to pass
In our bleak clime save under double glass?   70
The moral east-wind of New England life
Would snip its gay luxuriance like a knife;
Mile-deep the glaciers brooded here, they say,
Through æons numb; we feel their chill to-day.
These foreign plants are but half-hardy still,
Die on a south, and on a north wall chill.
Had we stayed Puritans! *They* had some heat,
(Though whence derived I have my own conceit),
But you have long ago raked up their fires;
Where they had faith, you 've ten sham-Gothic spires. 80
Why more exotics? Try your native vines,
And in some thousand years you *may* have wines;
Your present grapes are harsh, all pulps and skins,
And want traditions of ancestral bins
That saved for evenings round the polished board
Old lava fires, the sun-steeped hillside's hoard.
Without a Past, you lack that southern wall
O'er which the vines of Poesy should crawl;
Still they 're your only hope: no midnight oil
Makes up for virtue wanting in the soil;   90
Manure them well and prune them; 't won't be France,
Nor Spain, nor Italy, but there's your chance.
You have one story-teller worth a score
Of dead Boccaccios,—nay, add twenty more,—
A hawthorn asking spring's most dainty breath,
And him you 're freezing pretty well to death.
However, since you say so, I will tease
My memory to a story by degrees,
Though you will cry, 'Enough!' I 'm well-nigh sure,
Ere I have dreamed through half my overture.   100
Stories were good for men who had no books,
(Fortunate race!) and built their nests like rooks
In lonely towers, to which the Jongleur brought

His pedler's-box of cheap and tawdry thought,
With here and there a fancy fit to see
Wrought in quaint grace in golden filigree,—
Some ring that with the Muse's finger yet
Is warm, like Aucassin and Nicolete;
The morning newspaper has spoilt his trade,
(For better or for worse, I leave unsaid),   110
And stories now, to suit a public nice,
Must be half epigram, half pleasant vice.

  "All tourists know Shebagog County: there
The summer idlers take their yearly stare,
Dress to see Nature in a well-bred way,
As 't were Italian opera, or play,
Encore the sunrise (if they 're out of bed),
And pat the Mighty Mother on the head:
These have I seen,—all things are good to see,—
And wondered much at their complacency.   120
This world's great show, that took in getting-up
Millions of years, they finish ere they sup;
Sights that God gleams through with soul-tingling force
They glance approvingly as things of course,
Say, 'That 's a grand rock,' 'This a pretty fall,'
Not thinking, 'Are we worthy?' What if all
The scornful landscape should turn round and say,
'This is a fool, and that a popinjay'?
I often wonder what the Mountain thinks
Of French boots creaking o'er his breathless brinks,   130
Or how the Sun would scare the chattering crowd,
If some fine day he chanced to think aloud.
I, who love Nature much as sinners can,
Love her where she most grandeur shows,—in man:
Here find I mountain, forest, cloud, and sun,
River and sea, and glows when day is done;
Nay, where she makes grotesques, and moulds in jest
The clown's cheap clay, I find unfading zest.
The natural instincts year by year retire,
As deer shrink northward from the settler's fire,   140
And he who loves the wild game-flavor more
Than city-feasts, where every man's a bore
To every other man, must seek it where
The steamer's throb and railway's iron blare

Have not yet startled with their punctual stir
The shy, wood-wandering brood of Character.

"There is a village, once the county town,
Through which the weekly mail rolled dustily down,
Where the courts sat, it may be, twice a year,
And the one tavern reeked with rustic cheer;   *150*
Cheeshogquesumscot erst, now Jethro hight,
Red-man and pale-face bore it equal spite.
The railway ruined it, the natives say,
That passed unwisely fifteen miles away,
And made a drain to which, with steady ooze,
Filtered away law, stage-coach, trade, and news.
The railway saved it: so at least think those
Who love old ways, old houses, old repose.
Of course the Tavern stayed: its genial host
Thought not of flitting more than did the post   *160*
On which high-hung the fading signboard creaks,
Inscribed, 'The Eagle Inn, by Ezra Weeks.'

"If in life's journey you should ever find
An inn medicinal for body and mind,
'T is sure to be some drowsy-looking house
Whose easy landlord has a bustling spouse:
He, if he like you, will not long forego
Some bottle deep in cobwebbed dust laid low,
That, since the War we used to call the 'Last,'
Has dozed and held its lang-syne memories fast: *170*
From him exhales that Indian-summer air
Of hazy, lazy welcome everywhere,
While with her toil the napery is white,
The china dustless, the keen knife-blades bright,
Salt dry as sand, and bread that seems as though
'T were rather sea-foam baked than vulgar dough.

"In our swift country, houses trim and white
Are pitched like tents, the lodging of a night;
Each on its bank of baked turf mounted high
Perches impatient o'er the roadside dry,   *180*
While the wronged landscape coldly stands aloof,
Refusing friendship with the upstart roof.
Not so the Eagle; on a grass-green swell

That toward the south with sweet concessions fell
It dwelt retired, and half had grown to be
As aboriginal as rock or tree.
It nestled close to earth, and seemed to brood
O'er homely thoughts in a half-conscious mood,
As by the peat that rather fades than burns
The smouldering grandam nods and knits by turns,   *190*
Happy, although her newest news were old
Ere the first hostile drum at Concord rolled.
If paint it e'er had known, it knew no more
Than yellow lichens spattered thickly o'er
That soft lead-gray, less dark beneath the eaves
Which the slow brush of wind and weather leaves.
The ample roof sloped backward to the ground,
And vassal lean-tos gathered thickly round,
Patched on, as sire or son had felt the need,
Like chance growths sprouting from the old roof's seed,   *200*
Just as about a yellow-pine-tree spring
Its rough-barked darlings in a filial ring.
But the great chimney was the central thought
Whose gravitation through the cluster wrought;
For 't is not styles far-fetched from Greece or Rome,
But just the Fireside, that can make a home;
None of your spindling things of modern style,
Like pins stuck through to stay the card-built pile,
It rose broad-shouldered, kindly, debonair,
Its warm breath whitening in the October air,   *210*
While on its front a heart in outline showed
The place it filled in that serene abode.

  "When first I chanced the Eagle to explore,
Ezra sat listless by the open door;
One chair careened him at an angle meet,
Another nursed his hugely slippered feet;
Upon a third reposed a shirt-sleeved arm,
And the whole man diffused tobacco's charm.
'Are you the landlord?' 'Wahl, I guess I be,'
Watching the smoke, he answered leisurely.   *220*
He was a stoutish man, and through the breast
Of his loose shirt there showed a brambly chest;
Streaked redly as a wind-foreboding morn,
His tanned cheeks curved to temples closely shorn;

Clean-shaved he was, save where a hedge of gray
Upon his brawny throat leaned every way
About an Adam's-apple, that beneath
Bulged like a boulder from a brambly heath.
The Western World's true child and nursling he,
Equipt with aptitudes enough for three: *230*
No eye like his to value horse or cow,
Or gauge the contents of a stack or mow;
He could foretell the weather at a word,
He knew the haunt of every beast and bird,
Or where a two-pound trout was sure to lie,
Waiting the flutter of his home-made fly;
Nay, once in autumns five, he had the luck
To drop at fair-play range a ten-tined buck;
Of sportsmen true he favored every whim,
But never cockney found a guide in him;   *240*
A natural man, with all his instincts fresh,
Not buzzing helpless in Reflection's mesh,
Firm on its feet stood his broad-shouldered mind,
As bluffly honest as a northwest wind;
Hard-headed and soft-hearted, you 'd scarce meet
A kindlier mixture of the shrewd and sweet;
Generous by birth, and ill at saying 'No,'
Yet in a bargain he was all men's foe,
Would yield no inch of vantage in a trade,
And give away ere nightfall all he made.   *250*

　　" 'Can I have lodging here?' once more I said.
He blew a whiff, and, leaning back his head,
'You come a piece through Bailey's woods, I s'pose,
Acrost a bridge where a big swamp-oak grows?
It don't grow, neither; it 's ben dead ten year,
Nor th' ain't a livin' creetur, fur nor near,
Can tell wut killed it; but I some misdoubt
'T was borers, there 's sech heaps on 'em about.
You did n' chance to run ag'inst my son,
A long, slab-sided youngster with a gun?   *260*
He 'd oughto ben back more 'n an hour ago,
An' brought some birds to dress for supper—sho!
There he comes now. 'Say, Obed, wut ye got?
(He 'll hev some upland plover like as not.)
Wal, them 's real nice uns, an 'll eat A 1,

Ef I can stop their bein' over-done;
Nothin' riles *me* (I pledge my fastin' word)
Like cookin' out the natur' of a bird;
(Obed, you pick 'em out o' sight an' sound,
Your ma'am don't love no feathers cluttrin' round);   270
Jes' scare 'em with the coals,—thet's *my* idee.'
Then, turning suddenly about on me,
'Wal, Square, I guess so. Callilate to stay?
I 'll ask Mis' Weeks; 'bout *thet* it's hern to say.'

"Well, there I lingered all October through,
In that sweet atmosphere of hazy blue,
So leisurely, so soothing, so forgiving,
That sometimes makes New England fit for living.
I watched the landscape, erst so granite glum,
Bloom like the south side of a ripening plum,   280
And each rock-maple on the hillside make
His ten days' sunset doubled in the lake;
The very stone walls draggling up the hills
Seemed touched, and wavered in their roundhead wills.
Ah! there's a deal of sugar in the sun!
Tap me in Indian summer, I should run
A juice to make rock-candy of,—but then
We get such weather scarce one year in ten.

"There was a parlor in the house, a room
To make you shudder with its prudish gloom.   290
The furniture stood round with such an air,
There seemed an old maid's ghost in every chair,
Which looked as it had scuttled to its place
And pulled extempore a Sunday face,
Too smugly proper for a world of sin,
Like boys on whom the minister comes in.
The table, fronting you with icy stare,
Strove to look witless that its legs were bare,
While the black sofa with its horse-hair pall
Gloomed like a bier for Comfort's funeral.   300
Each piece appeared to do its chilly best
To seem an utter stranger to the rest,
As if acquaintanceship were deadly sin,
Like Britons meeting in a foreign inn.
Two portraits graced the wall in grimmest truth,

Mister and Mistress W. in their youth,—
New England youth, that seems a sort of pill,
Half wish-I-dared, half Edwards on the Will,
Bitter to swallow, and which leaves a trace
Of Calvinistic colic on the face.   310
Between them, o'er the mantel, hung in state
Solomon's temple, done in copperplate;
Invention pure, but meant, we may presume,
To give some Scripture sanction to the room.
Facing this last, two samplers you might see,
Each, with its urn and stiffly weeping tree,
Devoted to some memory long ago
More faded than their lines of worsted woe;
Cut paper decked their frames against the flies,
Though none e'er dared an entrance who were wise,   320
And bushed asparagus in fading green
Added its shiver to the franklin clean.

"When first arrived, I chilled a half-hour there,
Nor dared deflower with use a single chair;
I caught no cold, yet flying pains could find
For weeks in me,—a rheumatism of mind.
One thing alone imprisoned there had power
To hold me in the place that long half-hour:
A scutcheon this, a helm-surmounted shield,
Three griffins argent on a sable field;   330
A relic of the shipwrecked past was here,
And Ezra held some Old-World lumber dear.
Nay, do not smile; I love this kind of thing,
These cooped traditions with a broken wing,
This freehold nook in Fancy's pipe-blown ball,
This less than nothing that is more than all!
Have I not seen sweet natures kept alive
Amid the humdrum of your business hive,
Undowered spinsters shielded from all harms,
By airy incomes from a coat of arms?"   340

He paused a moment, and his features took
The flitting sweetness of that inward look
I hinted at before; but, scarcely seen,
It shrank for shelter 'neath his harder mien,
And, rapping his black pipe of ashes clear,

He went on with a self-derisive sneer:
"No doubt we make a part of God's design,
And break the forest-path for feet divine;
To furnish foothold for this grand prevision
Is good, and yet—to be the mere transition,　　　350
That, you will say, is also good, though I
Scarce like to feed the ogre By-and-By.
Raw edges rasp my nerves; my taste is wooed
By things that are, not going to be, good,
Though were I what I dreamed two lustres gone,
I'd stay to help the Consummation on,
Whether a new Rome than the old more fair,
Or a deadflat of rascal-ruled despair;
But *my* skull somehow never closed the suture
That seems to knit yours firmly with the future,　　　360
So you 'll excuse me if I 'm sometimes fain
To tie the Past's warm nightcap o'er my brain;
I 'm quite aware 't is not in fashion here,
But then your northeast winds are *so* severe!

　　"But to my story: though 't is truly naught
But a few hints in Memory's sketchbook caught,
And which may claim a value on the score
Of calling back some scenery now no more.
Shall I confess? The tavern's only Lar
Seemed (be not shocked!) its homely-featured bar.　　370
Here dozed a fire of beechen logs, that bred
Strange fancies in its embers golden-red,
And nursed the loggerhead whose hissing dip,
Timed by nice instinct, creamed the mug of flip
That made from mouth to mouth its genial round,
Nor left one nature wholly winter-bound;
Hence dropt the tinkling coal all mellow-ripe
For Uncle Reuben's talk-extinguished pipe;
Hence rayed the heat, as from an indoor sun,
That wooed forth many a shoot of rustic fun.　　　380
Here Ezra ruled as king by right divine;
No other face had such a wholesome shine,
No laugh like his so full of honest cheer;
Above the rest it crowed like Chanticleer.

　　"In this one room his dame you never saw,
Where reigned by custom old a Salic law;

Here coatless lolled he on his throne of oak,
And every tongue paused midway if he spoke.
Due mirth he loved, yet was his sway severe;
No blear-eyed driveller got his stagger here; 390
'Measure was happiness; who wanted more,
Must buy his ruin at the Deacon's store;'
None but his lodgers after ten could stay,
Nor after nine on eves of Sabbath-day.
He had his favorites and his pensioners,
The same that gypsy Nature owns for hers:
Loose-ended souls, whose skills bring scanty gold,
And whom the poor-house catches when they 're old;
Rude country-minstrels, men who doctor kine,
Or graft, and, out of scions ten, save nine; 400
Creatures of genius they, but never meant
To keep step with the civic regiment.
These Ezra welcomed, feeling in his mind
Perhaps some motions of the vagrant kind;
These paid no money, yet for them he drew
Special Jamaica from a tap they knew,
And, for their feelings, chalked behind the door
With solemn face a visionary score.
This thawed to life in Uncle Reuben's throat
A torpid shoal of jest and anecdote, 410
Like those queer fish that doze the droughts away,
And wait for moisture, wrapped in sun-baked clay;
This warmed the one-eyed fiddler to his task,
Perched in the corner on an empty cask,
By whose shrill art rapt suddenly, some boor
Rattled a double-shuffle on the floor;
'Hull's Victory' was, indeed, the favorite air,
Though 'Yankee Doodle' claimed its proper share.

" 'T was there I caught from Uncle Reuben's lips,
In dribbling monologue 'twixt whiffs and sips, 420
The story I so long have tried to tell;
The humor coarse, the persons common,—well,
From Nature only do I love to paint,
Whether she send a satyr or a saint;
To me Sincerity 's the one thing good,
Soiled though she be and lost to maidenhood.
Quompegan is a town some ten miles south

From Jethro, at Nagumscot river-mouth,
A seaport town, and makes its title good
With lumber and dried fish and eastern wood.   430
Here Deacon Bitters dwelt and kept the Store,
The richest man for many a mile of shore;
In little less than everything dealt he,
From meeting-houses to a chest of tea;
So dextrous therewithal a flint to skin,
He could make profit on a single pin;
In business strict, to bring the balance true
He had been known to bite a fig in two,
And change a board-nail for a shingle-nail.
All that he had he ready held for sale,   440
His house, his tomb, whate'er the law allows,
And he had gladly parted with his spouse.
His one ambition still to get and get,
He would arrest your very ghost for debt.
His store looked righteous, should the Parson come,
But in a dark back-room he peddled rum,
And eased Ma'am Conscience, if she e'er would scold,
By christening it with water ere he sold.
A small, dry man he was, who wore a queue,
And one white neckcloth all the week-days through,— 450
On Monday white, by Saturday as dun
As that worn homeward by the prodigal son.
His frosted earlocks, striped with foxy brown,
Were braided up to hide a desert crown;
His coat was brownish, black perhaps of yore;
In summer-time a banyan loose he wore;
His trousers short, through many a season true,
Made no pretence to hide his stockings blue;
A waistcoat buff his chief adornment was,
Its porcelain buttons rimmed with dusky brass.   460
A deacon he, you saw it in each limb,
And well he knew to deacon-off a hymn,
Or lead the choir through all its wandering woes
With voice that gathered unction in his nose,
Wherein a constant snuffle you might hear,
As if with him 't were winter all the year.
At pew-head sat he with decorous pains,
In sermon-time could foot his weekly gains,
Or, with closed eyes and heaven-abstracted air,

Could plan a new investment in long-prayer. 470
A pious man, and thrifty too, he made
The psalms and prophets partners in his trade,
And in his orthodoxy straitened more
As it enlarged the business at his store;
He honored Moses, but, when gain he planned,
Had his own notion of the Promised Land.

"Soon as the winter made the sledding good,
From far around the farmers hauled him wood,
For all the trade had gathered 'neath his thumb.
He paid in groceries and New England rum, 480
Making two profits with a conscience clear,—
Cheap all he bought, and all he paid with dear.
With his own mete-wand measuring every load,
Each somehow had diminished on the road;
An honest cord in Jethro still would fail
By a good foot upon the Deacon's scale,
And, more to abate the price, his gimlet eye
Would pierce to cat-sticks that none else could spy;
Yet none dared grumble, for no farmer yet
But New Year found him in the Deacon's debt. 490

"While the first snow was mealy under feet,
A team drawled creaking down Quompegan street.
Two cords of oak weighed down the grinding sled,
And cornstalk fodder rustled overhead;
The oxen's muzzles, as they shouldered through,
Were silver-fringed; the driver's own was blue
As the coarse frock that swung below his knee.
Behind his load for shelter waded he;
His mittened hands now on his chest he beat,
Now stamped the stiffened cowhides of his feet, 500
Hushed as a ghost's; his armpit scarce could hold
The walnut whipstock slippery-bright with cold.
What wonder if, the tavern as he past,
He looked and longed, and stayed his beasts at last,
Who patient stood and veiled themselves in steam
While he explored the bar-room's ruddy gleam?

"Before the fire, in want of thought profound,
There sat a brother-townsman weather-bound:

A sturdy churl, crisp-headed, bristly-eared,
Red as a pepper; 'twixt coarse brows and beard   510
His eyes lay ambushed, on the watch for fools,
Clear, gray, and glittering like two bay-edged pools;
A shifty creature, with a turn for fun,
Could swap a poor horse for a better one,—
He 'd a high-stepper always in his stall;
Liked far and near, and dreaded therewithal.
To him the in-comer, 'Perez, how d 'ye do?'
'Jest as I 'm mind to, Obed; how do you?'
Then, his eyes twinkling such swift gleams as run
Along the levelled barrel of a gun   520
Brought to his shoulder by a man you know
Will bring his game down, he continued, 'So,
I s'pose you 're haulin' wood? But you 're too late;
The Deacon's off; Old Splitfoot could n't wait;
He made a bee-line las' night in the storm
To where he won't need wood to keep him warm.
'Fore this he 's treasurer of a fund to train
Young imps as missionaries; hopes to gain
That way a contract that he has in view
For fireproof pitchforks of a pattern new.   530
It must have tickled him, all drawbacks weighed,
To think he stuck the Old One in a trade;
His soul, to start with, was n't worth a carrot,
And all he 'd left 'ould hardly serve to swear at.'

   "By this time Obed had his wits thawed out,
And, looking at the other half in doubt,
Took off his fox-skin cap to scratch his head,
Donned it again, and drawled forth, 'Mean he 's dead?'
'Jesso; he 's dead and t' other *d* that follers
With folks that never love a thing but dollars.   540
He pulled up stakes last evening, fair and square,
And ever since there 's been a row Down There.
The minute the old chap arrived, you see,
Comes the Boss-devil to him, and says he,
"What are you good at? Little enough, I fear;
We callilate to make folks useful here."
"Well," says old Bitters, "I expect I can
Scale a fair load of wood with e'er a man."
"Wood we don't deal in; but perhaps you 'll suit,
Because we buy our brimstone by the foot: 550

Here, take this measurin'-rod, as smooth as sin,
And keep a reckonin' of what loads comes in.
You 'll not want business, for we need a lot
To keep the Yankees that you send us hot;
At firin' up they 're barely half as spry
As Spaniards or Italians, though they 're dry;
At first we have to let the draught on stronger,
But, heat 'em through, they seem to hold it longer."

" 'Bitters he took the rod, and pretty soon
A teamster comes, whistling an ex-psalm tune.   560
A likelier chap you would n't ask to see,
No different, but his limp, from you or me'—
'No different, Perez! Don't your memory fail?
Why, where in thunder was his horns and tail?'
'They 're only worn by some old-fashioned pokes;
They mostly aim at looking just like folks.
Sech things are scarce as queues and top-boots here;
'T would spoil their usefulness to look too queer.
Ef you could always know 'em when they come,
They 'd get no purchase on you: now be mum.   570
On come the teamster, smart as Davy Crockett,
Jinglin' the red-hot coppers in his pocket,
And clost behind, ('t was gold-dust, you 'd ha' sworn),
A load of sulphur yallower 'n seed-corn;
To see it wasted as it is Down There
Would make a Friction-Match Co. tear its hair!
"Hold on!" says Bitters, "stop right where you be;
You can't go in athout a pass from me."
"All right," says t' other, "only step round smart;
I must be home by noon-time with the cart."   580
Bitters goes round it sharp-eyed as a rat,
Then with a scrap of paper on his hat
Pretends to cipher. "By the public staff,
That load scarce rises twelve foot and a half."
"There 's fourteen foot and over," says the driver,
"Worth twenty dollars, ef it 's worth a stiver;
Good fourth-proof brimstone, that 'll make 'em squirm,—
I leave it to the Headman of the Firm;
After we masure it, we always lay
Some on to allow for settlin' by the way.   590
Imp and full-grown, I 've carted sulphur here,
And gi'n fair satisfaction, thirty year."

With that they fell to quarrellin' so loud
That in five minutes they had drawed a crowd,
And afore long the Boss, who heard the row,
Comes elbowin' in with "What's to pay here now?"
Both parties heard, the measurin'-rod he takes,
And of the load a careful survey makes.
"Sence I have bossed the business here," says he,
"No fairer load was ever seen by me."   600
Then, turnin' to the Deacon, "You mean cus,
None of your old Quompegan tricks with us!
They won't do here: we 're plain old-fashioned folks,
And don't quite understand that kind o' jokes.
I know this teamster, and his pa afore him,
And the hard-working Mrs. D. that bore him;
He would n't soil his conscience with a lie,
Though he might get the custom-house thereby.
Here, constable, take Bitters by the queue,
And clap him into furnace ninety-two,   610
And try this brimstone on him; if he 's bright,
He 'll find the masure honest afore night.
He is n't worth his fuel, and I 'll bet
The parish oven has to take him yet!" '

    "This is my tale, heard twenty years ago
From Uncle Reuben, as the logs burned low,
Touching the walls and ceiling with that bloom
That makes a rose's calyx of a room.
I could not give his language, wherethrough ran
The gamy flavor of the bookless man   620
Who shapes a word before the fancy cools,
As lonely Crusoe improvised his tools.
I liked the tale,—'t was like so many told
By Rutebeuf and his brother Trouvères bold;
Nor were the hearers much unlike to theirs,
Men unsophisticate, rude-nerved as bears.
Ezra is gone and his large-hearted kind,
The landlords of the hospitable mind;
Good Warriner of Springfield was the last;
An inn is now a vision of the past;   630
One yet-surviving host my mind recalls,—
You 'll find him if you go to Trenton Falls."

TO THE DANDELION

Dear common flower, that grow'st beside the way,
Fringing the dusty road with harmless gold,
    First pledge of blithesome May,
Which children pluck, and, full of pride uphold,
    High-hearted buccaneers, o'erjoyed that they
An Eldorado in the grass have found,
    Which not the rich earth's ample round
    May match in wealth, thou art more dear to me
Than all the prouder summer-blooms may be.

Gold such as thine ne'er drew the Spanish prow   10
Through the primeval hush of Indian seas,
    Nor wrinkled the lean brow
Of age, to rob the lover's heart of ease;
    'T is the Spring's largess, which she scatters now
To rich and poor alike, with lavish hand,
    Though most hearts never understand
    To take it at God's value, but pass by
The offered wealth with unrewarded eye.

Thou art my tropics and mine Italy;
To look at thee unlocks a warmer clime;   20
    The eyes thou givest me
Are in the heart, and heed not space or time:
    Not in mid June the golden-cuirassed bee
Feels a more summer-like warm ravishment
    In the white lily's breezy tent,
    His fragrant Sybaris, than I, when first
From the dark green thy yellow circles burst.

Then think I of deep shadows on the grass,
Of meadows where in sun the cattle graze,
    Where, as the breezes pass,   30
The gleaming rushes lean a thousand ways,
    Of leaves that slumber in a cloudy mass,
Or whiten in the wind, of waters blue
    That from the distance sparkle through
    Some woodland gap, and of a sky above,
Where one white cloud like a stray lamb doth move.

My childhood's earliest thoughts are linked with thee;
The sight of thee calls back the robin's song,
   Who, from the dark old tree
Beside the door, sang clearly all day long,   40
   And I, secure in childish piety,
Listened as if I heard an angel sing
    With news from heaven, which he could bring
Fresh every day to my untainted ears
When birds and flowers and I were happy peers.

How like a prodigal doth nature seem,
When thou, for all thy gold, so common art!
   Thou teachest me to deem
More sacredly of every human heart,
   Since each reflects in joy its scanty gleam   50
Of heaven, and could some wondrous secret show,
    Did we but pay the love we owe,
   And with a child's undoubting wisdom look
On all these living pages of God's book.

AUSPEX

My heart, I cannot still it,
Nest that had song-birds in it;
And when the last shall go,
The dreary days, to fill it,
Instead of lark or linnet,
Shall whirl dead leaves and snow.

Had they been swallows only,
Without the passion stronger
That skyward longs and sings,—
Woe 's me, I shall be lonely   10
When I can feel no longer
The impatience of their wings!

A moment, sweet delusion,
Like birds the brown leaves hover;
But it will not be long

Before their wild confusion
Fall wavering down to cover
The poet and his song.

THE CATHEDRAL

Far through the memory shines a happy day,
Cloudless of care, down-shod to every sense,
And simply perfect from its own resource,
As to a bee the new campanula's
Illuminate seclusion swung in air.
Such days are not the prey of setting suns,
Nor ever blurred with mist of afterthought;
Like words made magical by poets dead,
Wherein the music of all meaning is
The sense hath garnered or the soul devined,   10
They mingle with our life's ethereal part,
Sweetening and gathering sweetness evermore,
By beauty's franchise disenthralled of time.

I can recall, nay, they are present still,
Parts of myself, the perfume of my mind,
Days that seem farther off than Homer's now
Ere yet the child had loudened to the boy,
And I, recluse from playmates, found perforce
Companionship in things that not denied
Nor granted wholly; as is Nature's wont,   20
Who, safe in uncontaminate reserve,
Lets us mistake our longing for her love,
And mocks with various echo of ourselves.

These first sweet frauds upon our consciousness,
That blend the sensual with its imaged world,
These virginal cognitions, gifts of morn,
Ere life grow noisy, and slower-footed thought
Can overtake the rapture of the sense,
To thrust between ourselves and what we feel,
Have something in them secretly divine.   30
Vainly the eye, once schooled to serve the brain,

With pains deliberate studies to renew
The ideal vision: second-thoughts are prose;
For beauty's acme hath a term as brief
As the wave's poise before it break in pearl.
Our own breath dims the mirror of the sense,
Looking too long and closely: at a flash
We snatch the essential grace of meaning out,
And that first passion beggars all behind,
Heirs of a tamer transport prepossessed.   40
Who, seeing once, has truly seen again
The gray vague of unsympathizing sea
That dragged his Fancy from her moorings back
To shores inhospitable of eldest time,
Till blank foreboding of earth-gendered powers,
Pitiless seignories in the elements,
Omnipotences blind that darkling smite,
Misgave him, and repaganized the world?
Yet, by some subtler touch of sympathy,
These primal apprehensions, dimly stirred,   50
Perplex the eye with pictures from within.
This hath made poets dream of lives foregone
In worlds fantastical, more fair than ours;
So Memory cheats us, glimpsing half-revealed.
Even as I write she tries her wonted spell
In that continuous redbreast boding rain:
The bird I hear sings not from yonder elm;
But the flown ecstasy my childhood heard
Is vocal in my mind, renewed by him,
Haply made sweeter by the accumulate thrill   60
That threads my undivided life and steals
A pathos from the years and graves between.

I know not how it is with other men,
Whom I but guess, deciphering myself;
For me, once felt is so felt nevermore.
The fleeting relish at sensation's brim
Had in it the best ferment of the wine.
One spring I knew as never any since:
All night the surges of the warm southwest
Boomed intermittent through the wallowing elms,   70
And brought a morning from the Gulf adrift,
Omnipotent with sunshine, whose quick charm

Startled with crocuses the sullen turf
And wiled the bluebird to his whiff of song:
One summer hour abides, what time I perched,
Dappled with noonday, under simmering leaves,
And pulled the pulpy oxhearts, while aloof
An oriole clattered and the robins shrilled,
Denouncing me an alien and a thief:
One morn of autumn lords it o'er the rest,   80
When in the lane I watched the ash-leaves fall,
Balancing softly earthward without wind,
Or twirling with directer impulse down
On those fallen yesterday, now barbed with frost,
While I grew pensive with the pensive year:
And once I learned how marvellous winter was,
When past the fence-rails, downy-gray with rime,
I creaked adventurous o'er the spangled crust
That made familiar fields seem far and strange
As those stark wastes that whiten endlessly   90
In ghastly solitude about the pole,
And gleam relentless to the unsetting sun:
Instant the candid chambers of my brain
Were painted with these sovran images;
And later visions seem but copies pale
From those unfading frescos of the past,
Which I, young savage, in my age of flint,
Gazed at, and dimly felt a power in me
Parted from Nature by the joy in her
That doubtfully revealed me to myself.   100
Thenceforward I must stand outside the gate;
And paradise was paradise the more,
Known once and barred against satiety.

What we call Nature, all outside ourselves,
Is but our own conceit of what we see,
Our own reaction upon what we feel;
The world 's a woman to our shifting mood,
Feeling with us, or making due pretence;
And therefore we the more persuade ourselves
To make all things our thought's confederates,   110
Conniving with us in whate'er we dream.
So when our Fancy seeks analogies,
Though she have hidden what she after finds,

She loves to cheat herself with feigned surprise.
I find my own complexion everywhere:
No rose, I doubt, was ever, like the first,
A marvel to the bush it dawned upon,
The rapture of its life made visible,
The mystery of its yearning realized,
As the first babe to the first woman born;   120
No falcon ever felt delight of wings
As when, an eyas, from the stolid cliff
Loosing himself, he followed his high heart
To swim on sunshine, masterless as wind;
And I believe the brown earth takes delight
In the new snowdrop looking back at her,
To think that by some vernal alchemy
It could transmute her darkness into pearl;
What is the buxom peony after that,
With its coarse constancy of hoyden blush?   130
What the full summer to that wonder new?

But, if in nothing else, in us there is
A sense fastidious hardly reconciled
To the poor makeshifts of life's scenery,
Where the same slide must double all its parts,
Shoved in for Tarsus and hitched back for Tyre.
I blame not in the soul this daintiness,
Rasher of surfeit than a humming-bird,
In things indifferent by sense purveyed;
It argues her an immortality   140
And dateless incomes of experience,
This unthrift housekeeping that will not brook
A dish warmed-over at the feast of life,
And finds Twice stale, served with whatever sauce.
Nor matters much how it may go with me
Who dwell in Grub Street and am proud to drudge
Where men, my betters, wet their crust with tears:
Use can make sweet the peach's shady side,
That only by reflection tastes of sun.

But she, my Princess, who will sometimes deign   150
My garret to illumine till the walls,
Narrow and dingy, scrawled with hackneyed thought
(Poor Richard slowly elbowing Plato out),

Dilate and drape themselves with tapestries
Nausikaa might have stooped o'er, while, between,
Mirrors, effaced in their own clearness, send
Her only image on through deepening deeps
With endless repercussion of delight,—
Bringer of life, witching each sense to soul,
That sometimes almost gives me to believe 160
I might have been a poet, gives at least
A brain desaxonized, an ear that makes
Music where none is, and a keener pang
Of exquisite surmise outleaping thought,—
Her will I pamper in her luxury:
No crumpled rose-leaf of too careless choice
Shall bring a northern nightmare to her dreams,
Vexing with sense of exile; hers shall be
The invitiate firstlings of experience,
Vibrations felt but once and felt life long: 170
Oh, more than half-way turn that Grecian front
Upon me, while with self-rebuke I spell,
On the plain fillet that confines thy hair
In conscious bounds of seeming unconstraint,
The *Naught in overplus*, thy race's badge!

One feast for her I secretly designed
In that Old World so strangely beautiful
To us the disinherited of eld,—
A day at Chartres, with no soul beside
To roil with pedant prate my joy serene 180
And make the minster shy of confidence.
I went, and, with the Saxon's pious care,
First ordered dinner at the pea-green inn,
The flies and I its only customers.
Eluding these, I loitered through the town,
With hope to take my minster unawares
In its grave solitude of memory.
A pretty burgh, and such as Fancy loves
For bygone grandeurs, faintly rumorous now
Upon the mind's horizon, as of storm 190
Brooding its dreamy thunders far aloof,
That mingle with our mood, but not disturb.
Its once grim bulwarks, tamed to lovers' walks,
Look down unwatchful on the sliding Eure,

Whose listless leisure suits the quiet place,
Lisping among his shallows homelike sounds
At Concord and by Bankside heard before.
Chance led me to a public pleasure-ground,
Where I grew kindly with the merry groups,
And blessed the Frenchman for his simple art   200
Of being domestic in the light of day.
His language has no word, we growl, for Home;
But he can find a fireside in the sun,
Play with his child, make love, and shriek his mind,
By throngs of strangers undisprivacied.
He makes his life a public gallery,
Nor feels himself till what he feels comes back
In manifold reflection from without;
While we, each pore alert with consciousness,
Hide our best selves as we had stolen them,   210
And each bystander a detective were,
Keen-eyed for every chink of undisguise.

So, musing o'er the problem which was best,—
A life wide-windowed, shining all abroad,
Or curtains drawn to shield from sight profane
The rites we pay to the mysterious I,—
With outward senses furloughed and head bowed
I followed some fine instinct in my feet,
Till, to unbend me from the loom of thought,
Looking up suddenly, I found mine eyes   220
Confronted with the minster's vast repose.
Silent and gray as forest-leaguered cliff
Left inland by the ocean's slow retreat,
That hears afar the breeze-borne rote and longs,
Remembering shocks of surf that clomb and fell,
Spume-sliding down the baffled decuman,
It rose before me, patiently remote
From the great tides of life it breasted once,
Hearing the noise of men as in a dream.
I stood before the triple northern port,   230
Where dedicated shapes of saints and kings,
Stern faces bleared with immemorial watch,
Looked down benignly grave and seemed to say,
Ye come and go incessant; we remain
Safe in the hallowed quiets of the past;

Be reverent, ye who flit and are forgot,
Of faith so nobly realized as this.
I seem to have heard it said by learnèd folk
Who drench you with æsthetics till you feel
As if all beauty were a ghastly bore,   240
The faucet to let loose a wash of words,
That Gothic is not Grecian, therefore worse;
But, being convinced by much experiment
How little inventiveness there is in man,
Grave copier of copies, I give thanks
For a new relish, careless to inquire
My pleasure's pedigree, if so it please,
Nobly, I mean, nor renegade to art.
The Grecian gluts me with its perfectness,
Unanswerable as Euclid, self-contained,   250
The one thing finished in this hasty world,
Forever finished, though the barbarous pit,
Fanatical on hearsay, stamp and shout
As if a miracle could be encored.
But ah! this other, this that never ends,
Still climbing, luring fancy still to climb,
As full of morals half-divined as life,
Graceful, grotesque, with ever new surprise
Of hazardous caprices sure to please,
Heavy as nightmare, airy-light as fern,   260
Imagination's very self in stone!
With one long sigh of infinite release
From pedantries past, present, or to come,
I looked, and owned myself a happy Goth.
Your blood is mine, ye architects of dream,
Builders of aspiration incomplete,
So more consummate, souls self-confident,
Who felt your own thought worthy of record
In monumental pomp! No Grecian drop
Rebukes these veins that leap with kindred thrill,   270
After long exile, to the mother-tongue.

Ovid in Pontus, puling for his Rome
Of men invirile and disnatured dames
That poison sucked from the Attic bloom decayed,
Shrank with a shudder from the blue-eyed race
Whose force rough-handed should renew the world,

And from the dregs of Romulus express
Such wine as Dante poured, or he who blew
Roland's vain blast, or sang the Campeador
In verse that clanks like armor in the charge,   280
Homeric juice, though brimmed in Odin's horn.
And they could build, if not the columned fane
That from the height gleamed seaward many-hued,
Something more friendly with their ruder skies:
The gray spire, molten now in driving mist,
Now lulled with the incommunicable blue;
The carvings touched to meaning new with snow,
Or commented with fleeting grace of shade;
The statues, motley as man's memory,
Partial as that, so mixed of true and false,   290
History and legend meeting with a kiss
Across this bound-mark where their realms confine;
The painted windows, freaking gloom with glow,
Dusking the sunshine which they seem to cheer,
Meet symbol of the senses and the soul,
And the whole pile, grim with the Northman's thought
Of life and death, and doom, life's equal fee,—
These were before me: and I gazed abashed,
Child of an age that lectures, not creates,
Plastering our swallow-nests on the awful Past,   300
And twittering round the work of larger men,
As we had builded what we but deface.
Far up the great bells wallowed in delight,
Tossing their clangors o'er the heedless town,
To call the worshippers who never came,
Or women mostly, in loath twos and threes.
I entered, reverent of whatever shrine
Guards piety and solace for my kind
Or gives the soul a moment's truce of God,
And shared decorous in the ancient rite   310
My sterner fathers held idolatrous.
The service over, I was tranced in thought:
Solemn the deepening vaults, and most to me,
Fresh from the fragile realm of deal and paint,
Or brick mock-pious with a marble front;
Solemn the lift of high-embowered roof,
The clustered stems that spread in boughs disleaved,
Through which the organ blew a dream of storm,

Though not more potent to sublime with awe
And shut the heart up in tranquility, 320
Than aisles to me familiar that o'erarch
The conscious silences of brooding woods,
Centurial shadows, cloisters of the elk:
Yet here was sense of undefined regret,
Irreparable loss, uncertain what:
Was all this grandeur but anachronism,
A shell divorced of its informing life,
Where the priest housed him like a hermit-crab,
An alien to that faith of elder days
That gathered round it this fair shape of stone? 330
Is old Religion but a spectre now,
Haunting the solitude of darkened minds,
Mocked out of memory by the sceptic day?
Is there no corner safe from peeping Doubt,
Since Gutenberg made thought cosmopolite
And stretched electric threads from mind to mind?
Nay, did Faith build this wonder? or did Fear,
That makes a fetish and misnames it God
(Blockish or metaphysic, matters not),
Contrive this coop to shut its tyrant in, 340
Appeased with playthings, that he might not harm?

I turned and saw a beldame on her knees;
With eyes astray, she told mechanic beads
Before some shrine of saintly womanhood,
Bribed intercessor with the far-off Judge:
Such my first thought, by kindlier soon rebuked,
Pleading for whatsoever touches life
With upward impulse: be He nowhere else,
God is in all that liberates and lifts,
In all that humbles, sweetens, and consoles: 350
Blessèd the natures shored on every side
With landmarks of hereditary thought!
Thrice happy they that wander not life long
Beyond near succor of the household faith,
The guarded fold that shelters, not confines!
Their steps find patience in familiar paths,
Printed with hope by loved feet gone before
Of parent, child, or lover, glorified
By simple magic of dividing Time.

My lids were moistened as the woman knelt,   360
And—was it will, or some vibration faint
Of sacred Nature, deeper than the will?—
My heart occultly felt itself in hers,
Through mutual intercession gently leagued.

Or was it not mere sympathy of brain?
A sweetness intellectually conceived
In simpler creeds to me impossible?
A juggle of that pity for ourselves
In others, which puts on such pretty masks
And snares self-love with bait of charity?   370
Something of all it might be, or of none:
Yet for a moment I was snatched away
And had the evidence of things not seen;
For one rapt moment; then it all came back,
This age that blots out life with question-marks,
This nineteenth century with its knife and glass
That make thought physical, and thrust far off
The Heaven, so neighborly with man of old,
To voids sparse-sown with alienated stars.

'T is irrecoverable, that ancient faith,   380
Homely and wholesome, suited to the time,
With rod or candy for child-minded men:
No theologic tube, with lens on lens
Of syllogism transparent, brings it near,—
At best resolving some new nebula,
Or blurring some fixed-star of hope to mist.
Science was Faith once; Faith were Science now,
Would she but lay her bow and arrows by
And arm her with the weapons of the time.
Nothing that keeps thought out is safe from thought.   390
For there 's no virgin-fort but self-respect,
And Truth defensive hath lost hold on God.
Shall we treat Him as if He were a child
That knew not his own purpose? nor dare trust
The Rock of Ages to their chemic tests,
Lest some day the all-sustaining base divine
Should fail from under us, dissolved in gas?
The armèd eye that with a glance discerns
In a dry blood-speck between ox and man

Stares helpless at this miracle called life, 400
This shaping potency behind the egg,
This circulation swift of deity,
Where suns and systems inconspicuous float
As the poor blood-disks in our mortal veins.
Each age must worship its own thought of God,
More or less earthy, clarifying still
With subsidence continuous of the dregs;
Nor saint nor sage could fix immutably
The fluent image of the unstable Best,
Still changing in their very hands that wrought: 410
To-day's eternal truth To-morrow proved
Frail as frost-landscapes on a window-pane.
Meanwhile Thou smiledst, inaccessible,
At Thought's own substance made a cage for Thought,
And Truth locked fast with her own master-key;
Nor didst Thou reck what image man might make
Of his own shadow on the flowing world;
The climbing instinct was enough for Thee.
Or wast Thou, then, an ebbing tide that left
Strewn with dead miracle those eldest shores, 420
For men to dry, and dryly lecture on,
Thyself thenceforth incapable of flood?
Idle who hopes with prophets to be snatched
By virtue in their mantles left below;
Shall the soul live on other men's report,
Herself a pleasing fable of herself?
Man cannot be God's outlaw if he would,
Nor so abscond him in the caves of sense
But Nature still shall search some crevice out
With messages of splendor from that Source 430
Which, dive he, soar he, baffles still and lures.
This life were brutish did we not sometimes
Have intimation clear of wider scope,
Hints of occasion infinite, to keep
The soul alert with noble discontent
And onward yearnings of unstilled desire;
Fruitless, except we now and then divined
A mystery of Purpose, gleaming through
The secular confusions of the world,
Whose will we darkly accomplish, doing ours. 440
No man can think nor in himself perceive,

Sometimes at waking, in the street sometimes,
Or on the hillside, always unforewarned,
A grace of being, finer than himself,
That beckons and is gone,—a larger life
Upon his own impinging, with swift glimpse
Of spacious circles luminous with mind,
To which the ethereal substance of his own
Seems but gross cloud to make that visible,
Touched to a sudden glory round the edge.   450
Who that hath known these visitations fleet
Would strive to make them trite and ritual?
I, that still pray at morning and at eve,
Loving those roots that feed us from the past,
And prizing more than Plato things I learned
At that best academe, a mother's knee,
Thrice in my life perhaps have truly prayed,
Thrice, stirred below my conscious self, have felt
That perfect disenthralment which is God;
Nor know I which to hold worst enemy,   460
Him who on speculation's windy waste
Would turn me loose, stript of the raiment warm
By Faith contrived against our nakedness,
Or him who, cruel-kind, would fain obscure,
With painted saints and paraphrase of God,
The soul's east-window of divine surprise.
Where others worship I but look and long;
For, though not recreant to my fathers' faith,
Its forms to me are weariness, and most
That drony vacuum of compulsory prayer,   470
Still pumping phrases for the Ineffable,
Though all the valves of memory gasp and wheeze.
Words that have drawn transcendent meanings up
From the best passion of all bygone time,
Steeped through with tears of triumph and remorse,
Sweet with all sainthood, cleansed in martyr-fires,
Can they, so consecrate and so inspired,
By repetition wane to vexing wind?
Alas! we cannot draw habitual breath
In the thin air of life's supremer heights,   480
We cannot make each meal a sacrament,
Nor with our tailors be disbodied souls,—
We men, too conscious of earth's comedy,

Who see two sides, with our posed selves debate,
And only for great stakes can be sublime!
Let us be thankful when, as I do here,
We can read Bethel on a pile of stones,
And, seeing where God *has* been, trust in Him.

Brave Peter Fischer there in Nuremberg,
Moulding Saint Sebald's miracles in bronze,   490
Put saint and stander-by in that quaint garb
Familiar to him in his daily walk,
Not doubting God could grant a miracle
Then and in Nuremberg, if so He would;
But never artist for three hundred years
Hath dared the contradiction ludicrous
Of supernatural in modern clothes.
Perhaps the deeper faith that is to come
Will see God rather in the strenuous doubt,
Than in the creed held as an infant's hand   500
Holds purposeless whatso is placed therein.

Say it is drift, not progress, none the less,
With the old sextant of the fathers' creed,
We shape our courses by new-risen stars,
And, still lip-loyal to what once was truth,
Smuggle new meanings under ancient names,
Unconscious perverts of the Jesuit, Time.
Change is the mask that all Continuance wears
To keep us youngsters harmlessly amused;
Meanwhile some ailing or more watchful child,   510
Sitting apart, sees the old eyes gleam out,
Stern, and yet soft with humorous pity too.
Whilere, men burnt men for a doubtful point,
As if the mind were quenchable with fire,
And Faith danced round them with her war-paint on,
Devoutly savage as an Iroquois;
Now Calvin and Servetus at one board
Snuff in grave sympathy a milder roast,
And o'er their claret settle Comte unread.
Fagot and stake were desperately sincere: 520
Our cooler martyrdoms are done in types;
And flames that shine in controversial eyes
Burn out no brains but his who kindles them.

This is no age to get cathedrals built:
Did God, then, wait for one in Bethlehem?
Worst is not yet: lo, where his coming looms,
Of earth's anarchic children latest born,
Democracy, a Titan who hath learned
To laugh at Jove's old-fashioned thunder-bolts,—
Could he not also forge them, if he would?   530
He, better skilled, with solvents merciless,
Loosened in air and borne on every wind,
Saps unperceived: the calm Olympian height
Of ancient order feels its bases yield,
And pale gods glance for help to gods as pale.
What will be left of good or worshipful,
Of spiritual secrets, mysteries,
Of fair religion's guarded heritage,
Heirlooms of soul, passed downward unprofaned
From eldest Ind? This Western giant coarse,   540
Scorning refinements which he lacks himself,
Loves not nor heeds the ancestral hierarchies,
Each rank dependent on the next above
In ordinary gradation fixed as fate.
King by mere manhood, nor allowing aught
Of holier unction than the sweat of toil;
In his own strength sufficient; called to solve,
On the rough edges of society,
Problems long sacred to the choicer few,
And improvise what elsewhere men receive   550
As gifts of deity; tough foundling reared
Where every man 's his own Melchisedek,
How make him reverent of a King of kings?
Or Judge self-made, executor of laws
By him not first discussed and voted on?
For him no tree of knowledge is forbid,
Or sweeter if forbid. How save the ark,
Or holy of holies, unprofaned a day
From his unscrupulous curiosity
That handles everything as if to buy,   560
Tossing aside what fabrics delicate
Suit not the rough-and-tumble of his ways?
What hope for those fine-nerved humanities
That made earth gracious once with gentler arts,
Now the rude hands have caught the trick of thought

And claim an equal suffrage with the brain?

The born disciple of an elder time,
(To me sufficient, friendlier than the new),
Who in my blood feel motions of the Past,
I thank benignant Nature most for this,—   570
A force of sympathy, or call it lack
Of character firm-planted, loosing me
From the pent chamber of habitual self
To dwell enlarged in alien modes of thought,
Haply distasteful, wholesomer for that,
And through imagination to possess,
As they were mine, the lives of other men.
This growth original of virgin soil,
By fascination felt in opposites,
Pleases and shocks, entices and perturbs.   580
In this brown-fisted rough, this shirt-sleeved Cid,
This backwoods Charlemagne of empires new,
Whose blundering heel instinctively finds out
The goutier foot of speechless dignities,
Who, meeting Cæsar's self, would slap his back,
Call him "Old Horse," and challenge to a drink,
My lungs draw braver air, my breast dilates
With ampler manhood, and I front both worlds,
Of sense and spirit, as my natural fiefs,
To shape and then reshape them as I will.   590
It was the first man's charter; why not mine?
How forfeit? when deposed in other hands?

Thou shudder'st, Ovid? Dost in him forebode
A new avatar of the large-limbed Goth,
To break, or seem to break, tradition's clue,
And chase to dreamland back thy gods dethroned?
I think man's soul dwells nearer to the east,
Nearer to morning's fountains than the sun;
Herself the source whence all tradition sprang,
Herself at once both labyrinth and clue.   600
The miracle fades out of history,
But faith and wonder and the primal earth
Are born into the world with every child.
Shall this self-maker with the prying eyes,
This creature disenchanted of respect

By the New World's new fiend, Publicity,
Whose testing thumb leaves everywhere its smutch,
Not one day feel within himself the need
Of loyalty to better than himself,
That shall ennoble him with the upward look?   610
Shall he not catch the Voice that wanders earth,
With spiritual summons, dreamed or heard,
As sometimes, just ere sleep seals up the sense,
We hear our mother call from deeps of Time,
And, waking, find it vision,—none the less
The benediction bides, old skies return,
And that unreal thing, preëminent,
Makes air and dream of all we see and feel?
Shall he divine no strength unmade of votes,
Inward, impregnable, found soon as sought,   620
Not cognizable of sense, o'er sense supreme?
Else were he desolate as none before.
His holy places may not be of stone,
Nor made with hands, yet fairer far than aught
By artist feigned or pious ardor reared,
Fit altars for who guards inviolate
God's chosen seat, the sacred form of man.
Doubtless his church will be no hospital
For superannuate forms and mumping shams,
No parlor where men issue policies   630
Of life-assurance on the Eternal Mind,
Nor his religion but an ambulance
To fetch life's wounded and malingerers in,
Scorned by the strong; yet he, unconscious heir
To the influence sweet of Athens and of Rome,
And old Judæa's gift of secret fire,
Spite of himself shall surely learn to know
And worship some ideal of himself,
Some divine thing, large-hearted, brotherly,
Not nice in trifles, a soft creditor,   640
Pleased with his world, and hating only cant.
And, if his Church be doubtful, it is sure
That, in a world, made for whatever else,
Not made for mere enjoyment, in a world
Of toil but half-requited, or, at best,
Paid in some futile currency of breath,
A world of incompleteness, sorrow swift

And consolation laggard, whatsoe'er
The form of building or the creed professed,
The Cross, bold type of shame to homage turned, 650
Of an unfinished life that sways the world,
Shall tower as sovereign emblem over all.

The kobold Thought moves with us when we shift
Our dwelling to escape him; perched aloft
On the first load of household-stuff he went;
For, where the mind goes, goes old furniture.
I, who to Chartres came to feed my eye
And give to Fancy one clear holiday,
Scarce saw the minster for the thoughts it stirred
Buzzing o'er past and future with vain quest. 660
Here once there stood a homely wooden church,
Which slow devotion nobly changed for this
That echoes vaguely to my modern steps.
By suffrage universal it was built,
As practised then, for all the country came
From far as Rouen, to give votes for God,
Each vote a block of stone securely laid
Obedient to the master's deep-mused plan.
Will what our ballots rear, responsible
To no grave forethought, stand so long as this? 670
Delight like this the eye of after days
Brightening with pride that here, at least, were men
Who meant and did the noblest thing they knew?
Can our religion cope with deeds like this?
We, too, build Gothic contract-shams, because
Our deacons have discovered that it pays,
And pews sell better under vaulted roofs
Of plaster painted like an Indian squaw.
Shall not that Western Goth, of whom we spoke,
So fiercely practical, so keen of eye, 680
Find out, some day, that nothing pays but God,
Served whether on the smoke-shut battle-field,
In work obscure done honestly, or vote
For truth unpopular, or faith maintained
To ruinous convictions, or good deeds
Wrought for good's sake, mindless of heaven or hell?
Shall he not learn that all prosperity,
Whose bases stretch not deeper than the sense,

Is but a trick of this world's atmosphere,
A desert-born mirage of spire and dome,   690
Or find too late, the Past's long lesson missed,
That dust the prophets shake from off their feet
Grows heavy to drag down both tower and wall?
I know not; but, sustained by sure belief
That man still rises level with the height
Of noblest opportunities, or makes
Such, if the time supply not, I can wait.
I gaze round on the windows, pride of France,
Each the bright gift of some mechanic guild
Who loved their city and thought gold well spent   700
To make her beautiful with piety;
I pause, transfigured by some stripe of bloom,
And my mind throngs with shining auguries,
Circle on circle, bright as seraphim,
With golden trumpets, silent, that await
The signal to blow news of good to men.

Then the revulsion came that always comes
After these dizzy elations of the mind:
And with a passionate pang of doubt I cried,
"O mountain-born, sweet with snow-filtered air   710
From uncontaminate wells of ether drawn
And never-broken secrecies of sky,
Freedom, with anguish won, misprized till lost,
They keep thee not who from thy sacred eyes
Catch the consuming lust of sensual good
And the brute's license of unfettered will.
Far from the popular shout and venal breath
Of Cleon blowing the mob's baser mind
To bubbles of wind-piloted conceit,
Thou shrinkest, gathering up thy skirts, to hide   720
In fortresses of solitary thought
And private virtue strong in self-restraint.
Must we too forfeit thee misunderstood,
Content with names, nor inly wise to know
That best things perish of their own excess,
And quality o'er-driven becomes defect?
Nay, is it thou indeed that we have glimpsed,
Or rather such illusion as of old
Through Athens glided menadlike and Rome,

A shape of vapor, mother of vain dreams 730
And mutinous traditions, specious plea
Of the glaived tyrant and long-memoried priest?"

I walked forth saddened; for all thought is sad,
And leaves a bitterish savor in the brain,
Tonic, it may be, not delectable,
And turned, reluctant, for a parting look
At those old weather-pitted images
Of bygone struggle, now so sternly calm.
About their shoulders sparrows had built nests,
And fluttered, chirping, from gray perch to perch, 740
Now on a mitre poising, now a crown,
Irreverently happy. While I thought
How confident they were, what careless hearts
Flew on those lightsome wings and shared the sun,
A larger shadow crossed; and looking up,
I saw where, nesting in the hoary towers,
The sparrow-hawk slid forth on noiseless air,
With sidelong head that watched the joy below,
Grim Norman baron o'er this clan of Kelts.
Enduring Nature, force conservative, 750
Indifferent to our noisy whims! Men prate
Of all heads to an equal grade cashiered
On level with the dullest, and expect
(Sick of no worse distemper than themselves)
A wondrous cure-all in equality;
They reason that To-morrow must be wise
Because To-day was not, nor Yesterday,
As if good days were shapen of themselves,
Not of the very lifeblood of men's souls;
Meanwhile, long-suffering, imperturbable, 760
Thou quietly complet'st thy syllogism,
And from the premise sparrow here below
Draw'st sure conclusion of the hawk above,
Pleased with the soft-billed songster, pleased no less
With the fierce beak of natures aquiline.

Thou beautiful Old Time, now hid away
In the Past's valley of Avilion,
Haply, like Arthur, till thy wound be healed,
Then to reclaim the sword and crown again!

Thrice beautiful to us; perchance less fair 770
To who possessed thee, as a mountain seems
To dwellers round its bases but a heap
Of barren obstacle that lairs the storm
And the avalanche's silent bolt holds back
Leashed with a hair,—meanwhile some far-off clown,
Hereditary delver of the plain,
Sees it an unmoved vision of repose,
Nest of the morning, and conjectures there
The dance of streams to idle shepherds' pipes,
And fairer habitations softly hung 780
On breezy slopes, or hid in valleys cool,
For happier men. No mortal ever dreams
That the scant isthmus he encamps upon
Between two oceans, one, the Stormy, passed,
And one, the Peaceful, yet to venture on,
Has been that future whereto prophets yearned
For the fulfilment of Earth's cheated hope,
Shall be that past which nerveless poets moan
As the lost opportunity of song.

O Power, more near my life than life itself 790
(Or what seems life to us in sense immured),
Even as the roots, shut in the darksome earth,
Share in the tree-tops' joyance, and conceive
Of sunshine and wide air and wingèd things
By sympathy of nature, so do I
Have evidence of Thee so far above,
Yet in and of me! Rather Thou the root
Invisibly sustaining, hid in light,
Not darkness, or in darkness made by us.
If sometimes I must hear good men debate 800
Of other witness of Thyself than Thou,
As if there needed any help of ours
To nurse Thy flickering life, that else must cease,
Blown out, as 't were a candle, by men's breath,
My soul shall not be taken in their snare,
To change her inward surety for their doubt
Muffled from sight in formal robes of proof:
While she can only feel herself through Thee,
I fear not Thy withdrawal; more I fear,
Seeing, to know Thee not, hoodwinked with dreams 810

Of signs and wonders, while, unnoticed, Thou,
Walking Thy garden still, commun'st with men,
Missed in the commonplace of miracle.

ODE RECITED AT THE HARVARD COMMEMORATION

I

    Weak-winged is song,
Nor aims at that clear-ethered height
Whither the brave deed climbs for light:
    We seem to do them wrong,
Bringing our robin's-leaf to deck their hearse
Who in warm life-blood wrote their nobler verse,
Our trivial song to honor those who come
With ears attuned to strenuous trump and drum,
And shaped in squadron-strophes their desire,
Live battle-odes whose lines were steel and fire: 10
    ,Yet sometimes feathered words are strong,
A gracious memory to buoy up and save
From Lethe's dreamless ooze, the common grave
    Of the unventurous throng.

II

To-day our Reverend Mother welcomes back
    Her wisest Scholars, those who understood
The deeper teaching of her mystic tome,
    And offered their fresh lives to make it good:
        No lore of Greece or Rome,
No science peddling with the names of things,   20
Or reading stars to find inglorious fates,
        Can lift our life with wings
Far from Death's idle gulf that for the many waits,
        And lengthen out our dates
With that clear fame whose memory sings
In manly hearts to come, and nerves them and dilates:
Nor such thy teaching, Mother of us all!
        Not such the trumpet-call
        Of thy diviner mood,
        That could thy sons entice   30
From happy homes and toils, the fruitful nest
Of those half-virtues which the world calls best,
        Into War's tumult rude;
        But rather far that stern device

The sponsors chose that round thy cradle stood
   In the dim, unventured wood,
    The VERITAS that lurks beneath
    The letter's unprolific sheath,
  Life of whate'er makes life worth living,
Seed-grain of high emprise, immortal food,   40
   One heavenly thing whereof earth hath the giving.

III

Many loved Truth, and lavished life's best oil
   Amid the dust of books to find her,
Content at last, for guerdon of their toil,
   With the cast mantle she hath left behind her.
    Many in sad faith sought for her,
    Many with crossed hands sighed for her;
    But these, our brothers, fought for her,
    At life's dear peril wrought for her,
    So loved her that they died for her,   50
    Tasting the raptured fleetness
    Of her divine completeness:
    Their higher instinct knew
Those love her best who to themselves are true,
And what they dare to dream of, dare to do; ·
    They followed her and found her
    Where all may hope to find,
Not in the ashes of the burnt-out mind,
But beautiful, with danger's sweetness round her.
    Where faith made whole with deed   60
    Breathes its awakening breath
    Into the lifeless creed,
    They saw her plumed and mailed,
    With sweet, stern face unveiled,
And all-repaying eyes, look proud on them in death.

IV

Our slender life runs rippling by, and glides
   Into the silent hollow of the past;
    What is there that abides
    To make the next age better for the last?
     Is earth too poor to give us   70
    Something to live for here that shall outlive us?
     Some more substantial boon

Than such as flows and ebbs with Fortune's fickle moon?
  The little that we see
  From doubt is never free;
  The little that we do
  Is but half-nobly true;
  With our laborious hiving
What men call treasure, and the gods call dross,
  Life seems a jest of Fate's contriving,   80
  Only secure in every one's conniving,
A long account of nothings paid with loss,
Where we poor puppets, jerked by unseen wires,
  After our little hour of strut and rave,
With all our pasteboard passions and desires,
Loves, hates, ambitions, and immortal fires,
  Are tossed pell-mell together in the grave.
  But stay! no age was e'er degenerate,
  Unless men held it at too cheap a rate,
  For in our likeness still we shape our fate.   90
   Ah, there is something here
  Unfathomed by the cynic's sneer,
  Something that gives our feeble light
  A high immunity from Night,
  Something that leaps life's narrow bars
To claim its birthright with the hosts of heaven;
  A seed of sunshine that can leaven
  Our earthly dullness with the beams of stars,
   And glorify our clay
  With light from fountains elder than the Day;   100
  A conscience more divine than we,
  A gladness fed with secret tears,
  A vexing, forward-reaching sense
  Of some more noble permanence;
   A light across the sea,
Which haunts the soul and will not let it be,
Still beaconing from the heights of undegenerate years.

v

  Whither leads the path
  To ampler fates that leads?
  Not down through flowery meads,   110
  To reap an aftermath

Of youth's vainglorious weeds,
　　But up the steep, amid the wrath
And shock of deadly-hostile creeds,
　　Where the world's best hope and stay
By battle's flashes gropes a desperate way,
And every turf the fierce foot clings to bleeds.
　　Peace hath her not ignoble wreath,
　　Ere yet the sharp, decisive word
Light the black lips of cannon, and the sword   120
　　　Dreams in its easeful sheath;
But some day the live coal behind the thought,
　　　Whether from Baäl's stone obscene,
　　　Or from the shrine serene
　　　Of God's pure altar brought,
Bursts up in flame; the war of tongue and pen
Learns with what deadly purpose it was fraught,
And, helpless in the fiery passion caught,
Shakes all the pillared state with shock of men:
Some day the soft Ideal that we wooed   130
Confronts us fiercely, foe-beset, pursued,
And cries reproachful: "Was it, then, my praise,
And not myself was loved? Prove now thy truth;
I claim of thee the promise of thy youth;
Give me thy life, or cower in empty phrase,
The victim of thy genius, not its mate!"
　　Life may be given in many ways,
　　And loyalty to Truth be sealed
As bravely in the closet as the field,
　　So bountiful is Fate;   140
　　　But then to stand beside her,
　　　When craven churls deride her,
To front a lie in arms and not to yield,
　　　This shows, methinks, God's plan
　　　And measure of a stalwart man,
　　　Limbed like the old heroic breeds,
　　　Who stands self-poised on manhood's solid earth,
　　Not forced to frame excuses for his birth,
Fed from within with all the strength he needs.

VI

Such was he, our Martyr-Chief,   150
　　Whom late the Nation he had led,
　　With ashes on her head,

Wept with the passion of an angry grief:
Forgive me, if from present things I turn
To speak what in my heart will beat and burn,
And hang my wreath on his world-honored urn.
    Nature, they say, doth dote,
    And cannot make a man
    Save on some worn-out plan,
    Repeating us by rote: 160
For him her Old-World moulds aside she threw,
    And, choosing sweet clay from the breast
    Of the unexhausted West,
With stuff untainted shaped a hero new,
Wise, steadfast in the strength of God, and true.
    How beautiful to see
Once more a shepherd of mankind indeed,
Who loved his charge, but never loved to lead;
One whose meek flock the people joyed to be,
    Not lured by any cheat of birth,   170
    But by his clear-grained human worth,
And brave old wisdom of sincerity!
    They knew that outward grace is dust;
    They could not choose but trust
In that sure-footed mind's unfaltering skill,
    And supple-tempered will
That bent like perfect steel to spring again and thrust.
    His was no lonely mountain-peak of mind,
    Thrusting to thin air o'er our cloudy bars,
    A sea-mark now, now lost in vapors blind;   180
    Broad prairie rather, genial, level-lined,
    Fruitful and friendly for all human kind,
Yet also nigh to heaven and loved of loftiest stars.
    Nothing of Europe here,
Or, then, of Europe fronting mornward still,
    Ere any names of Serf and Peer
    Could Nature's equal scheme deface
    And thwart her genial will;
    Here was a type of the true elder race,
And one of Plutarch's men talked with us face to face.   190
    I praise him not; it were too late;
And some innative weakness there must be
In him who condescends to victory
Such as the Present gives, and cannot wait,
    Safe in himself as in a fate.

So always firmly he:
He knew to bide his time,
And can his fame abide,
Still patient in his simple faith sublime,
　　　Till the wise years decide.　　　　　　　　200
　　Great captains, with their guns and drums,
　　　Disturb our judgment for the hour,
　　　　But at last silence comes;
　These all are gone, and, standing like a tower,
　　Our children shall behold his fame,
　　The kindly-earnest, brave, foreseeing man,
Sagacious, patient, dreading praise, not blame,
　New birth of our new soil, the first American.

VII

Long as man's hope insatiate can discern
　　Or only guess some more inspiring goal　　　210
　　Outside of Self, enduring as the pole,
Along whose course the flying axles burn
Of spirits bravely pitched, earth's manlier brood;
　　Long as below we cannot find
　　The meed that stills the inexorable mind;
So long this faith to some ideal Good,
Under whatever mortal names it masks,
Freedom, Law, Country, this ethereal mood
That thanks the Fates for their severer tasks,
　　Feeling its challenged pulses leap,　　　　220
　　While others skulk in subterfuges cheap,
And, set in Danger's van, has all the boon it asks,
　　Shall win man's praise and woman's love,
　　Shall be a wisdom that we set above
All other skills and gifts to culture dear,
　　A virtue round whose forehead we inwreathe
　　Laurels that with a living passion breathe
When other crowns grow, while we twine them, sear.
　　What brings us thronging these high rites to pay,
And seal these hours the noblest of our year,　　230
　　Save that our brothers found this better way?

VIII

We sit here in the Promised Land
That flows with Freedom's honey and milk;
But 't was they won it, sword in hand,

Making the nettle danger soft for us as silk.
 We welcome back our bravest and our best;—
 Ah me! not all! some come not with the rest,
Who went forth brave and bright as any here!
I strive to mix some gladness with my strain,
  But the sad strings complain,
  And will not please the ear:
I sweep them for a pæan, but they wane
  Again and yet again
Into a dirge, and die away, in pain.
In these brave ranks I only see the gaps,
Thinking of dear ones whom the dumb turf wraps,
Dark to the triumph which they died to gain:
  Fitlier may others greet the living,
  For me the past is unforgiving;
   I with uncovered head
   Salute the sacred dead,
Who went, and who return not.—Say not so!
'T is not the grapes of Canaan that repay,
But the high faith that failed not by the way;
Virtue treads paths that end not in the grave;
No ban of endless night exiles the brave;
  And to the saner mind
We rather seem the dead that stayed behind.
Blow, trumpets, all your exultations blow!
For never shall their aureoled presence lack:
I see them muster in a gleaming row,
With ever-youthful brows that nobler show;
We find in our dull road their shining track;
  In every nobler mood
We feel the orient of their spirit glow,
Part of our life's unalterable good,
Of all our saintlier aspiration;
  They come transfigured back,
Secure from change in their high-hearted ways,
Beautiful evermore, and with the rays
Of morn on their white Shields of Expectation!

IX

  But is there hope to save
 Even this ethereal essence from the grave?
 What ever 'scaped Oblivion's subtle wrong
Save a few clarion names, or golden threads of song?

Save a few clarion names, or golden threads of song?
        Before my musing eye
    The mighty ones of old sweep by,
Disvoicèd now and insubstantial things,
As noisy once as we; poor ghosts of kings,
Shadows of empire wholly gone to dust,   280
And many races, nameless long ago,
To darkness driven by that imperious gust
Of ever-rushing Time that here doth blow:
O visionary world, condition strange,
Where naught abiding is but only Change,
Where the deep-bolted stars themselves still shift and range!
    Shall we to more continuance make pretence?
Renown builds tombs; a life-estate is Wit;
        And, bit by bit,
The cunning years steal all from us but woe;   290
    Leaves are we, whose decays no harvest sow.
        But, when we vanish hence,
Shall they lie forceless in the dark below,
Save to make green their little length of sods,
Or deepen pansies for a year or two,
Who now to us are shining-sweet as gods?
Was dying all they had the skill to do?
That were not fruitless: but the Soul resents
Such short-lived service, as if blind events
Ruled without her, or earth could so endure;   300
She claims a more divine investiture
Of longer tenure than Fame's airy rents;
Whate'er she touches doth her nature share;
Her inspiration haunts the ennobled air,
        Gives eyes to mountains blind,
Ears to the deaf earth, voices to the wind,
And her clear trump sings succor everywhere
By lonely bivouacs to the wakeful mind;
For soul inherits all that soul could dare:
        Yea, Manhood hath a wider span   310
And larger privilege of life than man.
The single deed, the private sacrifice,
So radiant now through proudly-hidden tears,
Is covered up erelong from mortal eyes
With thoughtless drift of the deciduous years;
But that high privilege that makes all men peers,

That leap of heart whereby a people rise
    Up to a noble anger's height,
And, flamed on by the Fates, not shrink, but grow more bright,
    That swift validity in noble veins,   320
    Of choosing danger and disdaining shame,
        Of being set on flame
    By the pure fire that flies all contact base
But wraps its chosen with angelic might,
      These are imperishable gains,
    Sure as the sun, medicinal as light,
    These hold great futures in their lusty reins
And certify to earth a new imperial race.

x

    Who now shall sneer?
    Who dare again to say we trace   330
    Our lines to a plebeian race?
      Roundhead and Cavalier!
Dumb are those names erewhile in battle loud;
Dream-footed as the shadow of a cloud,
    They flit across the ear:
That is best blood that hath most iron in 't,
To edge resolve with, pouring without stint
    For what makes manhood dear.
    Tell us not of Plantagenets,
Hapsburgs, and Guelfs, whose thin bloods crawl   340
Down from some victor in a border-brawl!
    How poor their outworn coronets,
Matched with one leaf of that plain civic wreath
Our brave for honor's blazon shall bequeath,
    Through whose desert a rescued Nation sets
Her heel on treason, and the trumpet hears
Shout victory, tingling Europe's sullen ears
    With vain resentments and more vain regrets!

XI

    Not in anger, not in pride,
    Pure from passion's mixture rude   350
    Ever to base earth allied,
    But with far-heard gratitude,
    Still with heart and voice renewed,

To heroes living and dear martyrs dead,
The strain should close that consecrates our brave.
   Lift the heart and lift the head!
      Lofty be its mood and grave,
      Not without a martial ring,
      Not without a prouder tread
      And a peal of exultation: *360*
      Little right has he to sing
      Through whose heart in such an hour
      Beats no march of conscious power,
      Sweeps no tumult of elation!
      'T is no Man we celebrate,
      By his country's victories great,
   A hero half, and half the whim of Fate,
      But the pith and marrow of a Nation
      Drawing force from all her men,
      Highest, humblest, weakest, all,   *370*
      For her time of need, and then
      Pulsing it again through them,
   Till the basest can no longer cower,
   Feeling his soul spring up divinely tall,
   Touched but in passing by her mantle-hem.
   Come back, then, noble pride, for 't is her dower!
      How could poet ever tower,
      If his passions, hopes, and fears,
      If his triumphs and his tears,
      Kept not measure with his people?   *380*
Boom, cannon, boom to all the winds and waves!
Clash out, glad bells, from every rocking steeple!
Banners, adance with triumph, bend your staves!
      And from every mountain-peak
      Let beacon-fire to answering beacon speak,
      Katahdin tell Monadnock, Whiteface he,
And so leap on in light from sea to sea,
         Till the glad news be sent
         Across a kindling continent,
Making earth feel more firm and air breathe braver: *390*
"Be proud! for she is saved, and all have helped to save her!
      She that lifts up the manhood of the poor,
      She of the open soul and open door,
      With room about her hearth for all mankind!
      The fire is dreadful in her eyes no more;

From her bold front the helm she doth unbind,
Sends all her handmaid armies back to spin,
And bids her navies, that so lately hurled
Their crashing battle, hold their thunders in,
Swimming like birds of calm along the unharmful shore. *400*
No challenge sends she to the elder world,
That looked askance and hated; a light scorn
Plays o'er her mouth, as round her mighty knees
She calls her children back, and waits the morn
Of nobler day, enthroned between her subject seas."

XII

Bow down, dear Land, for thou hast found release!
   Thy God, in these distempered days,
   Hath taught thee the sure wisdom of His ways,
And through thine enemies hath wrought thy peace!
   Bow down in prayer and praise! *410*
No poorest in thy borders but may now
Lift to the juster skies a man's enfranchised brow.
O Beautiful! my Country! ours once more!
Smoothing thy gold of war-dishevelled hair
O'er such sweet brows as never other wore,
   And letting thy set lips,
   Freed from wrath's pale eclipse,
The rosy edges of their smile lay bare,
What words divine of lover or of poet
Could tell our love and make thee know it, *420*
Among the Nations bright beyond compare?
   What were our lives without thee?
   What all our lives to save thee?
   We reck not what we gave thee;
   We will not dare to doubt thee,
But ask whatever else, and we will dare!

Longfellow

WHEN, in the celebrated experiment that *Practical Criticism* reports, I. A. Richards gave his class thirteen poems for critical discussion, he included one by Longfellow. We are not surprised that a greater percent of students regarded it more unfavorably than any other poem on the list, especially when we remember that the class was made up of persons well advanced in literary study. But when we also recall that these students' judgments on poetry showed a deplorable lack of taste and principle, we may pause at least a moment in hesitation. And we may wonder more when we see that the next two most unpopular poems were by D. H. Lawrence and Gerard Manley Hopkins.

Richards does right to warn that this ranking of the poets is a rough estimate in which we cannot put much reliance. Besides, the unfavorable response to Longfellow (92 percent) was so far ahead of that to his nearest competitor (Lawrence at 66 percent) that it puts him almost in a class by himself. Also, the reasons given for dislike were not all the same. Yet I cannot help thinking that there is some significance, if only a precautionary one, in the fact that Longfellow is grouped with poets that most of us would regard as his indisputable superiors. When we turn to the favorable response (which Richards differentiates from the unfavorable because of a noncommital group), Longfellow keeps even more impressive company. Again he is least popular (5 percent), followed by Lawrence (19 percent), Donne (30 percent), Hopkins (31 percent), and Hardy (also 31 percent). Furthermore, except for Edna St. Vincent Millay and Alfred Noyes (whose reputations have hardly stood better than Longfellow's) the most popular poems on either list were written by poets of slight or dubious fame.* There are only two important inconsistencies. Christina Rossetti ranks fourth most popular on the favorable list and fourth least popular on the unfavorable list, and the Reverend G. A. Studdert Kennedy (who styled himself "Woodbine Willie") ranks second most popular on the favorable list and fifth least popular—along with Donne and Hardy!—on the unfavorable list.

* For those who would like the complete ranking (which is given by numbers rather than by names in Richards' appendix) here it is in order of increasing popularity: Favorable— Longfellow (5%), Lawrence (19%), Donne (30%), Hopkins (31%), Hardy (31%), G. H. Luce (37%), Wilfred R. Childe (44%), Phillip J. Bailey (45%), Noyes (48%), Rossetti (51%), Millay (52%), Kennedy (53%), J. D. C. Pellew (54%). Unfavorable—Longfellow (92%), Lawrence (66%), Hopkins (59%), Rossetti (43%), Donne (42%), Kennedy (42%), Hardy (42%), Noyes (41%), Bailey (37%), Luce (36%), Millay (35%), Childe (33%), Pellew (31%).

Though during his lifetime critics frequently grouped Longfellow with the literary immortals, they did so on the basis of approval. What strikes one about the grouping made by Richards' students is that, in addition to the fact that anonymity of the poets avoided prejudice, Longfellow was classed with Lawrence, Hopkins, Donne, and Hardy because along with them he was disliked so much. Yet while the grouping by Richards causes the bigger shock, the reputation that Longfellow held among his contemporaries has cast a more pervasive shadow over anyone who writes about him today. Together the two pieces of evidence raise questions about our anti-Longfellowism that ought to make us humble; and though this essay does not pretend to give final answers, it may persuade some that Longfellow is not the sink of poetical iniquity that we have conventionally come to describe him.

The charges brought against Longfellow are widely enough disseminated for us to neglect their systematic recital. Every literary historian also knows that the better critics always had reservations about his poetical accomplishments. Against these charges and as a supplement to these reservations there developed early, as Clarence Gohdes has shown with nicety, a strategy of defense. The convention for handling Longfellow, he writes, was established early. "One believed it to be a duty to undermine the uncritical regard for the poet by analyzing his defects and then to find merits which more plebeian tastes had perhaps not discovered."

This kind of defense, less well known than the attack, deserves some citation as a preliminary to what will follow, for the defenders of Longfellow (of whom I admit myself to be one) have built upon it further. Most make their stand for a part of the poetry, yielding what remains to the enemy. Thus recently the longer narratives have received a certain emphasis, a revival of the defense of certain nineteenth-century critics. But using the same kind of strategy, in 1907 George Saintsbury had tried to placate the enemy by yielding them the narratives, and made a valiant effort to save the short poems as constituting the markedly best of Longfellow's work. At about the same time Paul Elmer More had sought to restrict defense to an even more limited field, the sonnets. He declared that our poet was "a peer among the great sonnet writers of England"—rather blithely disregarding his shrewd counsel earlier in the same essay when he warned, "Let us not blunt or pervert our taste by ignoring distinctions." Also at the same time, the centennial of Longfellow's birth, William Dean Howells had discriminated between the didactic and non-didactic. In some poems he found no didacticism, in some he argued a blend of didacticism with poetry, and in still others he confessed its extrusive presence but advised readers to omit the several stanzas where it appeared.

These several strategies of divide and *reconquer* had, as the material from Mr. Gohdes shows, been anticipated by critics of the mid-nineteenth century. Anticipated too is another defense, going back at least as far as E. C. Stedman in 1885, who urged a difference between those poems of Longfellow which were written for the "primary class" and those written for the "upper form." In the *Cambridge History of American Literature* W. P. Trent makes a distinction along somewhat similar lines in speaking of the "double appeal" of Longfellow. Recently in the best essay on Longfellow since his centenary Norman Holmes Pearson makes further exploration under the title *Both Longfellows*. He comments: "What is chiefly disturbing in Longfellow's poems is his confusion of audiences, the frequency with which a poem for the court is turned by simile into a poem for the people. To serve both at once is a democratic concept, but it makes for awkward poetical relationships."

There have also been other defenses of a more general nature, sometimes used by these same critics. Thus Saintsbury and More undertake a broader line of battle in their unashamed support of Longfellow for his genteelness. "Sentiment, when it becomes (as it has rather a tendency to become), sentimentalism, is not the best of things," writes the first; "but it is at any rate better than the cheap and childish paradox, and much better than the banal brutality, which have been sometimes offered in its place." Longfellow, suggests More, had the "inward serenity and unvexed faith which it is the mission of the poet to bestow." And as always there is the historical argument to fall back upon. Even Odell Shepard, who since his editing of a volume of Longfellow in 1934 has become a good deal more stringent in his evaluation, recently warned that "not to know Longfellow, or to be contemptuous of him, is to lose some part of one's national heritage."

But neither the historical nor the moralistic arguments are very persuasive. The first fails when we think of such contemporaries of Longfellow as Emerson, Hawthorne, and Melville, the second when we think of the deeper morality exhibited by these and many authors of any time. The selection of certain genres of our poet's work promises more, and has indeed much in common with the method followed for at least one other poet in this book. But it seems to me that for Longfellow the divisions proposed are too sharp. Also, except in *Both Longfellows* they disappoint by the generality of their literary concern and the tendency to get away from a literary estimate into other modes of criticism.

As with our other schoolroom poets, we experience a lack of detailed literary evaluation of Longfellow. We have had witnesses in plenty that no other poet quite duplicates Longfellow's sweetness of sound and tone; but we have also heard that he is meretricious and stupidly bland. In the 1920's G. R. Elliott attempted a certain re-establishment of Longfellow's reputation by pointing parallels (hardly convincing) between some of his poems and those of the poetic idols of that decade. A good many others have reminded us that Longfellow showed craftsmanship—he did understand, remarks Mr. Shepard, "the elementary but oft neglected fact that a poet must make poems"—but they have seldom specified how that craftsmanship functioned.

At the outset of any study of Longfellow and all the way along, we must recognize that as a poet he had fully pledged his work in the interest of morality. To this in itself we cannot object, unless we are willing to dispense with most classics and the best modern literature. But negatively we question the profoundness of his moral view, and positively we object to the manner of fulfilling the pledge: an open didacticism which frequently seems to relegate the other parts of the poem to no more than a shifty preparation for a lesson. Though along with Howells we may point to many nondidactic poems or suggest the avoidance of the didactic parts, in so doing we avoid the issue. The didactic poems are so many and didacticism permeates the tone of the writings so thoroughly that we cannot overlook it.

Another kind of solution is advanced by Mr. Pearson in his essay. Extending the view that some of Longfellow's poems are for "the court of Cambridge and of the Harvard Yard" and some for "the middle classes and the populace," we may possibly look further for solution in the method by which Longfellow handles his didacticism. To what extent was he able to produce art to which both court and populace might respond? Much art has always functioned adequately for several levels of experience; and though our tendency is to rule out this possibility for the nineteenth century, some doubt remains whether we should. Howells urged of Longfellow that first he charms and then teaches. The Harvard Yard, it may be suggested, took pleasure in metaphor and the common reader in message. But not to make this separation absolute, the Yard also felt the integration of form and content, and the street was aware of it too in the sense that it took Longfellow's messages to its heart in a way in which it did not take the unadorned sermon (whether in poetry or prose).

Completely realized, a poem by Longfellow moves in three stages, of which *Snow-Flakes* (p. 222) furnishes an excellent example both as demonstration of method and of good poetry. In this poem each stanza marks a stage. The first gives us the scene:

> Out of the bosom of the Air,
>> Out of the cloud-folds of her garments shaken,
> Over the woodlands brown and bare . . .

With the second we have our analogy, in which the relation to man is explored:

> Even as our cloudy fancies take
> Suddenly shape in some divine expression,
> Even as the troubled heart doth make
> In the white countenance confession,
> The troubled sky reveals
> The grief it feels.

Elsewhere Longfellow does not always explore that relationship as fully as he might, and when he does explore it fully, the itemization of particulars sometimes gives us the effect of a mechanical formula. But in *Snow-Flakes* the relevance seems right, with exactly enough to hold the stanza to the scene and with further exploration adequately anticipated in the word "grief." That further exploration moves from analogy to statement, the third stage of the poem:

> This is the poem of the air . . .
> Now whispered and revealed
> To wood and field.

In this stanza Longfellow has stayed close to the original elements of his scene and has not let his statement become exhortation. He has muted his method. As Mr. Pearson says, though there is a simile in the second stanza, "the similitude which relates our fancies and our heart to the heavens is not insisted on and is itself actually enveloped in a congeries of metaphors by which man, physical nature, the atmosphere, and God become inextricably interwoven." But the essential method is still there with its elements of scene, analogy, and statement.

In contrast to *Snow-Flakes*, the poem *The Rainy Day* shows this method at its worst with a mechanical preservation of the points of analogy and with a hortatory statement that bursts through scene and analogy to a goal of moral insistency. The first stanza is fair, the second dubious, the third bad. Yet Longfellow, though we may deplore the result, was working just as soundly in his poetic medium. The contemporary reader of Longfellow, no matter how keen his literary sensibility, could quite honorably have a poetic pleasure in the lyric that our remoteness from his time will not allow us.

Other instances of the method much more happy for us than *The Rainy Day* are *The Building of the Ship* and *In the Churchyard at Cambridge*. Both these have clearly defined stages, and both show a third stage of statement that is hortatory in the extreme. In the former poem the analogical part presents bride and bridegroom in terms of the marriage of the ship to the sea, with some symbolic undertone of the sea as life and death. A statement for the bride—"Sail forth into the sea of life" —follows. Then, with what seems a calculated shock, this domestic advice is capped by the political exhortation, "Thou, too, sail on, O Ship of State!" The daring of the sudden shift, which was a revision of the original draft, justifies the structural transgression.

The poem with which Richards deals, *In the Churchyard at Cambridge* (p. 223), presents the analogical stage in terms of questions: Was the manner of the lady's burial a sign of vanity or humility? We receive no answer now, and it is foolish of us to expect one in the hereafter.

> Ah, you will then have other cares,
> In your own shortcomings and despairs,
> In your own secret sins and terrors!

Here is the statement—one which Richards calls "extremely urbane, rather witty, and *slightly* whimsical," and one which rises pertinently from the scene and its implications. Longfellow has thoroughly utilized his method to produce a poem of moral, as well as formal, charm.

A great many of the poems do not move through all three stages and in omitting the last stage avoid a danger always implicit in it. With classical brevity and poise a stanza from one of the *Tales of a Wayside Inn* shows what happens:

> Ships that pass in the night, and speak each other in passing,
> Only a signal shown and a distant voice in the darkness;
> So on the ocean of life, we pass and speak one another,
> Only a look and a voice, then darkness again and a silence.

Though the exact balancing of parts may here seem to be as mechanical as in *The Rainy Day* (made possibly worse by the intrusive "so"), there is a difference. For here the poet does not force the analogy, and going on to analogy he also remains in the scene. But more than this the analogy makes an extension with the word "silence." Silence existed in the scene of the passing ships but was not expressed; now added suddenly it throws a tremendous weight of pathos into the condition of man.

On a larger scale *Seaweed* (p. 224) gives further insight into Longfellow's work in two stages. It would be wrong to dismiss the last four stanzas as "worse than valueless"; and certainly they are not, as they have been declared, "homiletic." Longfellow could have made a homily ("out of chaotic experience the poet achieves the serenity of art"), and with fuller cognizance of materials and meter than my statement shows he might have stayed within the bounds of his poem. What current taste really objects to in the poem is not the analogy but the tendency to make it

mechanical. On my part I should like the poem much better if Long-
fellow from the third stanza had gone immediately to the eighth, suddenly
presenting poetry as having come to the repose on the beach that had been
anticipated for the seaweed in the earlier part of the scene:

> When descends on the Atlantic
>   The gigantic
> Storm-wind of the equinox,
> Landward in his wrath he scourges
>   The toiling surges,
> Laden with seaweed from the rocks:
>
> From Bermuda's reefs; from edges
>   Of sunken ledges,
> In some far-off, bright Azore;
> From Bahama, and the dashing,
>   Silver-flashing
> Surges of San Salvador;
>
> From the tumbling surf, that buries
>   The Orkneyan skerries,
> Answering the hoarse Hebrides;
> And from wrecks of ships, and drifting
>   Spars, uplifting
> On the desolate, rainy seas;—
>
> Ever drifting, drifting, drifting
>   On the shifting
> Currents of the restless heart;
> Till at length in books recorded,
>   They, like hoarded
> Household words, no more depart.

Yet with a response less chronologically restricted, we might prefer—
even ought to prefer—the poem just as its author wrote it. If we read the
poem right, we do not forget the pervasive rhythm and imagery of the
first four stanzas in the analogy of the last four. And though we may
complain with Rudolph Von Abele that Longfellow does not show an
awareness of the connotations of seaweed, with its grotesqueness as a
symbol of an ultimate poetic good, it is likely that the poet had the same
degree of whimsicality in treating it that Richards found in the tone of
In the Churchyard. Longfellow's age took comfort in extensive moral
explanation and was uneasy when wit was forced to its attention; our

age is hot for wit and boggles at direct moral intent. But though the emphasis is reversed, it is likely that the best readers in each age expect both elements.

One reason for the good repute which Longfellow's sonnets enjoy is probably that the form almost automatically limits the poet to a two-stage movement. Again we face the difficulty of too great adherence to formula, though at his best Longfellow manages to overcome it by a balanced admixture of precision and variety. The sonnet *Nature*, though it may terrify us with its hackneyed "as . . . so," belongs with those that surmount the limitations. It is instructive to compare this with its probable source, Leigh Hunt's translation of Filicaja's sonnet on providence, for the Hunt-Filicaja sonnet lacks the concreteness of Longfellow's scene. Because of this difference, *Nature* excels in effect as it moves from scene to analogy by close correspondence. It remains concrete while at the same time it expands into abstraction. The first sonnet of the *Divina Commedia* sequence (p. 225) yields an even more assayable richness. Again we have the careful correspondence in the laying down of the burden, in the prayer, and in the quietness:

> So, as I enter here from day to day,
>> And leave my burden at this minster gate,
>> Kneeling in prayer, and not ashamed to pray,
> The tumult of the time disconsolate
>> To inarticulate murmurs dies away,
>> While the eternal ages watch and wait.

But with this sonnet the analogy remains an image, a restraint which heightens the effect in a fashion unusual in Longfellow. His refusal to designate his translation as a translation and to tie down the "time disconsolate" to the Civil War contrasts notably with his openness of application in such a poem as *Seaweed*. A further merit lies in the surprising but relevant expansion of the details of the image. The "noises of the world" are more than fulfilled in the "tumult of the time," and the image of the cathedral heightened in the idea of eternity. Though one may be repulsed by the digressive didacticism of the phrase "and not ashamed to pray," even that detail is not a gratuitous intrusion. Besides it should be just as easy to forgive an extraneous moral as it is to forgive an occasional display of rhetoric, wit, and biography for their own sakes.

Still another kind of the two-stage poem may be touched upon, a kind which does not make the clear division of the "as . . . so," but which does clearly utilize the two elements of scene and analogy. The "carillon" stanzas of *The Belfry of Bruges* shift from chimes to poetry, yet we are brought back to the scene again, and the analogy is half dismissed with the stanza beginning "Thus dreamed I." In the second part of the poem, which though metrically much less distinctive should not be omitted as it is generally in anthologies, the first part is led away from even farther. In this passage of countersuggestion a new vision induced by the bells is interrupted by the sound of drums and of the workaday world. But the poet records only his sense perception: "Lo! the shadow of the belfry crossed the sun-illumined square."

In *The Fire of Drift-Wood* (p. 226) the two stages, though apparent, are closely blended. The conversation of the friends at the old farmhouse, presented as scene in the first seven stanzas, later becomes analogy for the image of the fire. That image first appears in the eighth stanza:

> Oft died the words upon our lips,
> As suddenly, from out the fire
> Built of the wreck of stranded ships,
> The flames would leap and then expire.

Here it is simile if the "as" may be read both comparatively and temporally; but rather than ending the poem with analogy, the extension in the next three stanzas makes it become the real scene, while the former scene becomes the analogical element. Talk turns to the sea and its perils, all merged in "The long-lost ventures of the heart, That send no answers back again." In the last stanza we have what might be argued as the third stage of hortatory statement. Yet since the poet addresses the fire and the occupants of the room, we should more properly regard the stanza as the final (and impressive) expression of the analogy:

> O flames that glowed! O hearts that yearned!
> They were indeed too much akin,
> The drift-wood fire without that burned,
> The thoughts that burned and glowed within.

Again the reader will sense a shy whimsicality in the phrase "too much," which without mocking the analogical method still offers its use here in a mood of restraint.

The two-stage poem does not have the immediate dangers of the three-stage poem that ends in homily. But both groups have their virtues. That cannot be said for most of the poems which (also two-stage) move directly from scene to statement. Here the poet's haste toward exhortation and impatience with his materials destroy any poetic effect that may occur elsewhere in the poem. The link betwen the lesson taught by the village blacksmith and the details of his life is tantalizingly tenuous, if it exists at all. When as in *Gaspar Becerra* the connection is close, it repels by its flatness. Even if there is no great haste toward statement and if the poet, once arrived there, lingers over his message, we still have the essential abruptness of *The Arsenal at Springfield*. With such poems as these less poetry appears than when the poem, openly didactic from beginning to end, makes no pretense of scene except as stage property. But there too we suffer from a sense of either pastiche, as *A Psalm of Life*, or flat allegory, as *Excelsior*. Since critics have copiously recorded their hurt from poems of this sort, there is no reason for further indulgence in these pages.

In the consideration of Longfellow's method a final kind of poem deserves mention, for it too operates loosely within the pattern of the three stages. That, of course, is the poem which functions only in the stage of scene, which does not enter the second stage of analogy or the third of statement at all. There are not many of these poems by Longfellow, but there are some. Among them I should count as successes *The Skeleton in Armor*, *My Lost Youth*, *Aftermath*, and *The Tide Rises, the Tide Falls*. Agreement would be pretty general that we are much happier with these poems than with the bulk of Longfellow, and the obvious temptation is to separate them out from the other poems and to admire them as the fragments which have survived the wreck of the poet's reputation. But to yield to such a temptation would raise difficult questions in criticism. *Snow-Flakes*, a three-stage poem, must be admitted to be as fine an achievement as the "purer" poem, *The Tide Rises*. *The Legend Beautiful*, which is an interesting example of the two-stage poem, shows as much poetical finish if not quite so immediate effectiveness as *The Skeleton in Armor*. The presence or absence of analogy and statement does not in itself determine success or failure. Indeed, I would go a step farther than this, though with some caution, and say that when Longfellow works well in analogy and statement he produces poetry that being more complex carries overtones of poetical effectiveness that his one-stage poems do not.

At his best in the one-stage poems Longfellow shows the same sort of structural sense that he shows in his poems of two or three stages, and in doing this bears out much of the argument made for his poetical craftsmanship there. The play upon the images of predatory and nonpredatory birds in *The Skeleton in Armor* is evidence of this view. In revising *My Lost Youth* Longfellow discarded one stanza and rearranged the others to produce a three-part pattern in which pleasant nostalgia and poignant melancholy are reconciled by a joy that at least partially integrates conflicting experiences. In both *Aftermath* (p. 227) and *The Tide Rises* his scenes are weighted with meticulously controlled symbolic meaning. Of the first of these poems, which deserves more fame than it has, it should be remarked that in using the word "aftermath" Longfellow does so almost entirely with its original meaning of a late autumn crop in mind, for though the figurative meaning was known in his time, it was not common. The

overtones of old age, of a change of poetical yield, and of death were thus
presented more subtly to the nineteenth-century reader than they seem to
us today.

> Not the sweet, new grass with flowers
> Is this harvesting of ours;
> Not the upland clover bloom;
> But the rowen mixed with weeds,
> Tangled tufts from marsh and meads,
> Where the poppy drops its seeds
> In the silence and the gloom.

In the word "poppy" of the next to the last line, the poet, as we have seen
him doing in the lines on "ships that pass in the night," extends his mean-
ing with firm precision.

In our examination of Longfellow's method certain qualities have been
touched upon that call for direct comment. These have to do with image,
tone, and ideas. Of the first of them I shall not have much to say that is
favorable, except for what has already been said in discussing didacticism.
But my treatment of tone and ideas will be mostly eulogistic.

Two poems, highly prized as they are and indeed deserving of some
praise, exhibit a carelessness with imagery which one runs into throughout
the poetry. Thus *Mezzo Cammin* begins with an image of building "Some
tower of song with lofty parapet." Then, too anxious to make an extension
in personal terms and perhaps also too anxious to justify lack of accom-
plishment, Longfellow turns in the second half of the octet to abstractions.
Coming back to his image in the last six lines, the poet is now climbing a
hill: "Though, half-way up the hill, I see the Past . . ." You *can*, if you
work hard at it, integrate the image, and in *The Builders* Longfellow has
shown what he had in mind:

> Thus alone can we attain
> To those turrets, where the eye
> Sees the world as one vast plain
> And one boundless reach of sky.

But in working at it we feel that we are helping the poet out, and that he
has ultimately failed us through his looseness of concept.

Though it is far more skillful, another sonnet, *The Evening Star*, does
not deserve the grade of "best" that Saintsbury has given it. In this sonnet
the lady stands as the standard of comparison in the octet (the evening
star is "like a fair lady") and the star as the standard in the sestet (the
lady retires "as that fair planet"). But to prepare for the retirement of
the lady in the latter part, Longfellow has had to describe the retirement

of the star in the first part. In doing this, he strikes us as having manufactured details in the setting of the star for the main action of the last six lines.

On the other hand, this sense of empirical artistry does not occur in a great many of the poems. *Snow-Flakes, The Fire of Drift-Wood,* and *Seaweed,* to name a few that we have considered, do not have it. Also, poems which at first glance may appear to be awkwardly contrived for a formula do not always turn out to be that. In *Jugurtha* (p. 228), for example, Richard E. Amacher has shown how Longfellow, using material from Plutarch, changed it not to prepare an easy anticipation of his theme but to enrich the whole image. According to Plutarch the African monarch on the point of death cries out to Hercules. As against this in the poem he exclaims, "How cold are thy baths, Apollo!" The choice of Apollo, Mr. Amacher has written, is "doubly appropriate"—first, as the god of manliness and beauty, and second, as the god of sudden death. The choice is also natural for the poet of the second stanza in addressing his traditional patron:

> How cold are thy baths, Apollo!
> Cried the Poet, unknown, unbefriended . . .

"It is as terrible," comments Mr. Amacher, "for the poet to lose his poetic vision as it is for the monarch to lose his throne and life. The warmth, brightness, and magnificence of Apollo ends in a frosty chill for both."

But the fitness of image in *Jugurtha* ought not to obscure the humor of the poem. Though Longfellow has selected an incident of great pathos and one which could lend itself to tragedy, he is certainly aware of the wit of Jugurtha and the poet. He uses words of great potential import— "death," "vision," "dream of his life"—but he is content to envelop them in an exclamation of colloquial bravado, even though he does not shrug off the horror of the scene:

> . . . And the dream of his life was ended;
> How cold are thy baths, Apollo!

This kind of thing takes us back to Richards' characterization and allows us to claim for Longfellow a perfection of mood that exhibits a polished social tone, neither comic nor sentimental, but humanely ethical. This tone has mostly been neglected in treating our poet, though it ought to have more recognition in justice both to him and to his readers.

It has been recognized fully in one poem, *The Courtship of Miles Standish.* "Geniality," "comedy . . . of a perfection," "racy of New England," "frolicsome humor" are some of the words and phrases used by critics in describing this work. But they do not use such terms very often of Longfellow, and in reading *Miles Standish* with students I have sometimes found it hard to establish a sense of its quizzical treatment of the fathers of New England. Still, unless predispositions are very strong, one cannot avoid the comedy in *Miles Standish*. Comedy is obvious also in a great many other narrative pieces. *King Witlaff's Drinking-Horn*, with its story of the monks who upon the death of their abbot drink another toast to an opportunely new saint, treats mortality with an aggressively comic assurance. In *The Cobbler of Hagenau* and *The Monk of Casal-Maggiore* we have delightful stories of medieval life that demonstrate Longfellow's potentiality as a comic artist. This is not to say that he was a comic artist, but rather that he shows a pervasive geniality throughout much of his work. In parts of such idyls as *Evangeline* and *Elizabeth*, as well as in the nonnarrative poetry, geniality is also widely present.

We come back then to the judgment of Richards, who found in its tone the secret of the poem *In the Churchyard*. It had, he said, a "social, urbane, highly cultivated, self-confident, temperate and easy kind of humour." It was "not a grim warning, or an exhortation, but a cheerful realization of the situation, not in the least evangelical." When Hawthorne wrote to Longfellow on the *Tales of a Wayside Inn*, we also glimpse the same response: "It seems idle to tell you that I have read the Wayside Inn with great comfort and delight. I take vast satisfaction in your poetry and take very little in most other men's, except it be the grand old strains that have been sounding on through all my life." Hawthorne recognizes what is too commonly overlooked—that we make the wrong assumption in looking to Longfellow for "the grand old strains." The poet treats problems of morality with social winsomeness. But it is hard to put into words a precise measure of that process. In calling *The Children's Hour* a "jocund sketch," Alfred Kreymborg has emphasized the comic too much. Mr. Pearson, who labels it a "domestic conceit," comes closer to its center. A contemporary catches its true quality with less technical expression: "That joyous hour," wrote Holmes, "his song made doubly dear."

How much Longfellow was aware of this tone is hard to gauge. He does not ever have much to say in a critical vein, and his poems on poetry do not go much beyond a romantic or genteel Platonism in their concept of the origin or function of art. A remark on Dante in a letter of 1864 has pertinence: "What fools some critics make of themselves by insisting that Dante ought to keep himself up to his highest level. As if he did not know what he was about. Sometimes the sock, sometimes the buskin; the final result a real *commedia*." In his poem *The Singers* he accepts several purposes for poetry, whether its gift is to charm, strengthen, or teach, but the kind of poetry which he wrote is not well described by any of the three (which Longfellow glossed as lyric, epic, and devotional or didactic) or by a combination. Possibly his incomplete syntax in one stanza of *The Poet and His Songs* is significant of his own inability at self-appraisal and forbearance from it:

> His, and not his, are the lays
> He sings; and their fame
> Is his, and not his; and the praise
> And the pride of a name.

Even if he had conscious purpose, he probably did not have enough of it. As with Lowell, though less disastrously, he did not fully know where his best parts lay. There are certainly plenty of examples of lack of humor in his verses. Part of this undoubtedly comes from the climate of his time, as the fact that three of the best humorous narratives use settings of medieval Catholicism as against only one that uses the setting of New England Puritanism. Someone once gave him a pen "Made from a fetter of the Prisoner Bonnivard, of Chillon; the handle of wood from the Frigate Constitution, and bound with a circlet of gold, inset with three precious stones from Siberia, Ceylon, and Maine." Upon this strange conglomeration Longfellow wrote a poem in thanks. That such a gift could be given and received in all seriousness makes us wrinkle our noses at the tastelessness of the age and of its laureate. The event and poem are so remote that we have no means of measuring them except dismay.

Just as Longfellow many times misses that perfection of mood which can have poetic pleasure for us, so his placid faith in mankind and his lack of profundity will leave us with a sense of inadequacy. In part our response is sound, but in part we seem to be making demands upon the poet that we have no right to urge. Though Longfellow does not go deeply into human experience, he sees with a good deal of clarity and poise that life which comes to his view. Without prophetic insight, he has perceptive everyday understanding, and he is willing to use diverse materials which show considerably larger spread than we might expect from our judgment of the genteel predilections of his background.

Most of all, I suppose that we think of his use of European and American scene and legend, and we are apt to say that he avoided his own culture by using the first and that when he went to the second his method was to Europeanize native materials. Both charges have truth. Yet concerning his use of Europe we should not forget that pressure was greater in Longfellow's time than ours for native material. In going to Europe (though he was following in the footsteps of Irving) he was moving against the literary currents of his day. A number of passages in the *Tales of a Wayside Inn* show his awareness of the problem and the reasons for his solution.

We next think of Longfellow as a domestic poet, singing the joys and sorrows of the family circle. This too is a sound judgment, but like the others it leaves out much. Longfellow went well beyond. *The Seaside and the Fireside*, a title used for his volume in 1850, suggests that he had a larger view than of the home. Through his friendships, he wrote on many public figures in a variety of activities (the sequence *Three Friends of Mine*). Though inadequately, he concerned himself with slavery and the Civil War, he attempted the industrial scene (*The Ropewalk*), he wrote on literature from Chaucer to Bayard Taylor and on its past (*The Singers*) and future (*Possibilities*). We miss his dealing with natural fact, sensuous detail, and the life of the time as we see it through our greater perspective. All the same, we should remember him as almost like the periodical essayist in his constant search for subjects and his welcoming use of a large variety of material.

In not going deep and in keeping on a social level, he exemplifies the manner of the periodical essayist. Yet because of this he should not be branded as genteel. *The Falcon of Ser Federigo* (p. 228), derived from Boccaccio's *Decameron*, shows the extent of Longfellow's willingness to follow material which, though not sordid, is far from prettified. Boccaccio tells about the knight who kills his cherished falcon so that he may provide a worthy meal for his beloved lady; but after they eat he learns that she has visited him to secure the falcon for her son who in feverish sickness has set his heart on it. If there is any chance for recovery, the boy has lost it by the falcon's death.

Longfellow follows these particulars of the plot closely. Interestingly, in view of his tendency toward diffuseness and didacticism, he reduces the length of Boccaccio by about one-fifth and offers a homily of less seriousness than that of his source. It may be to Longfellow's disadvantage that he reduces the passages in which the characters talk about the psychological conflicts which the situation raises, though it seems more likely that he secures the same effect of conflict without Boccaccio's wordiness. Certainly the presentation of action in specific, concretely delineated scenes is to the American poet's advantage. Boccaccio has one rude touch that Longfellow omits—Federigo's dramatic casting of the falcon's feathers, feet, and beak before his lady when he tells her that they have eaten the bird. But perhaps Longfellow makes up for this omission by adding that a falcon has been carved upon the lady's favorite chair after her marriage to Federigo:

> The image of a falcon carved in wood,
> And underneath the inscription, with a date,
> "All things come round to him who will but wait."

That is Longfellow's urbane and half-cynical moral, reflecting upon the fate of the dead falcon and dead son as well as upon the good fortune of Ser Federigo and Monna Giovanna. Though I would not say that he does better than Boccaccio (for as he wrote of Chaucer, the imitator must always fall vanquished), I find this focus of his tale more lively than Boccaccio's trite extolling of love. Tennyson's treatment of the same story eleven years later shows further how Longfellow avoided what the taste of some in his audience would probably have wanted him to do. In *The Falcon* Tennyson has a servant instead of Ser Federigo kill the bird, allows neither the knight nor the lady to eat it, and promises that the son will recover. In regard to this boy's death, it may be added that Boccaccio raises a doubt as to its cause (the son dies "whether for chagrin that he could not have the bird or for that his disorder was e'en fated to bring him to that pass"), while Longfellow simply tells of the death as a direct consequence of the falcon's sacrifice for love. Finally, in the *Decameron* the wedding takes place after Monna Giovanna "had abidden awhile full of tears and affliction"; but Longfellow stipulates exactly three months.

Insistence here is still not upon depth, but upon humorous insight and awareness. As many have noticed and as Paul Elmer More has best phrased it, Longfellow lacks the "enigmatical dualism, the pathetic or terrible sense of transiency, that runs through the heart of the world." But this too we should at least qualify, or allow Howells to do it for us when he speaks of the poet's "spiritual intimacy, which owns us close akin, whether we are young or old, great or mean, so only we are mortal." There is, to find common ground, a pathetic sense of transiency exhibited in such poems as *Aftermath* and *The Tide Rises*, but there is not a terrible sense and not a full recognition of the urgency of human experience.

Lack of recognition, however, does not prove that there is no awareness. The "comfort" which Hawthorne found in Longfellow's poetry and which the poet himself consciously proposed is based upon an assumption of turbulence. We see it in many of his poems that have to do with poetry, and in this essay have glanced at it in *Seaweed*, in which the "wild emotion" reaches the repose of "hoarded household words," and in *Jugurtha*, which provides no resolution. But generally resolution is offered, whether implicitly in the early *Prelude* or explicitly and rather naïvely in the later *Epimetheus, or the Poet's Afterthought.* Our poet saw himself as moving from the early period of *Sturm und Drang* to the wisdom and balance of the elder Goethe. Unlike Goethe he neglected the affirmation of turbulence that is the basis of dynamic resolution, and in contrast with contemporary thought he does not urge turbulence as the major part of experience. Yet we should grant his awareness of it and admit that since his prevailing mood lies between pathos and comedy the aesthetic need of conflict is less great than it would be otherwise.

More than with any other poets, there is a temptation to rewrite the poems of the schoolroom poets. Some years ago Desmond Powell suggested that Whittier would appear to advantage by the selection and rearrangement of passages from poems rather than by the printing of whole poems. As noted in this essay, Howells proposed not reading the didactic tags with which many of Longfellow's poems end; and in discussing *Seaweed* I have mentioned personal disapproval for the structure of the poem as we have it and preference for a derived poem made up of the first, second, third, and eighth stanzas.

Though the reprinting of a selection of Longfellow's poems with some lines omitted and others rearranged might be a literary impertinence, it would present the poet to modern readers with less of the detritus of time's ebbing flood than he otherwise comes to us now. Probably some precedent could be found, if not directly, then in the publication of passages and gems since the beginning of bookmaking or in the cutting by which Shakespeare on the modern stage almost always is presented.

The kind of thing that one might do has already been indicated for *Seaweed*. In the *Serenade* (p. 235) from *The Spanish Student* I should like to drop the last stanza, which though not didactic seems anticlimactic because of its abstraction; and then I should propose a new order in what is left, exactly reversing the present sequence of stars, moon, wind to that of wind, moon, stars.

Wind of the summer night!
　　Where yonder woodbine creeps,
Fold, fold thy pinions light!
　　She sleeps!
My lady sleeps!
　　Sleeps!

Moon of the summer night!
　　Far down yon western steeps,
Sink, sink in silver light!
　　She sleeps!
My lady sleeps!
　　Sleeps!

Stars of the summer night!
　　Far in yon azure deeps,
Hide, hide your golden light!
　　She sleeps!
My lady sleeps!
　　Sleeps!

This change would take us from the more closely felt to the more distantly perceived, at the same time intensifying the singer's desire for his beloved.

Though I should hesitate to tamper with *Snow-Flakes* (p. 222), which Mr. Pearson has called "a fine minor achievement" (if not a major one), I would suggest dropping the second stanza with its "even as" and starting with the third stanza. "This is the poem of the air," the poet would bravely begin and then he would go to his scene and be done.

> This is the poem of the air,
>   Slowly in silent syllables recorded;
> This is the secret of despair,
>   Long in its cloudy bosom hoarded,
>   Now whispered and revealed
>   To wood and field.
>
> Out of the bosom of the Air,
>   Out of the cloud-folds of her garments shaken,
> Over the woodlands brown and bare,
>   Over the harvest-fields forsaken,
>   Silent, and soft, and slow
>   Descends the snow.

"Snow," here the last word of the last line, concentrates all the materials of the poem at the end, and with the firmness of that concentration creates a pleasing disharmony with the gentleness in rhythm and connotation of what leads to it.

One more such venture will probably suffice. This time I take a brief narrative, *Killed at the Ford* (p. 236) and end up with only twelve of its original thirty-seven lines. Omitting the first stanza because it seems a too early announcement of the outcome of the action, I print the first five lines of the second stanza, stopping abruptly with the word "song" and not going on to quote it. Then I suppress the actual shooting of the soldier in the third stanza and the vision of the fifth and final stanza, giving the result (the whole of the fourth):

> Only last night, as we rode along,
> Down the dark of the mountain gap,
> To visit the picket-guard at the ford,
> Little dreaming of any mishap,
> He was humming the words of some old song.
>
> We lifted him up to his saddle again,
> And through the mire and the mist and the rain

> Carried him back to the silent camp,
> And laid him as if asleep on his bed;
> And I saw by the light of the surgeon's lamp
> Two white roses upon his cheeks,
> And one, just over his heart, blood-red!

In doing this, the action has been cut to its bare essentials, and because the song is not quoted in the earlier part of the poem—with a suspension of rhyme anticipating the single unrhymed line of the last part—the final lines give a sudden illumination of what has gone before without suggesting a mere echo.

The revisions (however primitive the surgery) leave poems that would seem more acceptable to modern taste than the originals. In all the revisions there is a sharper sense of progress and suspense; when analogy has been allowed to remain, it is not laboriously expressed; and the lingering over descriptive detail has been halted. Yet having done this, we must remember that Longfellow revised and that these were not the revisions that he made. Have we improved the poems to accord with any firm aesthetic criterion? Or have we shown the same blundering provincialism (worse because it boasts a pseudo-belletristic rather than pseudo-moral superiority) that the infamous Thomas Bowdler exhibited in his edition of Shakespeare?

These revisions warn us how restricted our sensibility is. We can never perhaps fully understand why Longfellow and his contemporaries regarded their means of climax, use of analogy, and leisurely presentation as artistic values. But as I have tried to show in these essays, we can achieve a greater comprehension than we have, and for the satisfaction of our intelligence and feeling we owe it to ourselves to try. With all his faults Lowell still said that Donne "wrote more profound verses than any other English poet save one only," and with his faults Longfellow still strove to make his steps "keep pace" with Dante. Since Donne and Dante were the masters of Lowell and Longfellow, as fellow servants we should recognize our common bond.

SNOW-FLAKES

> Out of the bosom of the Air,
>   Out of the cloud-folds of her garments shaken,
> Over the woodlands brown and bare,
>   Over the harvest-fields forsaken,
>   Silent, and soft, and slow
>   Descends the snow.

Even as our cloudy fancies take
  Suddenly shape in some divine expression,
Even as the troubled heart doth make
  In the white countenance confession,   10
    The troubled sky reveals
    The grief it feels.

This is the poem of the air,
  Slowly in silent syllables recorded;
This is the secret of despair,
  Long in its cloudy bosom hoarded,
    Now whispered and revealed
    To wood and field.

IN THE CHURCHYARD AT CAMBRIDGE

In the village churchyard she lies,
Dust is in her beautiful eyes,
  No more she breathes, nor feels, nor stirs;
At her feet and at her head
Lies a slave to attend the dead,
  But their dust is white as hers.

Was she, a lady of high degree,
So much in love with the vanity
  And foolish pomp of this world of ours?
Or was it Christian charity,   10
And lowliness and humility,
  The richest and rarest of all dowers?

Who shall tell us? No one speaks;
No color shoots into those cheeks,
  Either of anger or of pride,
At the rude question we have asked;
Nor will the mystery be unmasked
  By those who are sleeping at her side.

Hereafter?—And do you think to look
On the terrible pages of that Book   20

To find her failings, faults, and errors?
Ah, you will then have other cares,
In your own shortcomings and despairs,
In your own secret sins and terrors!

SEAWEED

When descends on the Atlantic
 The gigantic
Storm-wind of the equinox,
Landward in his wrath he scourges
 The toiling surges,
Laden with seaweed from the rocks:

From Bermuda's reefs; from edges
 Of sunken ledges,
In some far-off, bright Azore;
From Bahama, and the dashing,   10
 Silver-flashing
Surges of San Salvador;

From the tumbling surf, that buries
 The Orkneyan skerries,
Answering the hoarse Hebrides;
And from wrecks of ships, and drifting
 Spars, uplifting
On the desolate, rainy seas;—

Ever drifting, drifting, drifting
 On the shifting   20
Currents of the restless main;
Till in sheltered coves, and reaches
 Of sandy beaches,
All have found repose again.

So when storms of wild emotion
 Strike the ocean
Of the poet's soul, erelong
From each cave and rocky fastness,
 In its vastness,
Floats some fragment of a song: 30

From the far-off isles enchanted,
  Heaven has planted
With the golden fruit of Truth;
From the flashing surf, whose vision
  Gleams Elysian
In the tropic clime of Youth;

From the strong Will, and the Endeavor
  That forever
Wrestle with the tides of Fate;
From the wreck of Hopes far-scattered,   40
  Tempest-shattered,
Floating waste and desolate;—

Ever drifting, drifting, drifting
  On the shifting
Currents of the restless heart;
Till at length in books recorded,
  They, like hoarded
Household words, no more depart.

DIVINA COMMEDIA, I

Oft have I seen at some cathedral door
  A laborer, pausing in the dust and heat,
  Lay down his burden, and with reverent feet
  Enter, and cross himself, and on the floor
Kneel to repeat his paternoster o'er;
  Far off the noises of the world retreat;
  The loud vociferations of the street
  Become an undistinguishable roar.
So, as I enter here from day to day,
  And leave my burden at this minster gate,
  Kneeling in prayer, and not ashamed to pray,
The tumult of the time disconsolate
  To inarticulate murmurs dies away,
  While the eternal ages watch and wait.

THE FIRE OF DRIFT-WOOD

DEVEREUX FARM, NEAR MARBLEHEAD

We sat within the farm-house old,
　Whose windows, looking o'er the bay,
Gave to the sea-breeze damp and cold
　An easy entrance, night and day.

Not far away we saw the port,
　The strange, old-fashioned, silent town,
The lighthouse, the dismantled fort,
　The wooden houses, quaint and brown.

We sat and talked until the night,
　Descending, filled the little room;　　　　　　10
Our faces faded from the sight,
　Our voices only broke the gloom.

We spake of many a vanished scene,
　Of what we once had thought and said,
Of what had been, and might have been,
　And who was changed, and who was dead;

And all that fills the hearts of friends,
　When first they feel, with secret pain,
Their lives thenceforth have separate ends,
　And never can be one again;　　　　　　　　20

The first slight swerving of the heart,
　That words are powerless to express,
And leave it still unsaid in part,
　Or say it in too great excess.

The very tones in which we spake
　Had something strange, I could but mark;
The leaves of memory seemed to make
　A mournful rustling in the dark.

Oft died the words upon our lips,
　As suddenly, from out the fire　　　　　　　　30
Built of the wreck of stranded ships,
　The flames would leap and then expire.

And, as their splendor flashed and failed,
  We thought of wrecks upon the main,
Of ships dismasted, that were hailed
  And sent no answer back again.

The windows, rattling in their frames,
  The ocean, roaring up the beach,
The gusty blast, the bickering flames,
  All mingled vaguely in our speech;   40

Until they made themselves a part
  Of fancies floating through the brain,
The long-lost ventures of the heart,
  That send no answers back again.

O flames that glowed! O hearts that yearned!
  They were indeed too much akin,
The drift-wood fire without that burned,
  The thoughts that burned and glowed within.

AFTERMATH

When the summer fields are mown,
When the birds are fledged and flown,
  And the dry leaves strew the path;
With the falling of the snow,
With the cawing of the crow,
Once again the fields we mow
  And gather in the aftermath.

Not the sweet, new grass with flowers
Is this harvesting of ours;
  Not the upland clover bloom;   10
But the rowen mixed with weeds,
Tangled tufts from marsh and meads,
Where the poppy drops its seeds
  In the silence and the gloom.

JUGURTHA

How cold are thy baths, Apollo!
  Cried the African monarch, the splendid,
As down to his death in the hollow
  Dark dungeons of Rome he descended,
  Uncrowned, unthroned, unattended;
How cold are thy baths, Apollo!

How cold are thy baths, Apollo!
  Cried the Poet, unknown, unbefriended,
As the vision, that lured him to follow,
  With the mist and the darkness blended,   10
  And the dream of his life was ended;
How cold are thy baths, Apollo!

THE FALCON OF SER FEDERIGO

One summer morning, when the sun was hot,
Weary with labor in his garden-plot,
On a rude bench beneath his cottage eaves,
Ser Federigo sat among the leaves
Of a huge vine, that, with its arms outspread,
Hung its delicious clusters overhead.
Below him, through the lovely valley, flowed
The river Arno, like a winding road,
And from its banks were lifted high in air
The spires and roofs of Florence called the Fair;   10
To him a marble tomb, that rose above
His wasted fortunes and his buried love.
For there, in banquet and in tournament,
His wealth had lavished been, his substance spent,
To woo and lose, since ill his wooing sped,
Monna Giovanna, who his rival wed,
Yet ever in his fancy reigned supreme,
The ideal woman of a young man's dream.

Then he withdrew, in poverty and pain,
To this small farm, the last of his domain,   20

His only comfort and his only care
To prune his vines, and plant the fig and pear;
His only forester and only guest
His falcon, faithful to him, when the rest,
Whose willing hands had found so light of yore
The brazen knocker of his palace door,
Had now no strength to lift the wooden latch,
That entrance gave beneath a roof of thatch.
Companion of his solitary ways,
Purveyor of his feasts on holidays,   30
On him this melancholy man bestowed
The love with which his nature overflowed.

And so the empty-handed years went round,
Vacant, though voiceful with prophetic sound,
And so, that summer morn, he sat and mused
With folded, patient hands, as he was used,
And dreamily before his half-closed sight
Floated the vision of his lost delight.
Beside him, motionless, the drowsy bird
Dreamed of the chase, and in his slumber heard   40
The sudden, scythe-like sweep of wings, that dare
The headlong plunge through eddying gulfs of air,
Then, starting broad awake upon his perch,
Tinkled his bells, like mass-bells in a church,
And looking at his master, seemed to say,
"Ser Federigo, shall we hunt today?"

Ser Federigo thought not of the chase;
The tender vision of her lovely face,
I will not say he seems to see, he sees
In the leaf-shadows of the trellises,   50
Herself, yet not herself; a lovely child
With flowing tresses, and eyes wide and wild,
Coming undaunted up the garden walk,
And looking not at him, but at the hawk.
"Beautiful falcon!" said he, "would that I
Might hold thee on my wrist, or see thee fly!"
The voice was hers, and made strange echoes start
Through all the haunted chambers of his heart,
As an æolian harp through gusty doors
Of some old ruin its wild music pours.   60

"Who is thy mother, my fair boy?" he said,
His hand laid softly on that shining head.
"Monna Giovanna. Will you let me stay
A little while, and with your falcon play?
We live there, just beyond your garden wall,
In the great house behind the poplars tall."

So he spake on; and Federigo heard
As from afar each softly uttered word,
And drifted onward through the golden gleams
And shadows of the misty sea of dreams,   70
As mariners becalmed through vapors drift,
And feel the sea beneath them sink and lift,
And hear far off the mournful breakers roar,
And voices calling faintly from the shore!
Then waking from his pleasant reveries,
He took the little boy upon his knees,
And told him stories of his gallant bird,
Till in their friendship he became a third.

Monna Giovanna, widowed in her prime,
Had come with friends to pass the summer time   80
In her grand villa, half-way up the hill,
O'erlooking Florence, but retired and still;
With iron gates, that opened through long lines
Of sacred ilex and centennial pines,
And terraced gardens, and broad steps of stone,
And sylvan deities, with moss o'ergrown,
And fountains palpitating in the heat,
And all Val d'Arno stretched beneath its feet.
Here in seclusion, as a widow may,
The lovely lady whiled the hours away,   90
Pacing in sable robes the statued hall,
Herself the stateliest statue among all,
And seeing more and more, with secret joy,
Her husband risen and living in her boy,
Till the lost sense of life returned again,
Not as delight, but as relief from pain.
Meanwhile the boy, rejoicing in his strength,
Stormed down the terraces from length to length;
The screaming peacock chased in hot pursuit,
And climbed the garden trellises for fruit.   100

But his chief pastime was to watch the flight,
Of a gerfalcon, soaring into sight,
Beyond the trees that fringed the garden wall,
Then downward stooping at some distant call;
And as he gazed full often wondered he
Who might the master of the falcon be,
Until that happy morning, when he found
Master and falcon in the cottage ground.

And now a shadow and a terror fell
On the great house, as if a passing-bell   110
Tolled from the tower, and filled each spacious room
With secret awe and preternatural gloom;
The petted boy grew ill, and day by day
Pined with mysterious malady away.
The mother's heart would not be comforted;
Her darling seemed to her already dead,
And often, sitting by the sufferer's side,
"What can I do to comfort thee?" she cried.
At first the silent lips made no reply,
But, moved at length by her importunate cry,   120
"Give me," he answered, with imploring tone,
"Ser Federigo's falcon for my own!"
No answer could the astonished mother make;
How could she ask, e'en for her darling's sake,
Such favor at a luckless lover's hand,
Well knowing that to ask was to command?
Well knowing, what all falconers confessed,
In all the land that falcon was the best,
The master's pride and passion and delight,
And the sole pursuivant of this poor knight.   130
But yet, for her child's sake, she could no less
Than give assent, to soothe his restlessness,
So promised, and then promising to keep
Her promise sacred, saw him fall asleep.

The morrow was a bright September morn;
The earth was beautiful as if new-born;
There was that nameless splendor everywhere,
That wild exhilaration in the air,
Which makes the passers in the city street
Congratulate each other as they meet.   140

Two lovely ladies, clothed in cloak and hood,
Passed through the garden gate into the wood,
Under the lustrous leaves, and through the sheen
Of dewy sunshine showering down between.
The one, close-hooded, had the attractive grace
Which sorrow sometimes lends a woman's face;
Her dark eyes moistened with the mists that roll
From the gulf-stream of passion in the soul;
The other with her hood thrown back, her hair
Making a golden glory in the air,   150
Her cheeks suffused with an auroral blush,
Her young heart singing louder than the thrush,
So walked, that morn, through mingled light and shade,
Each by the other's presence lovelier made,
Monna Giovanna and her bosom friend,
Intent upon their errand and its end.

They found Ser Federigo at his toil,
Like banished Adam, delving in the soil;
And when he looked and these fair women spied,
The garden suddenly was glorified;   160
His long-lost Eden was restored again,
And the strange river winding through the plain
No longer was the Arno to his eyes,
But the Euphrates watering Paradise!

Monna Giovanna raised her stately head,
And with fair words of salutation said:
"Ser Federigo, we come here as friends,
Hoping in this to make some poor amends
For past unkindness. I who ne'er before
Would even cross the threshold of your door,   170
I who in happier days such pride maintained,
Refused your banquets, and your gifts disdained,
This morning come, a self-invited guest,
To put your generous nature to the test,
And breakfast with you under your own vine."
To which he answered: "Poor desert of mine,
Not your unkindness call it, for if aught
Is good in me of feeling or of thought,
From you it comes, and this last grace outweighs
All sorrows, all regrets of other days."   180

And after further compliment and talk,
Among the asters in the garden walk
He left his guests; and to his cottage turned,
And as he entered for a moment yearned
For the lost splendors of the days of old,
The ruby glass, the silver and the gold,
And felt how piercing is the sting of pride,
By want embittered and intensified.
He looked about him for some means or way
To keep this unexpected holiday;   190
Searched every cupboard, and then searched again,
Summoned the maid, who came, but came in vain;
"The Signor did not hunt to-day," she said,
"There's nothing in the house but wine and bread."
Then suddenly the drowsy falcon shook
His little bells, with that sagacious look,
Which said, as plain as language to the ear,
"If anything is wanting, I am here!"

Yes, everything is wanting, gallant bird!
The master seized thee without further word.   200
Like thine own lure, he whirled thee round; ah me!
The pomp and flutter of brave falconry,
The bells, the jesses, the bright scarlet hood,
The flight and the pursuit o'er field and wood,
All these forevermore are ended now;
No longer victor, but the victim thou!

Then on the board a snow-white cloth he spread,
Laid on its wooden dish the loaf of bread,
Brought purple grapes with autumn sunshine hot,
The fragrant peach, the juicy bergamot;   210
Then in the midst a flask of wine he placed
And with autumnal flowers the banquet graced.
Ser Federigo, would not these suffice
Without thy falcon stuffed with cloves and spice?

When all was ready, and the courtly dame
With her companion to the cottage came,
Upon Ser Federigo's brain there fell
The wild enchantment of a magic spell!
The room they entered, mean and low and small,
Was changed into a sumptuous banquet-hall,   220

With fanfares by aerial trumpets blown;
The rustic chair she sat on was a throne;
He ate celestial food, and a divine
Flavor was given to his country wine,
And the poor falcon, fragrant with his spice,
A peacock was, or bird of paradise!

When the repast was ended, they arose
And passed again into the garden-close.
Then said the lady, "Far too well I know,
Remembering still the days of long ago,   230
Though you betray it not, with what surprise
You see me here in this familiar wise.
You have no children, and you cannot guess
What anguish, what unspeakable distress
A mother feels, whose child is lying ill,
Nor how her heart anticipates his will.
And yet for this, you see me lay aside
All womanly reserve and check of pride,
And ask the thing most precious in your sight,
Your falcon, your sole comfort and delight,   240
Which if you find it in your heart to give,
My poor, unhappy boy perchance may live."

Ser Federigo listens, and replies,
With tears of love and pity in his eyes;
"Alas, dear lady! there can be no task
So sweet to me, as giving when you ask.
One little hour ago, if I had known
This wish of yours, it would have been my own.
But thinking in what manner I could best
Do honor to the presence of my guest,   250
I deemed that nothing worthier could be
Than what most dear and precious was to me;
And so my gallant falcon breathed his last
To furnish forth this morning our repast."

In mute contrition, mingled with dismay,
The gentle lady turned her eyes away,
Grieving that he such sacrifice should make
And kill his falcon for a woman's sake,
Yet feeling in her heart a woman's pride,
That nothing she could ask for was denied;   260

Then took her leave, and passed out at the gate
With footstep slow and soul disconsolate.

Three days went by, and lo! a passing-bell
Tolled from the little chapel in the dell;
Ten strokes Ser Federigo heard, and said,
Breathing a prayer, "Alas! her child is dead!"
Three months went by; and lo! a merrier chime
Rang from the chapel bells at Christmas-time;
The cottage was deserted, and no more
Ser Federigo sat beside its door,   270
But now, with servitors to do his will,
In the grand villa, half-way up the hill,
Sat at the Christmas feast, and at his side
Monna Giovanna, his belovèd bride,
Never so beautiful, so kind, so fair,
Enthroned once more in the old rustic chair,
High-perched upon the back of which there stood
The image of a falcon carved in wood,
And underneath the inscription, with a date,
"All things come round to him who will but wait."   280

SERENADE

Stars of the summer night!
　　Far in yon azure deeps,
Hide, hide your golden light!
　　She sleeps!
My lady sleeps!
　　Sleeps!

Moon of the summer night!
　　Far down yon western steeps,
Sink, sink in silver light!
　　She sleeps!   10
My lady sleeps!
　　Sleeps!

Wind of the summer night!
   Where yonder woodbine creeps,
Fold, fold thy pinions light!
   She sleeps!
My lady sleeps!
   Sleeps!

Dreams of the summer night!
   Tell her, her lover keeps   20
Watch! while in slumbers light
   She sleeps!
My lady sleeps!
   Sleeps!

KILLED AT THE FORD

He is dead, the beautiful youth,
The heart of honor, the tongue of truth,
He, the life and light of us all,
Whose voice was blithe as a bugle-call,
Whom all eyes followed with one consent,
The cheer of whose laugh, and whose pleasant word,
Hushed all murmurs of discontent.

Only last night, as we rode along,
Down the dark of the mountain gap,
To visit the picket-guard at the ford,   10
Little dreaming of any mishap,
He was humming the words of some old song:
"Two red roses he had on his cap
And another he bore at the point of his sword."

Sudden and swift a whistling ball
Came out of a wood, and the voice was still;
Something I heard in the darkness fall,
And for a moment my blood grew chill;
I spake in a whisper, as he who speaks
In a room where some one is lying dead;   20
But he made no answer to what I said.

We lifted him up to his saddle again,
And through the mire and the mist and the rain
Carried him back to the silent camp,
And laid him as if asleep on his bed;
And I saw by the light of the surgeon's lamp
Two white roses upon his cheeks,
And one, just over his heart, blood-red!

And I saw in a vision how far and fleet
That fatal bullet went speeding forth,   30
Till it reached a town in the distant North,
Till it reached a house in a sunny street,
Till it reached a heart that ceased to beat
Without a murmur, without a cry;
And a bell was tolled, in that far-off town,
For one who had passed from cross to crown,
And the neighbors wondered that she should die.

Bibliographical Note

The primary purpose of these entries is to locate the writings of critics named throughout this work. It should be understood that these are not complete lists of the available criticism. Even so, the reader will probably find here the most helpful and stimulating material, though obviously several of the books and articles are cited only as bibliographical aids and not as recommendations.

THE SCHOOLROOM POETS

DUNCAN, JOSEPH E. *The Revival of Seventeenth-Century Metaphysical Poetry, Chiefly in England, 1800–1912.* Cambridge, Mass.: Privately printed, 1951.

STAUFFER, DONALD A. "A Hope for Poetry?" *The Hudson Review*, I (Winter, 1949), 573–79.

WELLS, HENRY W. *The American Way of Poetry.* New York: Columbia University Press, 1943.

BRYANT

BRYANT, WILLIAM CULLEN, II. "The Genesis of 'Thanatopsis,'" *New England Quarterly*, XXI (June, 1948), 163–84.

FOERSTER, NORMAN. *Nature in American Literature.* New York: The Macmillan Company, 1923.

LEGARÉ, HUGH SWINTON. Review, *Southern Review*, VIII (February, 1832), 443–62. Reprinted McDowell, *op. cit.*, 1935.

LEONARD, WILLIAM ELLERY. "Bryant and the Minor Poets," *The Cambridge History of American Literature*, I (1917; 1944 edition), 260–83.

McDOWELL, TREMAINE. *William Cullen Bryant: Representative Selections.* New York: American Book Company, 1935.

———. "Bryant's Practice in Composition and Revision," *PMLA*, LII (June, 1937), 474–502.

MORLEY, CHRISTOPHER. "Trade Winds," *Saturday Review of Literature*, ca. 1938.

POE, EDGAR ALLAN. Reviews, *Southern Literary Messenger*, 1837, and *Godey's Lady's Book*, 1846. Reprinted *The Complete Works*, ed. James A. Harrison, Volumes IX and XIII. New York: Thomas Y. Crowell & Company, 1902.

VAN DOREN, CARL. "The Growth of 'Thanatopsis,'" *Nation*, CI (October 7, 1915), 432–33.

WINTERS, YVOR. *In Defense of Reason*. Denver and New York: The Swallow Press & William Morrow and Company, 1947.

WHITTIER

MORE, PAUL ELMER. *Shelburne Essays*, Third and Eleventh Series. New York: Houghton Mifflin Company, 1921. Third Series first printed 1906.

PAYNE, WILLIAM MORTON. "Whittier," *The Cambridge History of American Literature*, II (1918; 1944 edition), 42–54.

POWELL, DESMOND. "Whittier," *American Literature*, IX (November, 1937), 335–42.

SCOTT, WINFIELD TOWNLEY. "Poetry in American: A New Consideration of Whittier's Verse," *New England Quarterly*, VII (June, 1934), 258–75.

———. *Mr. Whittier and Other Poems*. New York: The Macmillan Company, 1948.

STRONG, A. H. *American Poets and Their Theology*. Philadelphia: The Griffith and Rowland Press, 1916.

WENDELL, BARRETT. *A Literary History of America*. New York: Charles Scribners' Sons, 1928. First printed 1900.

HOLMES

ADKINS, NELSON F. " 'The Chambered Nautilus': Its Scientific and Poetic Backgrounds," *American Literature*, IX (January, 1938), 458–65.

ARMS, GEORGE. " 'To Fix the Image All Unveiled and Warm,' " *New England Quarterly*, XIX (December, 1946), 534–37.

CLARK, HARRY HAYDEN. "Dr. Holmes: A Re-interpretation," *New England Quarterly*, XII (March, 1939), 19–34.

HAYAKAWA, S. I. "The Boston Poet-Laureate: Oliver Wendell Holmes," *Studies in English Literature*, XVI (October, 1936), 572–92.

HAYAKAWA, S. I., and HOWARD MUMFORD JONES. *Oliver Wendell Holmes: Representative Selections*. New York: American Book Company, 1939.

KERN, ALEXANDER C. "Dr. Oliver Wendell Holmes Today," *University of Kansas City Review*, XIV (Spring, 1948), 191–99.

MORSE, J. T. *Life and Letters of Oliver Wendell Holmes*. Boston: Houghton, Mifflin and Company, 1896. Two volumes.

OBERNDORF, CLARENCE P., ed. *The Psychiatric Novels of Oliver Wendell Holmes*. New York: Columbia University Press, 1943.

PRITCHARD, JOHN P. *Return to the Fountains*. Durham: Duke University Press, 1942.

Stephen, Leslie. *Studies of a Biographer*, Volume ii. New York: G. P. Putnam's Sons, 1898.

Tilton, Eleanor M. *Amiable Autocrat: A Biography of Dr. Oliver Wendell Holmes*. New York: Henry Schuman, 1947.

Wendell, Barrett. See under "Whittier."

LOWELL

The anthologies cited early in the chapter are easily identifiable and require no entries.

Blair, Walter. "Lowell," *The Literature of the United States*, Volume i, ed. Walter Blair *et al*. Chicago: Scott, Foresman and Company, 1946.

Clark, Harry Hayden, and Norman Foerster. *James Russell Lowell: Representative Selections*. New York: American Book Company, 1947. The poems in this selection are substantially the same as those in Clark's *Major American Poets* (1936).

Clark, William Smith, ed. *Lowell: Essays, Poems and Letters*. New York: The Odyssey Press, 1948.

Foerster, Norman. See "Clark, Harry Hayden."

Greenslet, Ferris. *James Russell Lowell*. Boston: Houghton, Mifflin and Company, 1905.

Howard, Leon. *Victorian Knight-Errant: A Study of the Early Literary Career of James Russell Lowell*. Berkeley and Los Angeles: University of California Press, 1952.

James, Henry. *Essays in London and Elsewhere*. New York: Harper & Brothers, 1893.

Matthiessen, F. O. *American Renaissance*. New York: Oxford University Press, 1941.

Matthiessen, F. O., ed. *The Oxford Book of American Verse*. New York: Oxford University Press, 1950.

O'Connor, William Van. *Sense and Sensibility in Modern Poetry*. Chicago: University of Chicago Press, 1948.

Shepard, Odell. "The New England Triumvirate: Longfellow, Holmes, Lowell," *Literary History of the United States*, i, 1948, 587–606.

Smith, Thelma M., ed. *Uncollected Poems of James Russell Lowell*. Philadelphia: University of Pennsylvania Press, 1950.

Voss, Arthur. "James Russell Lowell," *University of Kansas City Review*, xv (Spring, 1949), 224–33.

———. "Backgrounds of Lowell's Satire in 'The Biglow Papers,'" *New England Quarterly*, xxiii (March, 1950), 47–64.

Wendell, Barrett. See under "Whittier."

LONGFELLOW

Amacher, Richard E. "Longfellow's *Jugurtha*," *The Explicator*, vi (February, 1948), 29.

Elliott, G. R. "Gentle Shades of Longfellow," *Southwest Review*, x (April, 1925), 34–52.

Gohdes, Clarence. *American Literature in Nineteenth-Century England.* New York: Columbia University Press, 1944.

Howells, William Dean. "The Art of Longfellow," *North American Review*, clxxxiv (March 1, 1907), 472–85.

Kreymborg, Alfred. *Our Singing Strength.* New York: Coward-McCann, Inc. 1929.

More, Paul Elmer. *Shelburne Essays*, Fifth Series. New York: G. P. Putnam's Sons, 1908.

Pearson, Norman Holmes. "Both Longfellows," *University of Kansas City Review*, xvi (Summer, 1950), 245–53.

Powell, Desmond. See under "Whittier."

Richards, I. A. *Practical Criticism.* New York: Harcourt, Brace and Company, 1929.

Saintsbury, George. *Prefaces and Essays.* London: The Macmillan Company, 1933.

Shepard, Odell. *Henry Wadsworth Longfellow: Representative Selections.* New York: American Book Company, 1934.

Shepard, Odell. See under "Lowell."

Stedman, E. C. *Poets of America.* Boston: Houghton, Mifflin and Company, 1892. First printed 1885.

Trent, William Peterfield. "Longfellow," *The Cambridge History of American Literature*, ii (1918; 1944 edition), 32–41.

Von Abele, Rudolph. "A Note on Longfellow's Poetic," *American Literature*, xxiv (March, 1952), 77–83.

Index

243

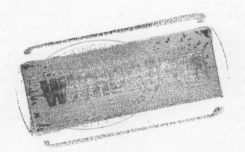